The
Mormon
Establishment

Books by Wallace Turner

Gamblers' Money: The New Force in American Life

The Mormon Establishment

The
Mormon
Establishment

Wallace Turner

Houghton Mifflin Company Boston

The Riverside Press Cambridge

1966

Second Printing   C

Contents

The
Mormon
Establishment

I

The Holy City
by the Dead Sea

THE BEST view is from the West, high above the floor of the desert. From there, at about ten miles distance, the city is displayed like a tapestry on the talus that slants up to the Wasatch Range. Once a great freshwater lake washed those cliffs; the dead sea in the distance is its corpse. The slope is gentle and yet the houses at the base of the rock are about 1000 feet higher than the wide streets downtown; and the even geometry of the precisely north-south and east-west streets pleases the eye as the plane turns into the approach to land.

That is the best view. The effect is heightened on one of those days when the temperature pattern has created a snow line about halfway up the mountains. Below the snow line the city sparkles and glistens. In the far distance the taller mountains hover mysteriously, and these will have snow on them even in late July. The buildings of the downtown area stand out, to give a different texture to this montage of wood and masonry against the mountains and snow. The dome of the capitol fits in place on its hill to the north, superior to its city but itself dominated by the timeless mountains.

But when the whitened mountain backdrop is most beautiful, the trees are dormant. The wind off the desert whistles through their bare branches and the wet snow clings there until the sun melts it. It is best to see this city in all its sea-

sons, to walk the street when the July sun pours through the
leaves and when the January snow is blowing, to savor the
smells of plant life in the spring and sample the goodness of
harvest in the autumn.

This strange and unusual city changes often. Yet it has a
continuity to it, and a central theme, a sense of unity with
the purposes for which it was founded. Washington, D.C.,
is a little like that. But this city does not exist to govern men.
It was not built here on the desert, on the bleak shores of a
dead sea, to provide a center from which the reins of government could reach out to check the actions of men. In a sense,
this is a Mecca, the holy place of a religion.

The city was built as a hiding place for the group of religious fanatics who followed a man named Brigham Young
across the plains and mountains, settling in a place where
he felt assured they could gather their strength and engage in the religious practices that they believed would benefit their souls. These were members of a religious congregation of such abiding faith as to make men marvel. They had
endured terrible things. They were the major part of what
had been a larger group, a group shattered by the killing of
its leader, Joseph Smith. They were riddled with heresy,
with fanaticism and with legend. Their leaders were even
then doing things secretly that would bring down the skies
on all of them. But they were a strong people. They believed, and they would overcome the obstacles before them.

They did overcome, and Salt Lake City is their monument.

This is the city where one of the world's major religions is
centered. It was belief in the divine inspiration of Joseph
Smith, Jr. that created Salt Lake City. Today perhaps less
than half of the city is Mormon by self-designation. An even
smaller number believes in the divine inspiration of Joseph,
the Prophet. But the Mormons run the place. It is their
city, just as Utah is their state. The patterns of life are set

by the Saints. Every important action taken in Salt Lake City is shaped by the realization that the Mormons own the town.

The history of the Saints is both a trap and a necessity for those who would understand them today. How can a man be understood without knowing the society from which he came? And his father's and his grandfather's societies? It is impossible in most cities to achieve a sense of the continuity between today's leaders and those who settled the town. It is as if one generation gradually put down the burdens, and utter strangers from the new generation picked them up. This is not true in Mormon country. The church has given the Latter-day Saints this continuity of yesterday and today with tomorrow.

One example will illustrate the point: The most important office in the Church of Jesus Christ of Latter-day Saints is the presidency. The president is the man longest in service as an apostle. The current president is David O. McKay, born in 1873, an apostle since 1906. He will be succeeded by Joseph Fielding Smith, born in 1876, an apostle since 1910. Joseph Fielding Smith is the son of Joseph F. Smith who was president of the church from 1901 to 1918. Joseph F. Smith was the son of Hyrum Smith who was the brother of the Prophet, Joseph Smith, Jr., the young man who told wondrous stories of visions of angels, of personal revelations from God. The Mormons believe that the Prophet Joseph was the means through which the true Gospel was restored to earth. They call their religion the Restored Gospel.

Thus one day—if he survives President McKay—the grandson of Hyrum Smith and the grandnephew of the Prophet will become the president of the church which his father and uncle founded with four other men on April 6, 1830, at Fayette, New York. Now that nucleus has grown to 2.5 millions. But this growth does not hide the unity of time and purpose in those relationships stretching from 1830 to the present. There is unity also in the realization that many of the people who make up the LDS church today are descendants of those who crossed the plains with Brigham Young. But there is a disunity, too, for the direct descendants of Joseph Smith are not there; they lead the Reorganized Church of Jesus Christ of Latter Day Saints in Independence, Missouri, a competing group. Theirs is a different story, a story of the *Book of Mormon* without Brigham Young.

In fewer than 150 years, this Utah church has become an important religious organization, a world church. It established this lovely city. It built a state in the desert where only wild things had existed prior to 1847. It developed a people who are unique in American society. To be born a Mormon is to be born with a second nationality. The duties required to maintain this connection are at least as demanding as those of the American citizen, and perhaps much more demanding.

Salt Lake City provides the greatest flowering of Mormonism. Yet, in widening waves, this religious force in American life is felt across the nation. A Mormon is governor of Michigan, and George Romney may become the Republican presidential candidate in 1968. Mormons are found in all walks of life—except those pathways that are dishonorable and shabby. Even there one may find men and women who were born into Mormonism, but have forsaken it.

The social order in Salt Lake City peels back like an onion on examination. The outer layer is that gorgeous scene from high above the desert or the marvelous, cool beauty of clear water running down the gutters of Main Street on a day when the temperature is knocking 100 degrees. This outer layer is the polite waitresses and the gentle cab drivers and the helpful hotel clerks and the lights on the spires of the old Temple at night. It is the lovely campus of Brigham Young University at Provo and the swelling voices of the Tabernacle Choir rolling through the hot summer night as its members rehearse for next Sunday's national radio broadcast.

A wise man will never lose the respect that these surface wonders give him for the religion that grew on the revelations of the Prophet Joseph. These are a wonderful people who live here, inheritors of those brave ones who conquered the desert and fought Satan and outmaneuvered the United States government.

Examination of this city, and of the system of life lived by the dominant people in it, causes questions, arouses wonder. Why is the west view of the Temple spoiled by the Hotel Utah behind it? Why is the church not only permitting but actually financing the construction of other buildings that will further hide the most famous Mormon building? One wonders about the social structure in Mormon country. What is life like behind the walls of those neat homes in Bountiful? And does the church leadership have the power to dictate who wins and who loses elections? Why does one find all those people in the former Montgomery Ward store reading microfilms of records of long-closed churches in Poland? Why are the streets so wide? How does it happen that Catholics own the *Salt Lake Tribune*, but the LDS church owns the *Deseret News*? What, anyway, is a "Deseret?" Do the Mormons still practice polygamy? What is that Beehive sign that appears all over and even is the name given to the main house where Brigham Young lived? What do the Mormons believe? Why won't they allow non-Members in the Temple? Why are there so few Negroes?

The answers make Salt Lake City more understandable, and indicate the intricate weaving of the fabric of life there —the Saints and their church interact continually with each other and with the gentiles and their non-church organizations. Much of Salt Lake City belongs entirely to the Saints. The physical things—the Temple, the Tabernacle, the real estate in strategic locations—are just a part of this.

In a deeper, and an intangible sense, the special moral flavor of the place and the sense of historical continuity derive from the Mormon church.

The western cities thrive on celebrations. They have people who specialize in the marking of Pioneer Sites, and in the creation of organizations called Sons and Daughters of Pioneers. The founders are just a step in time away from the people who live in cities all across the West, just as in Salt Lake City. But there is a difference. When those founders of other places are commemorated in centennial celebrations it is only another civic ceremony, with some names to be enshrined on a plaque. These founders may be represented by one or so descendants produced from some back eddy of life, but whatever mark the founders made usually has been erased long ago by their successors.

A far different rule applies to Salt Lake City and all of the Mormon country. One big event each year is the "Days of '47," which commemorates the arrival of the first group of settlers. Brigham Young—ill and weary from leading his band of refugees across the wilds to safety, told them: "This is the place." A whole group of statuary rises on the spot at the mouth of Emigrant Canyon where Young said those words. Another group, surmounted by Brigham's form, stands at the head of Main Street. A plaque on the stone base even carries the names of the first party, down to the names of three Negroes—carefully set apart, of course.

The "Days of '47" parade on July 24 each year celebrates the arrival on the edge of the Great Salt Lake at a place so isolated that Brigham Young considered his people would be able to live in safety from the increasing attacks which had disrupted their lives since the church was formed. This parade and celebration really is a Mormon historical binge, much in the same pattern year after year. Persons outside the church may take part. The non-Mormon J. Bracken Lee rides in the parade as mayor of Salt Lake City. The standard pieces are there: The Mormon Battalion, the floats entered by various wards and stakes, the marching bands from the Mormon towns. This is a Mormon day, a day of great historical recollection not just to Salt Lake City and the state of Utah, but to all Mormons everywhere, for it was on this day that the successful transplanting of Joseph Smith's doctrines was begun to the safety of the desert. So it is both a civic and a religious holiday. So much of life is governed by religion in Mormon country.

There is this part of Salt Lake City that the Mormons own —the history. They also have a great influence on the language. Words have special meaning in Salt Lake City, and one for a time feels the need of a translator. For example, "quorum" has no Robert's Rules of Order connotation here. It is a term applying to the organization of the LDS church, and is slowly losing currency in the influx of outsiders. In many cases, "council" is replacing "quorum" which was a favorite word in Joseph's placing of titles in the church. "President" is another word much used. David O. McKay is president of the church; but Joseph Fielding Smith is the president of the Council of the Twelve; and a lesser man may be president of a stake. A bishop administers a ward in his free time from his profession.

A stake is an administrative organization of up to ten wards. A ward may have 250 to 500 persons in it. The groupings of wards are considered to be the "stakes that hold up the tent of Zion." The wards are the smallest organizations, the congregations of Mormonism, the parishes. Not every ward has its own chapel, or meeting house. Frequently two or more wards will use one chapel, scheduling their functions at different hours.

There are other words that mean different things to the Saints than to the rest of us. "Sealed" for example is a word used in some of the highest rites of the church. The most sacred Mormon marriage ceremony can only be performed in the Temple, of which there are but thirteen in the world. A man and woman may be married in a home, a chapel, or wherever suits them, but they are married in Mormon eyes for "time and eternity" only when the ceremony is performed in a Temple. "Gentile" means non-Mormon. "Vicarious" has special significance. Vicarious baptism is performed for relatives long dead who had no opportunity to heed the Restored Gospel. "Endowment" is concerned with another Temple rite. "Improvement" has a connotation from "Mutual Improvement Association," which is a Mormon program of awesome proportions. It has more Eagle Scouts in Chicago than all the rest of Scouting has produced in the city. The Mormons operate much of the Boy Scout movement where they are strong. The Mutual Improvement Association is the vehicle.

One must understand, too, that the nickname "Mormon" is only reluctantly accepted. Theirs is the church of Latter-day Saints, and they prefer to be called Saints. They prefer to have the initials LDS used when an adjective is required. Today, when the public temper is perhaps better ready to accept them as Saints, they have grown accustomed to the nickname "Mormon" and accept it. When he discusses his religion, Governor Romney of Michigan will complain that "we should be called Saints, for that is the name of our religion. We have never called ourselves Mormons and that is not our name." Yet Senator Wallace F. Bennett, the member of a family that has become important in commercial life in Utah, wrote a book called *Why I Am a Mormon* which is sold through the church bookstores.

The nickname derives, of course, from the formal name of the book Joseph Smith produced as his translations from the Golden Plates. This is the *Book of Mormon*, which is named for one of the figures in it. The Saints accept the Christian Testaments as the word of God. One of their Articles of Faith, as set out by Joseph Smith, Jr., expresses the relationship of the Bible and the *Book of Mormon*: "We believe the Bible to be the Word of God as far as it is translated correctly; we also believe the Book of Mormon to be the Word of God."

This is a revealing statement of Mormon theology. It reflects the fundamental premise that other religions are corrupted versions of the true Gospel that Jesus Christ brought to mankind. This assurance is the core of the Saints' religious belief. Since for them the sum of life is the practice of their religion, they are able to carry to the business house or the wheatfield or wherever they go this assurance of knowing the proper course and of being on it.

A wise old man named Eric Hoffer once wrote a book called *The True Believer* between work shifts as a longshoreman on the docks of San Francisco Bay. He was not discussing the Mormons, but was discussing the sort of mental attitude one must have to try to overturn the patterns of life around him. However, his book is full of statements that could apply to the Saints. One of these is this:

"For men to plunge headlong into an undertaking of vast change, they must be intensely discontented, yet not destitute, and they must have the feeling that by the possession of some potent doctrine, infallible leader or some new technique they have access to a source of irresistible power."

The men who became Mormons fitted this description exactly. Their inheritors are not discontented, for they find their wellsprings in the potent doctrine that they believe has irresistible power.

Initial contact with the peculiar social order in Salt Lake City produces the feeling that all the Saints are well-to-do, that they are all well-read, that they all have successfully made the transition from the unquestioning and unknowing belief of their childhood indoctrination to the religious conviction created by study of history and the sciences. At first one finds no apostates. There is an absence of strong criticism of the LDS church or of its leadership. The machinery of discipline is unseen on the surface. No one ever expresses any fear of the church's disfavor, nor is there even the strong suggestion that the church is a powerful enemy.

These initial impressions, of course, are erroneous. There are many poor Saints, and the church created a great machine about thirty years ago to provide welfare payments and supplies for those in dire need. There is no in-group talk today that explains that the machine was created by a church president who opposed the public welfare programs initiated by the Rooseveltian social planners, but such was the case. The upper reaches of the church still are predominantly conservative in economics and politics.

Certainly, there is a control mechanism for dangerous heretics. There are many Saints who know little of literature except what they read from the flood of church material on matters of doctrine and approved histories. There is no formal index of books which Mormons should not read. But there are books which every Mormon knows he should stay away from.

One of these is a fascinating biography of Joseph Smith, called *No Man Knows My History.* It was written by Fawn M. Brodie who was not very well identified on the book cover when it was issued in 1945. It has continued to sell well in the years since. A copy was requested at the non-Mormon Zion's Bookstore in Salt Lake City. It was brought out from under the counter and put in a bag. The action was nearly surreptitious, but not so close as to permit certainty. Mrs. Brodie was born in Ogden. She grew up in a little mountain valley in the high country. Her uncle was an apostle before she was born. Today he is the president of the church, David O. McKay. When her book was published, and the Saints felt that it cast some reflections on the character of the founder of their religion, the Prophet Joseph, her uncle was one of the counselors to the then president, George Albert

Smith. In addition, her father was an assistant apostle. These are positions at the pinnacle.

The book was well received by critics who found that it shed some realistic light on the life and times of Joseph Smith. It was my introduction to the Prophet. The biography created understanding and some admiration. But it was very poorly received by the Mormons, and the top leadership found it to be an unfriendly book. This placed Apostle McKay in a difficult position. Was he somehow responsible for what his niece had written? Of course he was not, but the difficult position went beyond this. What was he to do? Was he to try to protect her right to produce a book that the church leaders felt was injurious to the memory of the Prophet Joseph? Was this book a heresy?

The end of it came in June, 1946, when Mrs. Fawn McKay Brodie, the niece of the present president of the LDS church, was excommunicated for heresy. Mrs. Brodie has maintained a silence on this subject in the years since. But the incident was disturbing to many in the church and to many who live beside the church in Salt Lake City and elsewhere.

It was not a question of Mrs. Brodie's being deprived of much by being "disfellowshipped," the term Mormons sometimes use to cover excommunication. It was quite clear, say those who knew her then, that she no longer subscribed to the doctrines of the LDS church. However, no companion effort was made by the church to comb through its membership lists and "disfellowship" those hundreds (or thousands) of others who were born and reared as Mormons but who had lost their faith.

What disturbed the critics of the action toward Mrs. Brodie was the demonstration at the highest levels of the church that the old days of strong authoritarian control of thought were not past. It meant that the church leaders were still willing to move with dispatch to attack anyone who

might raise questions that the leaders would rather see
ignored.

There are many implications for many people in Mrs.
Brodie's case. They raise questions for a politician. It is unlikely that the church would attempt to order a political figure to take a specific action on religious grounds, with excommunication as the alternative. Or is it? Is it possible
that the LDS church would attempt to bar a certain national
television broadcast from the TV stations in which it has an
interest? What if it were a biography of the Prophet Joseph
based on Mrs. Brodie's book?

In the decades since Mrs. Brodie was excommunicated
from the religion of her family, there have been indications
of a softening of attitude. Today, it is considered unlikely
that the course of excommunication would be followed. Another Mormon author, Mrs. Juanita Brooks of St. George,
Utah, has produced a book, *The Mountain Meadow Massacre*, which is far more damaging to the image of the early
Mormon leaders in Utah than anything Mrs. Brodie wrote.
The massacre occurred when immigrants from Arkansas,
traveling by wagon train to California, were killed by Mormons who had first disarmed them on pretensions of guiding
them through hostile Indian country. On signal, each Mormon killed the Gentiles he was riding beside. Women and
older children were murdered along with the men. Mrs.
Brooks documented all of this, but still she is a member in
good standing of the LDS church.

Perhaps the answer is that the treachery of the Mormon
murderers in Southern Utah in the nineteenth century is a
matter that can safely be ignored, with the knowledge that
it will become a part of the folklore and disappear from public awareness. But the examination of Joseph Smith as a
man, and the questioning of some of his actions in preparation of the *Book of Mormon* and the revelations he said he
received from God, falls into a different category. It may be

felt that Mrs. Brodie's book questions the divinity of his inspiration and thus undermines the foundations of the LDS church.

Or it may be that the Mormon leaders, on reflection, have decided it is foolish to kill flies with a sledgehammer.

But these incidents demonstrate the peculiarity of the Mormon attitude on history. Perhaps this is because the religion today is so near to its days of formation. Other religions count their age in centuries and the Mormon counts its in decades. It yet is possible for researchers to discover new facts and new documents about the founders of the LDS church, while who can make new discoveries about Jesus of Nazareth, or Mohammed? Perhaps it comes also from the fact that the practice of their religion requires a close examination of ancestral origins and a study of Mormon history. This creates a mass LDS historical awareness that makes the Saints overly sensitive to the dredging up of their collective past.

However, there is one aspect of the church's treatment of Mrs. Brodie that raises other questions. In 1946, the church produced and began to sell a pamphlet called "No Ma'am, That's Not History." It was written by Hugh Nibley, a leading Mormon historian. The attack was sarcastic and vicious. Dr. Nibley refers to her as "little Brodie" and consistently calls her just "Brodie," with no courtesy title such as "Mrs." Brodie as a mother and honorable woman was entitled to receive. This sixty-two-page pamphlet is on sale, in its sixth edition, in the church's Deseret Bookstores.

It seems plain that the intention was to destroy Mrs. Brodie's credibility with Mormons who might have known her, or might have known about her background and relationship to David O. McKay. It was an unfeeling assault. Dr. Nibley is more easily excused for doing it than are the church authorities for selling it—even now, decades later. Dr. Nibley's feelings can be understood—this woman had

attacked the foundations of his religious belief and he felt
compelled to answer her. But the church leadership,in effect
endorsed the attack by placing it on sale in the bookstores
it controls. This incident gives an opportunity for a look
into the workings of the minds of some of the leading Saints.

Such events are just as much a part of Salt Lake City's life
today as the beauty of the lights winking in the dusk and
the mountains soaring into the blue twilight beyond. The
story of the attack on Mrs. Brodie makes understandable the
statement of a courageous Gentile businessman:

"I just don't want to talk about them. In my position, they
could ruin me if they decided they wanted to do it. I can't
afford to get them mad at me."

For the student of Mormon affairs, the streets of Salt Lake
City are filled with fascination. The Temple Square is worth
several days' study. But many feel that it is gradually being
surrounded and obscured by buildings that hide its glories.
There is the old one-room log house in the corner of Temple
Square, protected from the weather by a stone pavilion.
The cabin was built in 1847 and was moved several times
until it came to this place as a relic for tourists' eyes. Today's
Saints must draw strength, too, from the realization that
their forefathers lived in such a place.

A clear stream of water runs in the gutters on Main Street.
Why is this? Where does it come from? It comes usually
from an opened fire hydrant up the street, and it runs there
because it is a tradition. In the early days, the Mormon irrigation ditches ran along the sides of the streets in Salt Lake
City and still do in residential sections of many of the Mormon towns.

On Main Street, just off Temple Square, a new building
has a stunning sculpture standing in a shaded alcove where
flowers are planted and a sense of coolness and refuge is created. Such places brighten the soul with escape from the
hot, bright sunlight at 4200-foot elevation in the desert in

summer. Why does the sculpture depict a flight of seagulls? Because a flight of seagulls once gobbled up an infestation of crickets that threatened the crops of the pioneer Mormons. Here is the story, as set out by Apostle Joseph Fielding Smith in his book, *Essentials of Church History*:

PLAGUE OF THE CRICKETS. The season was so far advanced when the pioneers arrived in the summer of 1847 that little resulted from the planting, except to obtain some seed potatoes. Their salvation depended on the success of their crops in 1848. They had built three sawmills in the mountains and one grist mill. Their planted fields consisted of five thousand one hundred and thirty-three acres, of which nearly nine hundred acres were planted in winter wheat. With the aid of irrigation, all things looked favorable, and it appeared that there would be fruitful harvest. The Saints were happy and their prospects were bright. They gave thanks to the Lord and in humility desired to serve him. In the months of May and June they were menaced by a danger as bad as the persecution of mobs. Myriads of crickets came down the mountain sides into the valley, like a vast army marshaled for battle, and began to destroy the fields. From one they would pass to another, and in a few moments leave a field as barren as a desert waste. Something had to be done, or the inhabitants would perish. The community was aroused and every soul entered the unequal conflict. Trenches were dug around the fields and filled with water, in the hope of stopping the ravages of the pest, but without result. Fire was equally unavailing. The attempt was made to beat them back with clubs, brooms and other improvised weapons, but nothing that man could do was able to stop the steady onward march of the voracious crickets. The settlers were helpless before them.

THE MIRACLE OF THE GULLS. When all seemed lost, and the Saints were giving up in despair, the heavens became clouded with gulls, which hovered over the fields, uttering their plaintive scream. Was this a new evil come upon them? Such were the thoughts of some who expected that what the

crickets left the gulls would destroy; but not so, the gulls in
countless battalions descended and began to devour the
crickets, waging a battle for the preservation of the crops.
They ate, they gorged upon the pest, and then flying to the
streams would drink and vomit and again return to the battle
front. This took place day by day until the crickets were destroyed. The people gave thanks, for this was to them a miracle. Surely the Lord was merciful and had sent the gulls as
angels of mercy for their salvation. Since that time, the gull
has been looked upon by the Latter-day Saints almost as a
sacred deliverer. Laws have been passed for the protection
of these birds, and the wanton killing of one would be considered a crime of great magnitude.

(In addition to the sculpture at the office building on
Main Street, another monument commemorates the gulls.
This one is in Temple Square and is the work of Mahonri M.
Young, who was a grandson of Brigham Young. It was
placed in the Temple block in 1913, during the administration
of LDS President Joseph F. Smith, whose son wrote the passages quoted above.)

Much that is Mormon is revealed in the choice of words,
the images used and the thought set out in Apostle Smith's
account of the gulls. There is the desire of the Mormons to
serve God, and their gratitude for his blessings. They work
together, in planting, or in killing crickets and they are happy
—humbly happy, which is an attitude highly prized by the
leaders of the Saints.

Menace appeared suddenly. To demonstrate the magnitude of the danger, it was compared with mobs, for mobs are
the *bête noire* of the Saints' history. Mobs ran them out of
Missouri; mobs murdered Joseph and Hyrum Smith. The
menace of the crickets was met by joint action—and by
God's help. Although they were overwhelmed, they resisted
bravely and with great energy. But they were helpless alone

and survived only because God helped them, another manifestation that the Saints are His chosen ones.

Even as the miracle appeared overhead, ready to occur, the Mormons still feared it was but another of the afflictions to be put upon them. However, instead of being "myriads" or "armies" as were the evil crickets, the good gulls were "countless battalions." In the subconscious of the Mormon, "battalion" is a beneficent word, since it brings up pictures of the Mormon Battalion marching in the "Days of '47" parades, and recalls the history of the actual Mormon Battalion.

The actual Mormon Battalion was enlisted in the U.S. Army in 1846 and was marched west. This was a great financial coup for Brigham Young, for it caused the United States government to take his men west at its expense, and also gave the others in the Mormon party a considerable sum of money from the uniform allowance and advances in pay at enlistment. Of course, these Mormon men had to march across the wilds to the Pacific; those who pay the cost of social and economic advancement are rarely those who reap the benefit. The story, told to all Mormon children, and reiterated annually in the parade, gives a favorable connotation to "battalion."

Thus as one moves about the streets of this bright, clean city between the mountain and the desert, images of the past are reflected constantly in the events and structures of today. There also is a tendency of the people of today to have a personal involvement with the events and passions of the past. One finds this in surprising places, such as a small two-chair barber shop with one barber. The shop displays pictures of Joseph Smith and Emma Smith, his wife, on the wall over the mirrors.

A completely charming man holds forth there. He is James D. Wardle and he is a devout believer in the *Book of Mor-*

mon. He is a devout church member. But his church is the
Reorganized Church of Jesus Christ of Latter Day Saints.
This is a separate fragment of the church started in 1830 by
the Prophet Joseph. This one has headquarters in Independence, Missouri.

The Wardle family have been Reorganized LDS for three
generations—four, when one counts Wardle's children—and
the complexities of life for such a family in Salt Lake City
stagger the imagination. What does one do? How does one
have a social life? Does not the outcast feeling become overwhelming?

Wardle's grandparents were English converts who came
in the 1850s. As he talks of it, the listener can visualize what
happened.

"They were converted to one thing and found something
else here. The doctrines of blood atonement and polygamy
disturbed them. They quit the church and the Avenging
Angels went after them, and they escaped and finally came
back here to live. They became Josephites and we've been
that ever since. I really enjoy needling them."

The "them," even a newcomer to Salt Lake City would
realize, means the LDS Mormons. But what is "blood atonement" and who are the Avenging Angels and Josephites?
And why the picture of Emma Smith? Isn't that unusual?

The Blood Atonement doctrine was based on interpretations of Mormon theology in Brigham Young's time in which
it was argued that some sins were such grievous transgres-
sions of doctrine that they could only be atoned by spilling
the blood of the sinner. Brigham preached sermons in which
he urged the truth of this doctrine. Some observers argue
that today this is the basic reason that Utah retains the op-
tion of death by a firing squad in capital punishment cases.
A Brigham Young sermon is quoted by Professor Thomas
F. O'Dea as explaining the doctrine of Blood Atonement in
these words:

"There are sins that men commit for which they cannot receive forgiveness in this world, or in that which is to come,
and if they had their eyes open to see their true condition,
they would be perfectly willing to have their blood spilt upon
the ground, that the smoke thereof might ascend to heaven
as an offering for their sins."

Wardle, the barber, was saying that his grandparents
didn't think much of this idea. The practice has gone out of
style in Salt Lake City today, as has the idea of the Avenging
Angels who appeared to have existed to help erring Saints get
"their eyes open to see their true condition." Wardle said
that he was told as a boy that when his grandparents decided
to leave the LDS church, they fled and ambushed the Avenging Angels sent to deal with them. There was no shooting,
but the Wardle party warned that there would be the next
time. Eventually, the Wardles were able to come back to
Salt Lake City to live, and to become Josephites.

This is not the place to describe the great schism in Mormon ranks over the introduction of polygamy. But "Brigham-
ites" were the Utah Mormons (and their out-of-state connections) who today are in the majority while "Josephites" were
the non-polygamous faction headed by Joseph Smith III.
He was the son of the Prophet and Emma Smith, and became
president of the Reorganized Church in 1860. Emma Smith
is honored by the Reorganized Church as the only wife of
the Prophet. This is why Wardle had her picture hanging in
his shop alongside the much more familiar picture of the
Prophet.

The seriousness and great danger for his family in those
trying times almost escapes notice as Wardle tells of it. He
is a happy man, continually smiling. He gestures with his
scissors and comb as he talks, looking with his black mustache and steel-rimmed spectacles like a young Groucho
Marx. His mother? The question is like one that Clarence
Darrow might have asked William Jennings Bryan in that

examination in the Scopes trial. Where did a Josephite find
a wife in Salt Lake City?

Well, he explained, his father married a girl reared in a
solid Brighamite family, and she was converted from the LDS
to the Reorganized LDS church. He smiled. His own wife,
Wardle explained, he met in a skating rink and she, too, was
from a Brighamite family. They were married in a civil
service in a private home and she attempted to carry on her
LDS ties in spite of her husband's almost continual nagging
to get her to change. He smiled. When they had been
married five years, she changed to the Reorganized
Church. Their son has been brought up in the Reorganized
Church.

Wardle said—cheerfully, with the constant smile beneath
the startling mustache, waving the shears and comb—that
he had found lifelong entertainment in heckling his religious cousins, the Saints who surround him. He said he felt
he had been fortunate in his profession, for he could run his
own barber shop, and survive on the earnings, while if he
had been employed by someone else in Salt Lake City he believed he would have been required to trim his sails to the
Saints' disapproval of his religious views.

With great happiness he told of the time he got possession
of a book of Temple Recommends. These are the forms
which in a sense are tickets of admission that permit the certified faithful Saints to enter one of their Temples. One must
understand that not just any Mormon can go into a Temple.
One must be recommended for admittance by his bishop,
who is the head of his ward, and by the stake president, who
will be the head of as many as ten wards. They must find
that he has been tithing, has not been smoking, or drinking,
or using tea or coffee or violating any of the other rules by
which the Saints are supposed to live. If the bishop and the
stake president find the Saint worthy, they sign a form called

a "Recommend" and it becomes his admission slip to the Temples.

Since Gentiles are excluded from the Mormon Temples, anti-Mormons keep trying to get in. Wardle, even though he is a devout believer in the Gospel as Restored through Joseph Smith, is considered by the Saints to be a Gentile. He would not be admitted to the Temple, no matter what documents he showed. When he got possession—mysteriously—of the printed set of Recommends he spread them among acquaintances, for Wardle is too well known in Salt Lake City ever to hope to sneak through in a party of the devout.

The Temple rites are too complex to be explained at this point, but it should be understood that they are at the heart of the religion that has been developed in Salt Lake City. The very center of much of the believers' commitment is reiterated symbolically in these ceremonies. A Mormon's visit to the Temple is not like a tourist climbing the Washington monument; it is a religious act, just as the visit to Mecca involves the performance of acts that have great religious significance to the Muslim. Unbelievers are unwelcome in either ceremony.

One of the men who had tried to use the purloined Recommends was in Wardle's shop. He told a little of what had happened. He said "we got part way through and something upset them. I've always thought they were looking for us. When they found us, we were very emphatically invited to leave." Wardle said later that someone in the invading group boasted to his LDS girl friend what was to happen, and she told officials of the church. They were watching carefully in each party of Mormons who passed through for some unusual reaction to ceremonies that the gate crashers had thought they could observe without detection.

Wardle's shop appears to be a center for people who feel oppressed by the heavy concentration of Saints around them.

He said the single Reorganized LDS church in Salt Lake City has about 100 families in it, and that almost all of them are converts from the Utah church, either in this generation or an earlier one as in his case.

Thus even this hotbed of resistance to the LDS domination of the city and state has its roots within the organization that it opposes. This is one of the great powers of the doctrine that was set in motion by Joseph Smith: It can arouse the minds of men.

The long years of desert isolation, and the long hours of discussion of the ins-and-outs of doctrine have also created a tendency to argue and a yearning to talk. This causes interviews with Mormons to take much longer than anticipated. First, sometimes, there is a need to break past the reserve, but when this is done the talk pours out, and the goodwill overwhelms. The Mormons are at heart a kind and gentle people who shy from strangers only because their history tells them that they run great risk of being hurt. Time spent in these conversations with them is always worthwhile.

One summer day I was in Farmington, north of Salt Lake City, trying to see the district attorney, who was not around, when I heard the name of Nephi Taylor. Now this is a name to create questions. The *Book of Mormon* begins with the words, "I, Nephi, having been born of goodly parents . . ." The name is a purely Mormon name. The Taylor family for two generations was among the most important in the church.

When Joseph and Hyrum Smith were murdered in the jail in Carthage, Illinois, a young Mormon also held there was wounded. This was John Taylor, who followed Brigham Young as president of the Saints, and spent almost his entire term of office in flight from the federal authorities who wanted to punish him as a polygamist. He had many wives and children. One of his sons was John W. Taylor, a handsome man whose piercing eyes look out from pictures of the Twelve Apostles of that period.

John W. Taylor was removed from the Council of Twelve Apostles and eventually was expelled from the church in an excommunication proceeding because he refused to stop preaching and urging polygamy. He was instrumental in helping the growth of the polygamist colonies in Mexico where Governor George Romney was born. He died not long after his excommunication, and some Mormon historians hint that he was not really excommunicated. They suggest that a show was staged to satisfy the federal authorities in order to protect the church's relative safety when Utah had achieved statehood.

Nephi Taylor is the son of John W. Taylor and the grandson of John Taylor. He was running an American Oil Company service station on a back road a few miles north of Farmington. It was a neat place, and a lovely brick house stood a few hundred feet away on a knoll where its windows gave a view of the desert stretching toward the Great Salt Lake. This is a country of small farm holdings and of farmers who work hard, go to the meeting house on Sunday, and live the rural form of Mormonism which is far different from life in Salt Lake City. Nephi Taylor had been a ward bishop and a lifelong practicing member of his family's religion. He and his wife sat in a rear corner of the service station building, eating a lunch she had prepared and brought over from their home on the knoll.

What did I want? he asked. Now you don't tell a man: "I want to talk to you because your name tells me you are a historical oddity who could perhaps help me better to understand these people to whom you belong." But I think this is what he understood after we had exchanged a few sentences.

He looked remarkably like the picture of his father. He was a very handsome man in his late fifties, with the same

deep-set and penetrating eyes and chiseled face, tanned by
the sun. His hair was gray, and was cut just long enough to
rest in neat waves on his head. After the beginning in which
he accepted me, he was polite in the short and curt way of
people in the back country and was not offended by my hesitant questions about his family history.

Nephi Taylor said he was born in Colonia Juarez, Mexico.
He did not soon talk about his father's plural wives, but he
was the child of one of them, a girl who grew up in the same
neighborhood where he now runs a service station. She
brought him back there when his father died, and it was
there that he grew up and met his wife and married to settle
and rear a family with her. Thus he has lived in a monogamous marriage which was a style last practiced in his family
line in the early nineteenth century. They have four children: A doctor of philosophy who teaches at Utah State University at Logan, a representative for a publishing house,
a daughter married to a holder of a doctorate in engineering,
and a third son who was on a Mormon mission to England.

As he finished his dinner, he asked me to go for a ride with
him. He took his car and we drove into Farmington, a small
county seat town. He turned down a back street where the
irrigation ditch ran full of clear, cool water and the tree
branches shaded the wide street. He drove into a drive-
way and went to the door where a woman gave him the keys
to her car. We drove back to the service station in it. He
drove it directly onto the hoist and continued to talk with
me as he started to service it. His conversation was broken
when his sleeve was poured full of warm engine oil as he
drained the crankcase. He made no complaint of this. But
he remarked on it.

He impressed me as a fine man, a kind and courteous gen-
tleman. His horizon seemed to be the church, his wife, his
children and his service station.

He said he was eight years old when his father died. He

had two sisters younger, one sister and a brother older. When his mother brought them back to her home near Farmington, there was no resentment of their polygamous background that he could remember. His mother's father was an English convert to Mormonism who had crossed the continent in a handcart company in the 1850s and had not resented his daughter's marriage to John W. Taylor.

This farm girl was one of six wives of the handsome young church leader. She bore five children, and the other five wives had a total of 31. One of the other wives' sons, Samuel W. Taylor, was the author of a book about the family called *Family Kingdom*.

What was Nephi Taylor's feeling about the treatment given to his father by the church? Did he feel it was proper to have his father removed as an apostle for having ignored the order against taking more plural wives? He began by saying, "I don't know how much I'm supposed to tell you."

"I can't say that my father was ever disfellowshipped," he said, using the Mormon euphemism for excommunicated. "He brought up his family to be within the church."

Perhaps the historians are right who suspect that John W. Taylor never left his church, but was made an example to satisfy the United States Senate committee that was trying to decide whether Reed Smoot, a Mormon apostle, was fit to serve in the Senate.

Fragments of history like Nephi Taylor and James D. Wardle abound in Utah. They pop up at unexpected places. Theological arguments turn up strangely, too. One day at lunch, in a dining room at the University of Utah, a conversation turned suddenly from community betterment work to polygamy.

Within moments this man was trotting out the "Josephite" arguments that Joseph Smith never really expounded the polygamy doctrine, that actually it was an invention of Brigham Young and some of the other leaders of those early days who wanted to have several wives. It turned out that he, like Wardle, was brought up in the Reorganized LDS church.

This argument shocks the senses as one sits in that glass-walled room and looks out at the city from the other view, from the east, toward the desert and the gradually shrinking Great Salt Lake. One of the remarkable pleasures in looking at this beautiful city is to realize that it is built because of the belief in the visions and statements of Joseph Smith.

But if one of the main reasons that the city was built was a reason falsely ascribed to the Prophet Joseph, a new and entirely foreign element is thrown into the historical equations. It was assumed that the Mormons came to the desert to hide to practice polygamy and to get away from persecutions elsewhere. It was assumed that they had polygamy because they believed God ordered them to do so, issuing the order through Joseph Smith. The revelation, dated July 12, 1843, says in its first paragraph:

> Verily, thus saith the Lord unto you my servant Joseph, that inasmuch as you have inquired of my hand to know and understand wherein I, the Lord, justified my servants Abraham, Isaac, and Jacob, as also Moses, David and Solomon, my servants, as touching the principle and doctrine of their having many wives and concubines—

If this didn't come from the Prophet, where did it come from?

The answer that the Reorganized LDS church gives, and all the others who believe the *Book of Mormon* but disbelieve that God ordered polygamy, is that it came from Brigham Young. He just wanted to have polygamy, the luncheon companion argued, and they blamed it on the dead prophet, claiming that he set down the revelation secretly before he was murdered. Joseph died in 1844; polygamy was announced publicly in 1852.

The argument has been largely discredited by historians. But it shocked the mind to sit and think—as the eye moved over the city—that all of this might have been built by a dedicated people who were swindled by Brigham Young. And when that thought was discarded as entertaining but false, it was equally provoking to realize that the argument could be made seriously now, long years after it had lost any real meaning.

At about that point my friend was using the argument that Joseph Smith's legal wife, Emma, had borne several children and that the prophet was a sexually potent male—"why, she was even pregnant when he was killed. Yet, there is no record of any children by him born to any of the plural wives they talk about." (In her book, Mrs. Brodie had a picture of a man she suggested was the child of Joseph and a plural wife.)

And what of Brigham Young? No historian seriously questions but that it was the personal force and shrewd management of this one-time glazier that kept the biggest piece of the shattered religious organization alive after Joseph Smith was killed. It was Young who was the force that moved the major fragment to Utah and led it for another three decades until it was firmly established on its present course when he died. When Brigham was gone, the church could waver and shift its positions, but it was firmly committed to the fundamentals of social doctrine that have sustained it—close control, unity of effort, singlemindedness about the absolute necessity of living a life in and for the church.

His footprints are all over Salt Lake City, with a monument here, a former home there, and his name on the old land plats on display in the museums. But not much is made of his grave, which is located in a small family cemetery about halfway up the hill where the state capitol stands. This plot of ground is about one building lot in size, with a few trees on it. There is a well-tended lawn, and the whole is surrounded by a decorative cast iron fence. Within the fence is another smaller plot, fenced also, and this is the grave of Brigham Young and some of his wives. There is a dusty parking lot on one side of this shaded yard, and a stately old home on the other. There is no marking, no indication beyond the legends on the headstones that the great figure of the Utah church lies buried here.

The front gate is locked, and sometimes people come there and shake it, incredulous that the grave site of this great figure is not open to inspection. But the gate is locked and while visitors are not excluded totally, neither is it made easy for them to see the grave of Brigham Young.

The contrast between this and the fuss that is made over the Beehive House heightens the impression. The Beehive House—named for the beehive-shaped cupola on its top—was the official residence for the pioneer president of the LDS church who also was the federally appointed governor of the territory of Deseret until the government decided it needed a Gentile in the job. ("Deseret" is a Mormon word meaning "honey-bee"—thus the beehive symbol.) Brigham lived in the house from 1854 until his death in 1877. It was restored by the church in 1961 and has become a favorite tourist attraction.

Pleasant Mormon ladies lead tours, showing the motley crews of tourists the wonders of Brigham's life. However, they avoid discussion of the plural marriages, if they can. They speak of the children who lived in the house and of the social functions that went on there. But no one speaks of a passageway to the Lion House, next door, where other of the church president's families lived, nor of the long-gone strange house that stood across the street. This was Amelia's Palace, a grotesque looking house built for Amelia Folsom Young in the 1870s when she was Brigham's favorite. He died before it was completed. The thing looked remarkably like the ornate wooden carvings of the great organ in the Tabernacle in Temple Square.

The Mormon ladies take the tourists through and tell them all the good things about Brigham. But they do not mention that he is buried on the hill a block away. The best supposition that I've heard to explain the lack of interest in promoting the grave as a tourist attraction is that only a few of his wives are buried there with him. The church today would just as soon not talk about plural marriage, anyway, and how is it to explain all the situations that the grave reminds tourists to ask questions about? Then there are descendants of President Young by wives not buried with him. How to deal with their probable requests that their grandmother's body be exhumed and placed with their grandfather, if the grave is to become a place much visited by outsiders. So in all probability no action will be taken to glorify the little graveyard.

Thus in that beautiful City of the Saints the Mormons have things they show off proudly and things they would just as soon no one saw, and things they don't want to talk about at all. This also is the home of the proudest and most widely known institution that the church controls, the Mormon Tabernacle Choir. This has been a staple of Sunday mornings on the CBS radio network, and is beginning to move into the television stations that the church controls. This was the way the choir looked for one particular radio broadcast:

It was a summer morning, about 8:15 A.M., and the crowds were pouring across the street and into the old Tabernacle in Temple Square. An overnight storm had not completely gone, but the air was clean and fresh, befitting a new year in the long chain of years since Brigham picked this site. The "Days of '47" parade had taken place the day before, marking the anniversary of settlement.

A group of Negro women crossed into the Temple grounds

from their hotel, their faces curious and at the same time defiant as they entered the holy place of a religious belief that denied them and their race equality at the altar.

Ushers, usually older men, stood at the doors and around the inside of the Tabernacle. They watched with experienced eye as the crowd poured in. At the west end of the building, a door was marked "Choir Members Only," and another was marked "General Authorities" for the top LDS leaders. The choir members passed through a room full of racks for stored music and out through velvet drapes to a great stage dominated by the ornate organ.

The women in black skirts and white shirtwaists were on the audience's left, and the men in dark suits and white shirts and dark bow ties were on the right. A balding man with a fringe of gray hair was at the organ—Alexander Schreiner. The choir director, Richard P. Condie, had his coat off and led the choir through a warm-up. At the left of the stage was a radio-TV control booth, which showed the picture carried by television to those close enough to see the picture on the monitor screen. There were three TV cameras in the Tabernacle, something symbolic of the change in religion and life since that day of July 24, 1847, when the first group arrived in the desert.

A few minutes before air time, the choir members were excused, to be summoned back by notes of the organ. A man named Richard Evans moved onto the platform. He is a former radio announcer who has worked with the choir since it became a network staple on Sundays. He has been one of the Apostles since 1953. He spoke briefly to the audience, warning of the sensitivity of the Tabernacle's marvelous acoustics, and then stood by the organ with his watch in hand.

On the second that the broadcast opened, he cued Condie, the choir director, then read his opening lines identifying the program, and sat down. Evans checked details by phone, busied himself with papers, and listened prayerfully as the choir sang "Columbia, The Gem of the Ocean." (After the broadcast, the choir was rehearsing this song again and again.)

As the song ended, Apostle Evans went to the microphone to call for a George Frederick Handel overture "by the organ in Temple Square."

When the choir sings, one is struck by the fact that the faces are of middle-class America. There are no beards or mustaches or strange haircuts among the men, although the women have a variety of the currently acceptable hair fashions. There are no Negroes.

The standard TV shot was from the camera in the rear of the Tabernacle. It covered all the dais—the choir, director and the old organ which dominates it all. The cut shots were to the organist, the director, and side views of the ranks of singers. They did not go to Apostle Evans until he read the message of the broadcast. This avoided giving him the appearance of being the star, which he does not want.

After the second song, on came the Apostle, with his rich, deep voice riding the low organ notes with the "spoken word." He wore dark-rimmed glasses and leaned into the microphone, holding his script beyond the microphone and out of camera range—a professional performance by a professional.

The "spoken word" that day was in praise of "the simple things, the routine, the in-between times" that separate the moments of great excitement in life. It was comforting, bland, absolutely inoffensive but somehow reassuring. It had more to do with the placidity of Mahatma Gandhi than with the near brutal personal force of Brigham Young who caused that Tabernacle to be built and whose voice once roared through it.

As Apostle Evans finished, he sat down again, and the organ filled a few moments and the choir began to sing. Evans went back to the microphone, watch in hand, and as the organ filled the seconds he began to read the close-out—"in the shadows of the everlasting hills . . . may peace be with you always . . . from the crossroads of the West . . . The Tabernacle in Temple Square."

Then the broadcast was over and the choir had to answer to Director Condie for its musical sins, and the visitors moved out into the square where Mormon priests stood ready to lead them on tours of the grounds. It was Sunday morning in a new year.

Of late, every year has been better for the Mormons than the last, and they expect that the next will keep up the pattern. The religion has provided a total way of life for its people and they have carried it to the ends of the earth.

So few Americans recognize what is being carried. They know so little about those dynamic, forceful, successful and peculiar people who are becoming so important in American life.

II

The Angel Moroni,
the Farm Boy, and the Book

ONE OF THE sparkling intellectual pleasures of visiting Salt
Lake City is to sit in a room high on the west side of the Hotel
Utah, overlooking Temple Square, and read the histories of
the religion founded by Joseph Smith, Jr. There before
one's eyes, is the Temple that is the central place of this vital
organization. The city stretches around it. In a corner of the
grounds is a marker from which property survey lines for this
section of the West are marked. The Church of Jesus Christ
of Latter-day Saints owns this hotel. In the basement,
near the coffee shop, is a room designated by a red neon sign:
"Mission Room." This is not a nightclub, or a bar, or even a
restaurant. It is the room where young men and women
who are ready to travel as Mormon missionaries around the
world go for their meals in the few days they spend seeing
the sights and holy places in Salt Lake City. Then they go
forth with their emotions peaked to fulfill the proselyting
obligations of their religion.

In the center of the street intersection below a group of
statuary commemorates the arrival here of the first immigrants; on the top spire of the old Temple stands a gilded
statue with a trumpet to its lips. This is the Angel Moroni,
a central supernatural figure in the story of Joseph Smith, Jr.
and the Gold Plates. It was Moroni who led the young
man to the place where the plates were hidden and who

tested him and instructed him. The Mormons believe that Moroni was the last in the long line of historians who produced the narrative which the Prophet Joseph translated from the Gold Plates.

It is charming and stimulating to the imagination to sit surrounded thus by the strength of the religion that the Prophet founded while reading his account of the first meeting with Moroni. An account published by the church as the prophet's own words describes his praying in his room in his father's home in Palmyra, New York, on September 21, 1823. He was then seventeen years old.

A portion of that account:

> While I was thus in the act of calling upon God, I discovered a light appearing in my room, which continued to increase until the room was lighter than at noonday, when immediately a personage appeared at my bedside, standing in the air, for his feet did not touch the floor.
>
> He had on a loose robe of most exquisite whiteness. It was a whiteness beyond anything earthly I had ever seen, nor do I believe that any earthly thing could be made to appear so exceedingly white and brilliant. His hands were naked, and his arms also, a little above the wrists, so, also, were his feet naked, as were his legs, a little above the ankles. His head and neck were bare. I could discover that he had no other clothing on but this robe, as it was open so that I could see into his bosom.
>
> Not only was his robe exceedingly white, but his whole person was glorious beyond description, and his countenance truly like lightning. The room was exceedingly light, but not so very bright as immediately around his person. When I first looked upon him I was afraid, but the fear soon left me.
>
> He called me by name, and said unto me that he was a messenger sent from the presence of God to me, and that his name was Moroni; that God had a work for me to do; and that my name should be had for good and evil among all

nations, kindreds and tongues, or that it should be both good and evil spoken of among all people.

He said there was a book deposited, written upon gold plates, giving an account of the former inhabitants of this continent, and the source from whence they sprang. He also said that the fulness of the everlasting Gospel was contained in it; as delivered by the Savior to the ancient inhabitants.

Also, that there were two stones in silver bows—and these stones, fastened to a breastplate, constituted what is called the Urim and Thummim—deposited with the plates; and the possession and use of these stones were what constituted "seers" in ancient or former times; and that God had prepared them for the purpose of translating the book.

Moroni talked further to the boy who then was able to watch as the angel went "right up into heaven." That night Moroni came back twice. The next day Joseph saw him again, and as directed went to the hill now called Cumorah and designated as a sacred place by the Mormons. He found the plates stored under a flat rock in a stone box, but did not try to bring them away. He was told that for four years he would be tested. He was to return each year to Cumorah. He did so.

On January 18, 1827, when he had just turned twenty-one, Joseph was married to Emma Hale. On September 22 of that year he received the plates and translated the *Book of Mormon* from them in the following years. He had the assistance of several intimates who copied the words as he dictated them from the divinely inspired visions he received.

There were many problems for the young man in this time. He began to receive revelations to help him meet them. For example, his first assistant in the translation was Martin Harris, who managed to lose the first 116 pages of manuscript. A revelation in the summer of 1828 warned Joseph that wicked men had acquired this manuscript, had made

alterations in it, and were just waiting for him to retranslate
the plates. Then they would use the altered manuscript to
show that there were variations so as to question Joseph's
divine inspiration.

The revelation showed Joseph a way out of this trap. He
said that God advised him thus:

> And now, verily I say unto you, that an account of those
> things that you have written, which have gone out of your
> hands, is engraven upon the plates of Nephi;
>
> Yea, and you remember it was said in those writings that
> a more particular account was given of these things upon
> the plates of Nephi.
>
> And now, because the account which is engraven upon the
> plates of Nephi is more particular concerning the things
> which, in my wisdom, I would bring to the knowledge of
> the people in this account—
>
> Therefore, you shall translate the engravings which are
> on the plates of Nephi, down even till you come to the reign
> of King Benjamin, or until you come to that which you have
> translated, which you have retained;
>
> And behold, you shall publish it as the record of Nephi;
> and thus I will confound those who have altered my words.
>
> I will not suffer that they shall destroy my work; yea, I
> will show unto them that my wisdom is greater than the
> cunning of the devil.
>
> Behold, they have only got a part, or an abridgment of
> the account of Nephi.

So the preparation of the *Book of Mormon* began again,
this time with the words, "I, Nephi . . ." Oliver Cowdery, a
school teacher, became the chief scribe. The book was finished in 1829 and the manuscript turned over to a printer
in Palmyra, New York, to produce 5000 copies. (One of
these came into the hands of a glazier named Brigham
Young; the effects of this were beyond calculation.)

When the plates were translated, the Angel Moroni took
them back, the Prophet Joseph said in 1838. But before

they were taken away, Joseph showed them to eleven people in two groups. First, they were shown to Oliver Cowdery, Martin Harris and David Whitmer. Then they were shown to Christian Whitmer, Jacob Whitmer, Peter Whitmer, Jr., John Whitmer, Hiram Page, Joseph Smith, Sr., Hyrum Smith and Samuel H. Smith.

By this time Joseph was living with the Whitmer family, in which Hiram Page was a brother-in-law. Thus the witnesses to the *Book of Mormon* were members of the Whitmer family, members of the Prophet's family, and his two associates in the production of the book, Oliver Cowdery and Martin Harris.

Two statements from these witnesses are printed in the beginning of the editions of the *Book of Mormon* circulated by the Saints. The statement signed by Cowdery, Whitmer and Harris is this:

Be it known unto all nations, kindreds, tongues, and people, unto whom this work shall come: That we, through the grace of God the Father, and our Lord Jesus Christ, have seen the plates which contain this record, which is a record of the people of Nephi, and also of the Lamanites, their brethren, and also of the people of Jared, who came from the tower of which hath been spoken; and we also know that they have been translated by the gift and power of God, for his voice hath declared it unto us; wherefore we know of a surety, that the work is true. And we also testify that we have seen the engravings which are upon the plates; and they have been shown unto us by the power of God, and not of man. And we declare with words of soberness, that an angel of God came down from heaven, and he brought and laid before our eyes, that we beheld and saw the plates, and the engravings thereon; and we know that it is by the grace of God the Father, and our Lord Jesus Christ, that we beheld and bear record that these things are true. And it is marvelous in our eyes. Nevertheless, the voice of the Lord commanded us that we should bear record of it; wherefore, to be obedient unto the commandments of God, we bear testimony of these things. And we know that if we are faithful in Christ, we shall rid our garments of the blood of all men, and be found spotless before the judgment-seat of Christ, and shall dwell with him eternally in the heavens. And the honor be to the Father, and to the Son, and to the Holy Ghost, which is one God. Amen.

That is called among Mormons "The Testimony of Three Witnesses." The other statement is headed "And Also the Testimony of Eight Witnesses." It is signed by the Smiths, the other Whitmers and Page. Their statement is as follows:

Be it known unto all nations, kindreds, tongues, and people, unto whom this work shall come, that Joseph Smith Jr., the translator of this work, has shewn unto us the plates of which hath been spoken, which have the appearance of gold; and as many of the leaves as the said Smith has translated, we did handle with our hands; and we also saw the engravings thereon, all of which has the appearance of ancient work, and of curious workmanship. And this we bear record with for we have seen and hefted, and know of a surety, that the said Smith has got the plates of which we have spoken. And we give our names unto the world, to witness unto the world that which we have seen; and we lie not, God bearing witness of it.

One of the worrisome details of this part of the narrative of Joseph Smith has been that Oliver Cowdery and Martin Harris and David Whitmer all dropped away from the church in the 1830s. In fact, by the late 1830s, only the members of the Smith family among the witnesses to the existence of the Gold Plates still remained in the church. But the Mormons point to statements by the witnesses in later years reiterating their belief in the truth of the Prophet Joseph's story, and to the fact that both Cowdery and Harris rejoined the church late in life.

However, these problems of apostasy in the early church

have little significance in our understanding of what it has become today. What does it matter whether Oliver Cowdery dropped away over the question of whether he should sell his property or turn it over to the church? Or whether he returned to the church and was headed for Salt Lake City in 1850 when he died? Or that he lamented leaving the place of honor that would have been his?

The religion of the Saints is like all others in at least one regard: It requires faith. It requires that the believer put away questions and accept in faith the answers given to him; otherwise, he is not a believer and has no faith. A Saint believes that Joseph Smith's story of the Golden Plates is true.

It is not the purpose here to disagree with Mormon doctrine, nor to puncture holes in the story of Joseph Smith and the Gold Plates. Many books have been written on all sides of those questions. Each of them makes someone happy and someone sad, but convinces very few. The hope is to convey an understanding of what the Saints believe, in support of the theory that this religious belief is what makes their particular brand of civilization different. That difference is what this book seeks to explore. For the Saints exist, whether or not Joseph Smith was a false prohpet. They have evolved a very complicated religion on the teachings that he gave them. It amounts to a complete way of life. All of the turnings of this theology are far too complicated for exploration here. The most we can achieve is to understand some of the fundamentals and the reasons for certain unusual aspects of Mormon life—unusual that is, when judged by the standards of the ordinary American.

The Saints have a "revealed religion," which means that it was unveiled to a leader, Joseph Smith, and did not evolve over long centuries as a mixture of custom and doctrine. In a sense it is a religion with a limited hierarchy, although we shall see that it has a strong authoritarian control on its members. It is a religious practice full of discriminations—against Negroes, against women, against backsliders, against heretics, against apostates, against so many things.

It is a difficult religion to live. One cannot smoke or drink alcohol or coffee or tea. He must give 10 per cent of his gross income to the bishop of his ward, and must meet many other financial demands. He must be ready to do any job that his bishop or stake president or the general authorities of the church ask him to do. As an example: A man was well-situated in his profession in Boston, where his future was assured in a comfortable and interesting position. The church has a business in Salt Lake City which it operates in his professional field. He was "asked" to come back to Salt Lake City to assume direction of the church-owned business. He came.

One underlying belief of the Saints is this: They are now living a mortal existence which was preceded by an existence in the spirit world and which will be followed by life in the spirit world. During this mortal life, a person may be able to improve his status in the spirit world, or he may be able to worsen it. Where some Christian sects have a doctrine of pre-ordination, i.e., that all the events of a person's life are established in Heaven before his birth, the Mormons have a doctrine of "free agency." They hold that a soul in its mortal existence is continually confronted with choices and that it is completely free to pick among the alternatives. Thus the mortal has a chance to better his soul in the spirit world, to enhance his exaltation in the Celestial Kingdom which follows life on earth.

A certain broad code of conduct is set out to govern the Saint in his mortal existence. The sum of this is that he must always strive for betterment.

"Every Mormon who went to church yesterday is struggling for upward reach," said a scholar who was reared as a Saint.

"Wo be unto him that is at ease in Zion!" warns the *Book of Mormon*.

Discussion of what these people believe must always be weighted with the understanding that, as in other religious groups, there is a wide variation. For example, two Mormons were asked if those souls in pre-mortal existence could have more than one life on earth—could they expect to inhabit two or more different bodies at different periods in time? One man said he didn't know, that he had never thought about it, while the other shook his head wisely and said there was no more than one mortal existence per soul.

It also must be remembered that the Prophet Joseph lived just fourteen years after he formed the church. He established it in 1830; he was shot to death in 1844 in a jail in Carthage, Illinois. In the interval, doctrine was just whatever revelation told him that it was. But much of the doctrine has been worked out in detail by his successors in the leadership of Zion. The most graphic illustration of this is the large number of *Book of Mormon* religious groups— one expert said they numbered seventy-four identifiable fragments. All of these have formed since the murder of the Prophet, and all have significant differences in doctrine, while each insists that its interpretation is the only one properly drawn from the Prophet's writings and revelations.

One student argues that there really were three different churches at different times during Joseph Smith's life. James D. Wardle, the Salt Lake City barber who is a member of one of the more important offshoots, the Reorganized LDS church, holds this position. Wardle said that in the early days, the church was made up of independent branches around upstate New York and in Ohio. This ended, he said, with the establishment of the authoritarian control of the central church at Kirtland, Ohio, and the attempt to relocate in the frontier region of western Missouri. The third phase was the politically oriented church which built a city at

Nauvoo, Illinois, where Joseph Smith established the Nauvoo Legion and called himself Lieutenant General Smith. Wardle said he believes that the Reorganized Church, with headquarters at Independence, Missouri, is an extension of the second period, while the Salt Lake City church is an extension of the third.

Joseph Smith had intended that his church would establish Zion in the western reaches of Missouri, in those days the frontier. He picked a site for a great temple while on a visit to Independence, Missouri. That part of Missouri has many historic Mormon sites. The country was described by John D. Lee in a book written while he was waiting to be shot for his part in a massacre of gentile travelers in Utah. Lee was one of Joseph Smith's close followers, and described the theological basis as he understood it for the selection of the area north and west of what is now Kansas City. He wrote:

> Adam-ondi-Ahman was at the point where Adam came and settled and blest his posterity after being driven from the Garden of Eden. This was revealed to the people through Joseph Smith, the Prophet. The Temple Block in Jackson County, Missouri, stands on the identical spot where once stood the Garden of Eden. When Adam and Eve were driven from the Garden they traveled in a northwesterly course until they came to a valley on the east side of Grand River. There they tarried for several years, and engaged in tilling the soil.

There were 63.43 acres in the original Temple Lot picked out by Joseph Smith. But he and his followers were driven away from the area before they got around to buying the land. They fought a series of pitched battles with the gentiles on the frontier, using everything from white oak staves to guns. Eventually, the property was acquired and its ownership has been in contention among the inheritors of the Prophet's church since. The Utah Mormons own about

40 per cent of it, and the Reorganized LDS church owns another similar amount, including the site of their Auditorium where their headquarters is located.

But the place where Joseph Smith stood when he dedicated this as the future site of his Temple is in the hands of the Church of Christ Temple Lot which was organized by Granville Hedrick, an early Mormon who quit and started a new branch in 1859. He was joined by others who objected to changes in doctrine they believed had been made in the years since Joseph's murder. The Hedrickite branch of Mormonism has about 3000 members and only a handful of churches. Ownership of the site was the object of a suit many years ago which has been widely read as *The Temple Lot Case* because of the vast amount of testimony it gives about the conflicting views of the fragments of Joseph's church. However, that ownership remains today in the hands of the Hedrickites. The Utah Mormons have no structures in the Temple Site tract, although they have a complex of buildings nearby from which they operate a mission.

One of the parlor games for non-Mormon historians of the Saints has been to try to guess what direction the church would have taken had Joseph not been killed. The Mormons went to Illinois, after disaster overtook them in Missouri. One theory is that this conflict came from Joseph's antislavery statements; another theory is that the Missourians feared economic and political destruction from the well-knit Mormon organization. One of the fights John D. Lee described was over the Mormon insistence on voting.

(In Montana in the 1960s, the communal religious colonies of the Hutterian Brethren have been the targets of animosities based on the fear that they will bring economic disaster to the small towns where they exist.)

After pitched battles with the Missourians, the main Mormon settlement went back across the state to Illinois, leaving Joseph and some of the others in jail in Liberty. They

escaped in 1839 to join the main body in Illinois. The legislature gave the Mormons a charter for a city, which they
called Nauvoo. For five years the Prophet Joseph held
forth there, growing more and more powerful. He was a
friend of Stephen A. Douglas and other leading citizens and
politicians. His religious following grew constantly from the
influx of new converts from the eastern United States and
from Europe.

It was during the early 1840s that polygamy began secretly
in high Mormon circles. At the same time, Joseph was incurring the anger of some of his financially ambitious followers by demanding that their aims be subordinated to his
plans for the church-controlled community of Nauvoo.

One of his critics was William Law, a Canadian who had
been an important figure in the church in Nauvoo before he
broke with the Prophet. The break, according to John D.
Lee as well as to some modern historians, was over the attempt by Joseph to seduce Mrs. Law to be one of his plural
wives. Law and others in Nauvoo were thoroughly disen-
chanted with Joseph, although Law looked upon him as a
fallen prophet, not a false prophet. Law still subscribed to
the religious doctrine which Joseph presented through the
Book of Mormon and revelations.

Law started a paper, the Nauvoo *Expositor*. It began to
tell the mass of unknowing Saints that their leaders were
practicing polygamy. Law and his associates also intended
to attack the Mormon prophet's establishment on other
grounds.

The Prophet Joseph called together his captive city council in Nauvoo. It was decided that the Nauvoo *Expositor*
was libelous and that the press should be destroyed. The
Mormon armed guard, the Nauvoo Legion, wrecked the
press, pied the type and burned every issue of the paper
that could be found. This was the act that signaled the end
of the peaceful Mormon interlude in Nauvoo. The apostates

who owned the paper immediately fanned up anti-Mormon feeling in Illinois. Joseph was told to surrender himself for trial, but he and Hyrum ran, crossing the flooded Mississippi in a rowboat. He reconsidered and they returned to surrender on June 24, 1844. They were held to trial on a charge of riot.

On June 27 a group of militia, Mormon haters to the last man, came into the jail and murdered Joseph and Hyrum Smith. The brothers were not precisely defenseless. Arms had been smuggled into the jail. Joseph fired a six-shooter into the mob, as its members fired back. First Hyrum was killed. He had a single shot pistol, which did no damage, but Joseph's shots wounded some of the murderous mob. Joseph was wounded. John Taylor and Willard Richards, both apostles, were also in the cell. Taylor, who was to become LDS president in 1880 and spend his declining years in flight from federal officers, was wounded, hit five times. Richards was grazed by a rifle ball, but was not seriously hurt.

The Prophet jumped to a window where he was hit by another rifle ball. He fell to the ground outside and was dragged so his back rested against a well curb. A colonel of the militia ordered four men to fire, and Joseph Smith was dead. Richards carried the body back into the jail, placing it beside Hyrum's body.

The initial phase of the history of the Saints was at an end. But the religion that he had started was so compelling, so strong, so vigorous that it has outlived Joseph Smith and has become a far more powerful agency in the lives of men than it was in his day.

With the leader gone and anti-Mormon forces gathering, the splintering away began, for the Mormons were not able to remain in Nauvoo. (One family which did was that of the Widow Emma Smith, who gave birth to the Prophet's fourth son, David, after the murder. She later married Major Lewis

Bidamon and reared Joseph Smith III to become the president of the anti-polygamous Reorganized LDS church. On her deathbed she still insisted she was Joseph's only wife and that the polygamy doctrine was a slander on his memory. It is strange to imagine her and her sons living out those years in the ruins of Nauvoo, seeing frequently the ruins of the great Temple that was built there and was burned by vandals after the Mormon Exodus.)

When Joseph and Hyrum were murdered, Brigham Young was the president of the Quorum of the Twelve Apostles. Sidney Rigdon, a former Disciples of Christ minister who had followed Joseph for many years, attempted to take over, but instead, it was voted that the Quorum of the Twelve would run the church. This was in August, 1844, and Brigham Young did not become president of the Church of Jesus Christ of Latter-day Saints until December 5, 1847, by which time he had established the pioneer colony on the edge of the Great Salt Lake.

In the interval, Rigdon had established a church of his own, which eventually fell under the direction of William Bickerton, a convert of Rigdon's. As the "Bickertonites," this group has grown until it has numerous churches in Pennsylvania, Ohio, Colorado and Michigan. It has had its greatest success among Italians reared as Roman Catholics. The *Book of Mormon* was translated into Italian to help in this effort.

A strange man named James J. Strang also arose out of the wreckage of those days. Strang had been in the church a few months before Joseph was killed, but he set up his own church for the "Strangites" on Beaver Island in Lake Michigan. He had himself crowned king in 1850, and served in the Michigan legislature. An enemy killed him in 1856.

There were other groups, but the two important ones were the LDS members who went with Brigham Young to the desert of the isolated West, and the Reorganization that stayed in Illinois with Joseph Smith III as president. This latter was a consolidation of the more conservative elements of the old Nauvoo church: It differed from the strange organization led by Brigham Young in the wilderness. Joseph III resisted polygamy, and established a church which today can fit comfortably into a community as easily as any of the other Protestant groups. He lived until 1914 and was succeeded in turn by his three sons—Dr. Frederick M. Smith, Israel A. Smith and W. Wallace Smith. All of the wildly different economic and social ideas that raged around Nauvoo were transplanted to Salt Lake City.

The Reorganized Church, in short, was the *Book of Mormon* without Brigham Young.

This examination is of the Utah church, and reference is made to other Mormon groups occasionally to make clear the inter-relationship of them all. One of these comparisons has fascinated me since I was able to talk to each of the men involved.

Today, W. Wallace Smith is the president of the Reorganized Church. He is a tall, kindly, hesitant man who talked gently in his office, totally without cant and even with an appearance of unease to questions about some aspects of his grandfather's theology and life. He was able to muster the introspection to describe what it was like to grow up as the grandson of the Prophet. He felt that it had left its mark on his personality, he said. Perhaps he had resisted too hard the pressure to be a leader in his family's church. But eventually he took the position of president as an inherited obligation. For many years while his father and his older brothers led the church, this man ran a hardware business. He seemed to remember those years fondly.

By contrast, Joseph Fielding Smith is the president of the Quorum of Twelve Apostles of the Utah church. He is the grandson of Hyrum Smith and is the official historian of his church. His personality is totally unlike that of his cousin. Joseph Fielding Smith is a completely assured man who has spent almost all of his adult life as an apostle of the church. His father, Joseph F. Smith, was born at Far West, Missouri, in the years when the Mormons thought they were at the Garden of Eden, and grew up to be the sixth president of the church. Joseph Fielding Smith expects to be the tenth president. To even ask him if he felt some difference from his fellows because of his lineage would be unthinkable. Would one ask this question of the Duke of Windsor?

Yet these are the grandsons of the brothers who died together at the jail at Carthage, Illinois.

The main party of the Nauvoo refugees ended up with Brigham Young, who took them to Nebraska where they spent the winter of 1847-48, moving on into the new colony at Salt Lake City on the heels of the first party.

By now Brigham was in control. He set about assigning jobs to his members, getting the irrigation ditches built, the town staked out, the Temple grounds bounded, and inaugurating the iron discipline on tithing and other of the necessities through which he was to build his colony. Civilization was 1100 miles to the east or 750 miles to the west. It was in the isolation of this wild and remote area of North America that the Mormons were to grow and prosper and become a strong people.

What was life like for the early Utah Mormons? Whole shelves of books have been written to answer that question. The essence of them, it seems to me, was that these people were willing to allow Brigham and his colleagues at the top of the church to tell them how they were to live, even down to whether or not they had to have plural wives, and where they were to settle, and what they were to grow, and what they were to do with it.

The matter of tithing occupied much of Brigham's thoughts. The land where the Hotel Utah now stands once was the Tithing Office. To it the Mormon elders were ex-

pected to come with their tithes—one tenth of all their income. Of course, Brigham found fault with what they did.
He was preaching once in the Bowery, which was a forerun-
ner of the Tabernacle in Temple Square, for the Tabernacle
was not completed until 1867. This passage was spoken in
1855, and described how he felt toward some cattle and
horses given as tithing payments:

"'Some were disposed to do right with their surplus property, and once in a while you would find a man who had a
cow that would kick a person's hat off, or eyes out, or the
wolves had eaten off her teats. You would once in a while
find a man who had a horse that he considered surplus, but
at the same time he had the ringbone, was broken-winded,
spavined in both legs, and had the pole evil at one end of
the neck and a fistula at the other, and both knees sprung."

In those early years, the Saints lived free of the corrupting
influence of the gentile world, too, and it was a difficult thing
for an outsider to get to Salt Lake City, although he usually
was treated gently when he arrived. One who made that
journey was Richard Francis Burton, the nineteenth-century English adventurer and seeker after the bizarre. He
said he went there because it was the capital of a religious
sect; but Burton spent much of his life collecting accounts
of strange sexual practices, and this would lead to the strong
suspicion that he was attracted to Salt Lake City by the
knowledge that the Mormons practiced polygamy. He left
St. Joseph, Missouri, August 7, 1860. He was nineteen days
in transit, covering more than 1136 miles, he estimated.

Burton spent twenty-four days in Salt Lake City. If his
aim was to find out about the sexual practices of the Mormons, he failed. He saw the town, described it in detail,
and gave some wrong dates here and there, as well as other
misinformation. He described the Endowment House
which then stood in Temple Square to serve as the site of the
high religious rites now performed in the Temples. Construc-

tion was well along on the Salt Lake City Temple. He
spoke of Brigham's domestic establishment, and of the control exercised over the town. Burton also described the
"Days of '47" celebration—even in 1860 a fixture. A favorite
toast, he said, was "we can rock the cradle of Liberty without Uncle Sam to help us." They had tried to become the
State of Deseret and had been rebuffed. Burton also made a
fool of himself with a prophecy, noting that "perhaps New
Zion has a prophet-making air." He said that "in two generations hence the Mormons in their present position will on
their own ground be more than a match for the Atlantic,
and combined with the Chinese will be dangerous to the
Pacific states."

But while people such as Burton and the federal troops
came and went, and while the Mormons were rushing
blindly into the practice of plural marriage, the theocracy
began to jell into the social and economic pattern from
which the present order developed.

At the heart of this order is the church—this fact can
never be ignored. Joseph Smith started the pattern on which
the Utah church grew by establishing the Aaronic and Melchizedek priesthoods. When Joseph was translating and
Oliver Cowdery writing down the dictation that was to be
the *Book of Mormon*, they had a religious experience of
great importance one day during a prayerful walk in the
woods. It was in May, 1829, they said later, that John the
Baptist appeared and put his hands on their heads to anoint
them into the Aaronic priesthood.

A statue based on this event stands in the Temple grounds
in Salt Lake City today. Joseph and Cowdery then baptized
each other, when John the Baptist had finished with them.
The Melchizedek priesthood was restored to earth soon
thereafter, the Mormons believe, but the event was not so
carefully recorded and the exact date is not known.

After the Mormons reached Salt Lake City, the rituals of

their church became formalized so that these two priesthoods are the main line of religious activity for men today.
Mormon boys become members of the Aaronic priesthood
at about twelve years and move through Deacon, twelve to
thirteen years of age, to Teacher, fourteen to fifteen years,
and Priest, sixteen to twenty years.

If they go on a mission, they are ordained elders before
leaving Salt Lake City, but otherwise will become elders at
about twenty. This is the first step of the Melchizedek Priesthood. Almost every devout Mormon adult male is an elder,
and they are so addressed formally, as contrasted to the
informal salutation—"Brother."

An elder will become a Seventy sometime in middle life,
and probably will become a High Priest in middle life. All
bishops and other officers have the rank of High Priest.
The bishop is the chief officer of the ward. The next administrative rank is stake president. These administer collec-
tions of wards, up to about ten at most in each stake, and
report to the General Authorities in Salt Lake City. The
stake president will have two assistants and an advisory
council of up to fifteen men.

The six ranks of the priesthood are organized into quorums
of different sizes. The Seventies, for example, have quorums
of no more than seventy each, with a quorum president.
These are considered to be totally religious groups, as dif-
ferentiated from the administrative groups such as the stake
presidency or High Council.

There are great numbers of jobs within the church at the
lower levels, as this brief recital makes clear. Each of the
priesthood quorums has a specific field of activity. The
Seventies, for example, are the missionaries, traditionally,
but this emphasis has shifted in recent years. The imposi-
tion of these tasks was begun in Brigham Young's time, as
was the institution of the strong controls that still exist. In
his time, the president of the church was virtually a law

unto himself in Utah, both in religious and worldly matters, for it was hard to find the line that divided them. Today, the president still is completely powerful in religious matters, but his authority over the greatly expanded church is shared with his colleagues at the top.

Thirty-eight men are the elite of the Church of Jesus Christ of Latter-day Saints. They are not only called "The General Authorities" but are looked upon as the source of power and control by the rank and file membership. Remember that at the Tabernacle, a door is marked "General Authorities." It leads to the stage where seats are provided for these men. These personages at the pinnacle are the only LDS officers who are paid. They get a living allowance which varies as to need. Bishops and the other lesser officers serve without pay. However, the bureaucracy of the church is paid.

At the peak is the first presidency, which is made up of the president and his counselors. Then come the Twelve Apostles, ranked in importance as to their seniority within that body. There are now twelve Assistant Apostles, added when the original smaller group was unable to meet the demands on them. The patriarch of the church, a hereditary position for a man of the Smith family, ranks next. Then rank the First Council or Seven Presidents of the Seventy, and the Presiding Bishopric, which is the presiding bishop and his two counselors.

For many years it has been the custom of the Mormons to hold semi-annual conferences. At each of these it is the practice for the audience—once representing the majority of the Saints right there present in the Tabernacle, but now just a relative few who manage to get to Salt Lake City and find a seat—to vote to "sustain" the General Authorities. The hands shoot up automatically when the question is asked.

In 1966, I attended the April conference in Salt Lake City and was able to watch the almost casual way this disposal of power is reaffirmed. President David O. McKay was then

greatly enfeebled by age and a stroke. He sat in the top row
of the tiers of seats for the General Authorities while his first
counselor, Hugh B. Brown, spoke, explaining that President
McKay was "presiding" while Brown was "conducting" the
meeting. Then the ninety-two-year-old man slowly moved
two or three steps to the rostrum, so aged and frail that one's
anxiety was increased lest he fall. He spoke slowly and indis-
tinctly and with great effort. Since his stroke at age ninety,
his once-powerful voice had faded. But he was still handsome
and straight as he stood erect at the rostrum, his waves of
gray hair set off nicely against his dark suit. One sensed the
radiations of divinely inspired leadership received from this
old man by his co-religionists in that building. Hugh Brown
asked if the church sustained David O. McKay as seer,
prophet and revelator.

"All in favor make it manifest," he said, looking out at the
packed Tabernacle. The thousands of hands shot up, for no
member would resist the implied instruction that he support
the chosen LDS leaders.

In fact, as the years have passed, it has become the most
serious of religious crimes to question the integrity or good
faith or power of the General Authorities. Illustrative of this
increasing reliance on control by the General Authorities is
the prominence given to one question among the ten that a
bishop is told to ask an applicant for a permit to visit the
Temple. The first question is:

"Are you morally clean and worthy to enter the Temple?"

The second question:

"Will you and do you sustain the General Authorities of
the Church, and will you live in accordance with the accepted rules and doctrines of the church?"

Here is the full list:

Do you have any connection, in sympathy or otherwise,
with any of the apostate groups or individuals who are run-

ning counter to the accepted rules and doctrines of the Church?

Are you a full tithe payer?

Are you exempt from paying tithes?

Do you keep the Word of Wisdom?

Do you always wear the regulation garments?

Will you earnestly strive to do your duty in the church, to attend your sacrament, priesthood, and other meetings, and to obey the rules, laws, and commandments of the Gospel?

Have you ever been denied a recommend to any Temple? If so, ascertain date of refusal, name of Bishop, Ward, Stake and obtain a clearance from previous Bishop before issuing recommend. [Apparently this second sentence is an instruction to the bishop.]

Have you ever been divorced?

Bear in mind that the bishop is asking this short list of questions of people he knows very well as members of his small congregation of no more than 500 people. But the importance of the questions becomes more obvious as they are studied and the context in which they are asked is understood. They require a Mormon to bind himself by promise to the theological control of the top leaders of the church, and by implication prevent him from questioning any religious action they take.

On the book of "Recommend" forms, the tickets of admission to the Temple, it is said:

"Members of the Church seeking recommends to the Temple are expected to be entirely honest in answering the inquiries of presiding officers. Any withholding of the truth, misrepresentation or deception would seriously impair the applicant's position, if not disqualify him, to receive the blessings which are promised to the true and faithful in the Temple of our Lord."

The questions need no special explanation, except for two points: The Word of Wisdom, and the "regulation garments."

The Word of Wisdom is what keeps Mormons from drinking alcohol or smoking tobacco. It was given as a revelation to Joseph Smith on February 27, 1833, when the Saints were in Kirtland, Ohio. It says

> that inasmuch as any man drinketh wine or strong drink among you, behold it is not good, neither meet in the sight of your Father, only in assembling yourselves together to offer up your sacraments before him.
>
> And, behold, this should be wine, yea, pure wine of the grape of the vine, of your own make.
>
> And, again, strong drinks are not for the belly, but for the washing of your bodies.
>
> And again, tobacco is not for the body, neither for the belly, and is not good for man, but is an herb for bruises and all sick cattle, to be used with judgment and skill.
>
> And again, hot drinks are not for the body or belly.

Although it is plain from the language (of which only a part is quoted) that the statements are only advice, the Utah church has given them the status of commandments. One cannot get into the Temple if he smokes or drinks. This means that a Mormon cannot have a marriage for "time and eternity," one of the centerpieces of his religion, unless he gives up alcohol and tobacco. Yet on the night before he was murdered, the Prophet Joseph and his fellows sat in the jail in Carthage, drinking wine they bought from one of the jailers.

The church information machinery has pushed hard on the anti-smoking campaign in recent years, although it has not been as effective with non-members as has that of the Seventh Day Adventists. The Mormons have, as an example, distributed anti-tobacco films made by the Brigham Young University staff. As the clinical data indicating health damage from smoking has come out of various agencies, the Mormons have proudly pointed to their longtime injunction to members against tobacco.

The "regulation garments" derive from the Temple ceremonies which include one called the "endowments" in
which a Saint receives a special suit of underwear, which the
devout will wear at all times. Originally, it is said, this was a
long-legged and long-armed union suit, but it has been ab-
breviated as styles changed. Both men and women wear the
garment awake and sleeping. Symbols are embroidered on
the underwear to remind the wearers of Temple obligations.
These garments are sold wherever Mormons live. In Mormon areas of Idaho or Utah, advertisements in newspapers
are common which call attention to Mormon undergarment
sales. The church in the early 1960s started a factory in Salt
Lake City which does nothing but weave these garments.
Since mid-1965 the LDS Women's Relief Society has been
the sole source of the garments. It has been said that the
older, extremely devout Mormons never remove their underwear, even keeping it on one ankle of a leg draped outside
the tub while bathing. However, such devotion to form is
not widespread.

Another fundamental of Mormon doctrine with wide sociological effect is the place of women within the church.
They historically are relegated to a second place status,
which of course was a certainty in the nineteenth-century
atmosphere of the days of organization of the church, and
was more certain during the days of plural marriage. (Nor
is this by any means unique among established religions in
the United States and elsewhere. In 1965, a bishop of the

Episcopal church, James A. Pike of San Francisco, was
placed in serious difficulty because he wanted to ordain a
woman as a deacon.) In many of these religions—including
the Mormon—changes have come, but still the Mormon
woman must rely on a man for her exaltation in the Celestial Kingdom.

Mormon theology holds that a soul is required, during
mortal existence, to do things that will increase its stature

in the after life. Membership in the church, for example, and baptism are required. Women can do these things. But women cannot become priests and can progress in that way only as the companion of their fathers or husbands.

Mormon religious writing is full of the assertion that men can become gods if they conduct themselves properly in mortal life. The wife of a god must be a goddess, but a Mormon woman could never achieve it on her own. So every Mormon wife is anxious that her husband attend his priesthood quorum meetings. Her joy is unbounded if he becomes a bishop or stake president, and if he should become one of the General Authorities—well, her place in the Celestial Kingdom is assured.

Historians have pointed out that this position in the hereafter also was a great selling point for the older Mormon dignitaries who were courting young girls in the plural marriage days. After all, how could a young bachelor compete for a girl's hand when the middle-aged Apostle could offer her a guarantee of preference in Heaven?

The practice of every devout man's being a priesthood member and the need for young men to meet the hot queries directed to them as missionaries has made the Mormons among the most avid mass scholars of their religion known anywhere.

Where the Catholics, as an example, will believe just as devoutly and resist snide statements from unbelievers more pugnaciously, they tend to leave the understanding of the ins and outs of doctrine to the priest who has a full-time responsibility for those matters. Each Mormon man—if he is a really serious practitioner of his priestly duties—becomes a nearly insatiable student of history and doctrine. Thus, when one asks a question of a typical Mormon priest about some obscure aspect of doctrine, he gets an answer. There is an assurance in the Mormon's heart that the answer exists, and that he knows it.

There are some matters they would just as soon not discuss, for any act of any of the past Mormon leaders is an act in the family of the practicing Mormon. If a president of the church did a thing he should not have done, most Mormons feel it is impolite to have it brought up. Moreover, they feel at a disadvantage because they cannot justify what happened, yet feel a sense of personal responsibility for it. One of these subjects is polygamy; another is the LDS doctrine that holds Negroes to be a defective people bearing God's punishment on Cain.

The Mormons are not troubled by many doubts—except for those who lose their faith in the truth of their church's doctrines. But a man who believes that he is truly a Saint has an assurance that is awesome. This is not to imply that he has overpowering conceit or is a boor; it is just that he is self-assured. He is sometimes very kind and gentle and helpful. But he also can be very determined that his view be accepted.

There is a cohesiveness to the membership, a strong singleness of mind and purpose that the inquirer soon discovers. Yet one hears of remarks made in a different vein within the family at meetings where only Mormons are present. One that I found surprising—even shocking—was reported to me by a member of a long-established Mormon family, a man with an impeccable reputation for veracity in Salt Lake City. He was quoting a Mormon bishop (dead for several years) who had presided at a meeting in a home. Doctrine had been discussed. The discussion turned to polygamy. Then it turned to the reasons why the church turned against polygamy. The doctrinal reasons were pursued. The bishop indicated that he doubted that God ever really wanted mankind to be polygamous. Then, someone asked, how on earth did we ever get into it. My informant said he heard the bishop say:

"I think Brother Joseph just had a weakness for women."

This statement would have caused a bishop to have been run out of Utah—or worse—a century ago. But today it could be made safely in the circumstances where it was made. I include it here to emphasize the point that there is a wide difference among members of the LDS church in the degree of acceptance of all the works of Joseph Smith and Brigham Young and the other leaders now gone. As a practical matter, they are fairly free to resist any doctrine such as the communism of the United Order of Enoch or the plural marriage doctrine or others which have been discarded, but still are printed in the books. They get in trouble when they begin to attack the wisdom and authority of the men who now are in the top positions in the church.

There is an amazing selflessness among the Mormons where their church is concerned. They are willing to do almost any task that can be named if it is a part of their religion. Doctors will work in canneries for the welfare program. Wealthy women will be standing at their side, dressed in blue jeans and with a bandanna holding their hair. A young Mormon teacher calls on people in Lansing, Michigan, as a part of his Aaronic priesthood duties; his father accompanies him when he can find the time away from night meetings that require the attendance of the governor of Michigan. When he was governor of Utah from 1957 to 1965, George Dewey Clyde also made calls as a Mormon priest.

A part of this selflessness comes from the strength of religious commitment, but also a part of it comes from the nature of the religious belief. The Mormon doctrine tells its believers that those duties they perform for the church contribute to their exaltation in the Celestial Paradise. A sort of quid pro quo understanding exists with God.

This has been one of the great strengths of the church for all the years since Brigham Young brought his small party to the desert. It has been able to make common identity be-

tween the problems of the world and the problems of the
soul; and in another place we will examine the minor crisis
that exists as the church tends more and more to use this
dynamism to solve little problems when it could try to solve
the big ones that are not now touched by the organized
church. Once Mormons built railroads and irrigation systems and fought back the desert and captured a whole region of the world for civilization, all in the name of God.
Today, what do they build?

Where Brigham Young organized a whole supply system
designed to permit families to walk across the prairies, plains
and mountains pushing a handcart, what exists today to
use this energy and marvelous organization? Where Brigham Young would import boatloads of converts from Den-
mark and send them off to settle Idaho, what is done with
the new blood of the church today?

In the days of Brigham Young, Joseph Smith and the
great names of the early church, life was just one struggle
after another to keep the church alive as an institution and
to prevent the destruction of its members as individuals.

This history of persecution from other men, including the
legal authorities of many of the areas where Mormons tried
to settle, and the history of near disaster from weather, crickets, and conflicts with each other have given the Mormons
a strong sense of need for unity, a reason for subordinating
the needs of the individual to the needs of the religious
group.

Historians claim that at times important members of the
church have been thrown to the wolves to save the rest of
the church. Mormons believe—and I agree with them—
that Joseph Smith knew when he returned across the swol-
len Mississippi River for trial in 1844 that he would never see
freedom again. But he also knew that unless he surrendered,
his people would be destroyed.

The main currents of Mormon tradition, religious belief,

and practice make individuals within the church formidable opponents.

First, they are true believers, shielded from harm by the doctrine. If they follow it, and disaster comes to them on earth, perhaps they will be doubly rewarded in the Celestial Paradise. This gives one a sense of rightness and determination, as the Saracens demonstrated to the Crusaders.

Second, they are equipped by training and by the lore of their people to consider that persons who argue against their beliefs are just anti-Mormon and thus are fundamentally evil. Such persons can be considered in the same light as those who killed Joseph and Hyrum.

Third, they believe that their religion provides all the answers. If a question arises, they need only get the proper guidance from their religious literature—or from one of their religious leaders—and the proper course will unfold itself.

These beliefs create assurance.

Finally, a Mormon generally comes from an area where there may be other Mormons, perhaps a majority in the circles where he moves. The doctrines are enunciated repeatedly to him, and all the phenomena of life are interpreted to him in terms of the doctrine. He is told that he is one of the chosen, that he is a Saint, that his people all are Saints, and that the Saints are the finest people anywhere in any age.

In his awareness of political affairs, he sees the leaders of the church courted by public figures. This assures him. He soon comes to know that his church is asked for its views before any important action is taken by the officials in the areas where the LDS is strong. It is pointed out to him that even candidates for the presidency of the United States call on the president of the Saints, hoping for his support.

If he is a Salt Lake City Mormon, he grows aware as he becomes an adult and travels that there is something unique about his town, that it has a flavor not found in other major

American cities. He may attribute this to the special favor
of God for the benefit of the Saints who live in Salt Lake
City. Perhaps the Saint is right. However, I think the reason for the different quality of Salt Lake City is explained
in other terms.

The special atmosphere which attracts me and which I
admire derives from the fact that this is not a branch town,
as even such cosmopolitan places as San Francisco have become. The great affairs of Denver may be decided by a
board of directors sitting somewhere else and weighing Denver's problems against those of the company and its investments in, say, Kansas City. Perhaps no one sits on that
board who can really make Denver's need felt, or who really
has great concern about what happens to Denver.

But Salt Lake City is the center place for the Saints, and
the men who direct that church are able to make their wills
felt in many great and small ways in the minds of the men
who sit on boards of directors. The church still is courted
by the industrialists who would open a plant, by the mining
combines who would dig holes in the bare mountains. And
since the church leaders are terribly interested in what happens to Salt Lake City, there is a different air about the developments there. Someone cares, and is able to make that
care felt.

This is no small thing.

III

"Zion Will Be Built"

A GREAT PART of the fascination in studying the Saints comes from unraveling the reasons behind certain customs and institutions that are unique. In Salt Lake City, and in other cities where the Mormons live in large numbers, these recurrent patterns of life are always visible. Many of them can be traced back to the way the LDS church is organized, or to the theology of the church, or to some custom that has grown up, based on the fact that most everyone in shouting distance was a member of the faith. This is a special flavor of oneness, of unity, of in-group control that the observer will sense within a short stay in Salt Lake City or Logan or Ogden. After a few days and a few visits, one becomes accustomed to finding the Mormon Tabernacle in the center of town, physically and sociologically. The small number of Negroes no longer is remarkable. The peculiar liquor laws of Utah fail to surprise after a time.

The Mormons built these cities where now they are so strong. They may today be fewer than a majority in Salt Lake City, yet this is their town. The Irish and French Canadian and Italian Catholics took Boston from their predecessors; the Mormons created Salt Lake City. And since the Mormons were acting on Holy Orders when they moved to the shores of the Great Salt Lake, the actions taken in those early days were for religious reasons. Where ordinary life today is affected by those actions, a religious cast is given to quite ordinary and non-religious acts.

For example, the Saints went to the desert with a feeling that they were living up to the Articles of Faith that Joseph Smith wrote for them during the years just before his death. One of these statements of belief is referred to in Mormon circles as "The Gathering." It derives from the opening words of Article 10 of this creed.

The entire Article is as follows:

"We believe in the literal gathering of Israel and in the restoration of the Ten Tribes; that Zion will be built upon this (the American) continent; that Christ will reign personally upon the earth; and, that the earth will be renewed and receive its paradisiacal glory."

The theological matters involved here are related both to the Hebrew tribal histories that make up the narrative of much of the Old Testament, as well as to the writings of Joseph Smith and the *Book of Mormon*, which the Saints believe to be a history of a group of Israelites who came to the North American continent. The essence of the first thought before the first semicolon of the quotation above was that Mormons believe that the descendants of Israel will be gathered together. This creates a problem, for few Mormons are descended from Jacob who was renamed Israel when he wrestled and won with the Angel from whom he wanted a blessing.

However, the Mormon scholar and apostle, James E. Talmage, explained it thus:

"The name Israel, thus held with commendable pride by the remnant of a once mighty nation, was used in a figurative manner to designate the covenant people who constituted the Church of Christ; and in that sense it is still employed."

So the answer is simple: The members of the Church of Jesus Christ of Latter-day Saints are members of the nation

of Israel. It is in the "literal gathering" of these people that
a Mormon believes.

This is the central theological reason the Mormons lived
close together from the time Joseph Smith explained the doctrines until they began to break away from their desert
empire in the twentieth century. The idea was that they
were to be gathered together as quickly as they became believers, and were to live together.

Moreover, in the time of Brigham Young and the settlement of the desert, the church needed as many of its followers as it could get moved to Utah. It needed them for the
thoroughly practical reason that it needed people to popu-
late the empty places. As a consequence, there were the
great migrations from Europe, particularly England, and
from the eastern United States.

Some of the most stirring stories of Mormon heroism seem
to me to come from that early concept of The Gathering.
The handcart companies . . . Now there is a tale to chill
one's blood! The institution of this method of immigration
—like so much else in early Utah Mormon history—was
dictated by Brigham Young who in turn was driven to it by
the economic problems in meeting what he said was "the
will of the Lord." It was the will of the Lord that missionaries be sent abroad. It was the will of the Lord that they
have great success. It was the will of the Lord that the converts come to Utah.

This proselyting in Europe had gone on long before the
Brigham Young faction transplanted the *Book of Mormon*
to the desert. The immigration of converts from Europe
had begun long before Joseph Smith was killed. The mission in England was started in 1837, and from it some of the
great church leaders of the late nineteenth century emerged,
the product of conversions. A mission in Scandinavia was
established in 1849, at a time when the transplantation to
Salt Lake City was having trouble. Between 1840 and 1846,

said Dr. Thomas F. O'Dea in his great sociological examination, *The Mormons,** 4750 converts sailed from Liverpool
for the United States, headed for Nauvoo. For a time, it was
a problem to place the Europeans when the church was disrupted after Joseph's murder. But when the move had been
made to Salt Lake City, the patterns were then set up for
colonization in the Mountain West.

Initially, they bought wagons and draught animals at the
end of the riverboat trip in the upper Plains, then made the
trip west to the presence of Brigham Young who made settlement assignments. The Perpetual Emigration Fund, a
Mormon financial trust set up to help move the members
left behind in the Midwest in 1846, came to be used to help
the European immigrants. This fund was very important in
the Mormon immigrations.

In 1849 there were about 6000 persons in the valley of the
Great Salt Lake, and by 1852 there were about 20,000 according to Dr. Leonard J. Arrington, a leading economic
historian who has written much about the economic foundations of the LDS church. The big push for gathering the British converts was in full operation in the early
1850s. It is significant that before they ever left England in
specially chartered Mormon ships, the converts were listed
by occupation. Many of them paid their own way, and
some were brought by the Perpetual Emigration Fund. In
1853, Professor Arrington found, 2312 immigrants came
under auspices of the Fund. Of these, the church paid for
400 who were supposed to pay later; 955 went at their own
expense and 1000 were in "ten pound" companies. The
church had found it could bring over an immigrant for about
ten British pounds, if he would do a little for himself. It
was very highly organized and planned.

But by the late 1850s, it became apparent that various
financial and agricultural reverses, plus the heavy drains of

* The University of Chicago Press, Chicago and London, 1957

the cost of helping immigrants, had made it impossible for
this system to continue. So Brigham Young unveiled his
new plan.

"We cannot afford to purchase wagons and teams as in
times past," he said. "I am consequently thrown back upon
my old plan—to make hand-carts, and let the emigration foot
it, and draw upon them the necessary supplies, having a cow
or two for every ten. They can come just as quick, if not
quicker, and much cheaper—can start earlier and escape
the prevailing sickness which annually lays so many of our
brethren in the dust."

He was impressed that the carts could be made without
iron, and that one would serve a family, or two carts "if the
family be large." When the church president reached his
decision, the disciplined believers immediately began to
implement it. Hundreds signed up in Europe to take part
in the experiment. After all, the heads of the church had
announced in a General Epistle in 1856 the theological basis
for all of this. They had pointed out that the idea was to
"deliver the honest poor, the pauper, if you please, from the
thraldom of ages, from localities where poverty is a crime
and beggary an offence against the law, where every avenue
to rise in the scale of being to any degree of respectable joy-
ous existence it forever closed, and place them in a land
where honest labor and industry meet a suitable reward,
where the higher walks of life are open to the humblest and
poorest. . . ."

So the church leaders, having explained the aim, put out
the order:

"Let them come on foot, with hand-carts or wheelbarrows;
let them gird up their loins and walk through, and nothing
shall hinder or stay them."

Almost nothing, that is, except starvation, illness and
death!

So, inspired by the belief in The Gathering of Israel, these hundreds came across the sea and across from the eastern ports to Iowa City where the handcarts were made, with the theory that each would serve four or five persons with about 100 pounds of food, clothing and equipment. They were organized into companies of about 100 carts each. About twenty were assigned to each tent, and there was a wagon and ox team for each twenty carts. They went first to Florence, Nebraska, and rested there where the first refugees from Nauvoo had established quarters in 1847. Then they started bravely across the plains, mountains, rivers and wild country. The first companies arrived safely in Salt Lake City in September, 1856. Wilford Woodruff, the apostle who was to become the president of the church forced to deal with the polygamy problem decades later, was deeply thrilled by the arrival. He wrote:

"As I gazed upon the scene, meditating upon the future result, it looked to me like the first hoisting of the floodgates of deliverance to the oppressed millions. We can now say to the poor and honest in heart, come home to Zion, for the way is prepared."

But, as it turned out, the way was not so well prepared after all. Of the five companies started from Iowa City that summer of 1856, the last two were started much too late. They were caught in the early winter. Of the over 1000 persons in the two companies, more than 200 died. Even this was not so bad as it might have been, for a special rescue company found the immigrant parties, huddled and waiting for death, and took them to Salt Lake City.

Brigham Young still favored the continuance of this plan, but factors worked against him. In 1857, only 480 persons came west by handcart, said Dr. Arrington in his major economic study of the early Mormons.* In 1858 troubles on another front with the federal government stopped the migrations. President James Buchanan sent troops to Utah

* *The Great Basin Kingdom*, Harvard University Press, Cambridge, 1958.

to take control of the area from the church. In 1859 and
1860 there came only three last handcart companies with a
total of 584 passengers.

Dr. Arrington said that about 3000 persons pushed or
pulled 662 handcarts from Iowa City in the period 1856-
1860 while the conventional wagon trains brought 5200
immigrants. Beginning in 1861, teams and wagons were
sent from Salt Lake City to the end of the advancing railroad, so that by 1869, there had been 1913 wagons sent out
for the round trip. The railroad was finished by June, 1869,
and the immigrants came to The Gathering by steam engine.

There were perhaps as many as 90,000 Europeans who
came to the United States before 1900 because of their conversion to the LDS church, Dr. O'Dea has estimated. About
70,000 came during the thirty years of Brigham Young's
presidency, ending in 1877. Most were from England, but
the second largest number was from Scandinavia. Today
one sees signs of this in the Scandinavian names in telephone
books in Mormon areas. A summer's day walk down any
street in Salt Lake City's business district shows a constant
parade of blondes with blue eyes and skins tanned golden
brown under the sun of the high desert.

These floods of immigrants came to the American West
under the Mormon ideal of The Gathering. Their children
are important in the church today, and the strength of the
Saints draws much from this group of converts in the last
half of the nineteenth century. They came because it was
"the will of the Lord." They also needed to be near the Temples.

While the Mormons still flourished at Nauvoo, Joseph
Smith introduced the Temple rites, using the great Temple
that the church constructed in Illinois and then had to
leave for the vandals to destroy. These Temple rites have
been attacked many times over the years, just as have so

many of the other Mormon religious practices. A part of this
derives from resentment that the Temples are closed to all
but the devout, practicing Mormons. A part comes from the
desire among some persons to destroy the LDS religion for
any of the many reasons that have aroused hatreds among
non-Believers. The things that go on in the Mormon Temples today are not scandalous, or disorderly, or in any way
disreputable. They are the central acts of faith among the
Saints, and as such should have the respect that any person
gives to the religious belief of another.

There are some responsibilities and privileges for the
Saint that can be fulfilled only in the Temple. If he wants
to be "sealed for time and eternity" to the woman of his
choice, he can have this ceremony performed only in the
Temple. A marriage performed anywhere that a civil marriage can be performed will suffice to permit a man and
woman to live together in honor and decency in the eyes of
the Saints; but if they expect to live together in the life after
death, they must be sealed for time and eternity by a Mormon priest in the Temple.

In a church booklet called *Latter-day Saint Temples*, the
Mormons explain briefly some of the uses of the Temples. It
is said that the Temple Endowment

> . . . comprises a course of instruction relating to the jour-
> ney of man from the creation, through the Garden of Eden,
> his struggle when driven out into the world, and the exalta-
> tion to which he may attain. Rooms and representations
> symbolic of these various periods and stations are found in
> modern temples.
>
> The ordinances of the endowment embody certain obliga-
> tions of chastity, charity, consecration and service. Blessings
> are pronounced conditioned upon faithful observance of
> these obligations.
>
> In every detail the endowment is uplifting and sanctify-

ing, obligating him who receives it to moral, religious and patriotic endeavor.

A Saint must go to the Temple for his endowment rites. This is a complex ceremony, with a playlet performed full of allegory and explanation, and in which the Mormon is clothed in special garments and where his body is anointed with oil. The ceremony is calculated to give the Saint a feeling of his place in eternity and an understanding of his religion. The Mormon spokesmen who attempt valiantly to explain their church to the outside world explain that the endowment rites are the Saint's commitment to God and Christ and the commitment of these deities to the individual Saint.

In addition to these rites, the Temples are also the site of the vicarious baptisms and marriages for the dead. Now this has been a central part of the LDS religious practice for a long time and in the last few years has become even more important. It is the main religious activity today for hundreds of the Saints who pour into the former Montgomery Ward store building on Main Street in Salt Lake City. There they strain their eyes reading microfilmed records from all over the world. This is the headquarters of the Genealogical Society which is a branch of the LDS church. This organization will be described in detail, for it is one of the highly interesting manifestations of the adaptation of LDS belief to modern conditions.

The vicarious ceremonies of sealing in marriage and of baptism of persons dead are similar to those same ceremonies for living persons. The language is the same, except that the words "for and in behalf of" are inserted into the ritual. To understand the reasons for these rites and their significance to the Saints, one must understand some more of the theology as it was expounded by Joseph Smith and his successors.

First, there is a pre-mortal state, in which there are blessed spirits which surround God. There are other cursed spirits —perhaps a third of the original number—which are consigned to perdition for having taken the side of the Devil in a struggle with God.

When a person is born, one of these blessed spirits inhabits his body and is his soul. He may better or worsen the situation in the Celestial Kingdom for his soul—this spirit—by the way he conducts himself on earth. This is the Mormon doctrine of Free Agency as opposed to the pre-ordination doctrine of some other religions. It is from this as much as from any other theological source that the limitless upward striving of the Saints comes. There is no limit, they believe, to the ultimate benefits one can achieve in life after death through good works while on earth in the mortal state; therefore, an intelligent and believing Saint works hard all his life that he may have a greater degree of glory in the Celestial Kingdom.

"We believe that everyone will be saved," said Governor George Romney, a devout Mormon. "The question is the degree of exaltation that a man can win for himself in his life on earth."

But what of those persons who were not born in time to be exposed to the Restored Gospel of Joseph Smith? What of those marriages that were performed between people who now will be separated in the Spirit World? The answer: Vicarious baptisms, vicarious sealings for time and eternity.

There are indications from various sources that there was some fumbling around with these theological devices at different times, but today the pattern is set: A relative researches genealogical records and discovers an unbaptized ancestor. He proposes the ancestor for baptism, and the ceremony is performed in the Temple. The ancestor is assured of eternal glory as a baptized member of the LDS church. The procedure is similar for a marriage for "time and eternity" for ancestral stock discovered in the genealogical files. A vicarious ceremony is performed with a live couple standing in for the ancestors. Mormon elders living where Temples are located spend much time in such ceremonies.

Now to turn back to The Gathering concept and to understand a significant switch in church direction that came about at the turn of the century. It became obvious to the LDS leaders that they could not "gather" all the converts into the desert behind the Rocky mountains, even if they stretched them from Idaho to the San Fernando Valley. Also, the church was suffering financially, as an aftermath of the great struggle over polygamy, and could not buy up the lands necessary to settle the new flocks of immigrants. So they told the converts to stay at home.

But how was one to practice his religion if he had no Temple at hand? Few would be able to get to Utah, where four Temples had been constructed. What to do? The church began building Temples around the world. For the Temple is a necessity if a Mormon is to be completely square with his church. But even aside from the ordinances and ceremonies, the Temples have a place. David O. McKay, the Mormon president, wrote at the time of the dedication of a Temple in Oakland, California, in 1964:

> Our Temples have a special place in the Church aside from the ordinances given and performed within. They are lights upon a hill. Their light should not be hidden. A Temple exerts or should exert a continuous influence upon the people, especially the youth. . . .
>
> We must teach young people to live so that they can enter the house of God and make convenants, the dearest and most sacred in all the world. In youth they should take cognizance of the fact that they will have to control their appe-

tites and their passions if they would enter the Temple worthily.

Preparation for the Temple is during youth, not just when they go to the bishop for their Temple recommends. This is what is meant by having the house of God as a light to the church. It is one of the greatest means of character building in the church.

So the Temple has become extremely important in the LDS church. It was important in the beginning also. Joseph Smith caused the building of a Temple in Kirtland, Ohio, now owned by the Reorganized LDS church. The vandals burned down the one in Nauvoo. But in 1853, six years after the first Saints arrived in Salt Lake City, Brigham Young had them started on the beautiful old Temple that now stands in Temple Square and is the center of Mormonism today.

It took an even forty years to build this structure, and it cost about $4 million, which is of course an estimate. Much of the work was done in lieu of tithing. While it was being built, three other Temples were started and completed. One is at St. George, built between 1871 and 1877 in Southern Utah where Brigham liked to spend a few winter months each year; one at Logan, built between 1877 and 1884, in the beautiful Cache Valley a few miles south of the Idaho border; and one at Manti, built between 1877 and 1888. These sufficed as long as the ideal of The Gathering was followed, but when this became unfeasible, some other steps had to be taken to allow Mormons in other lands to have access to the Temples and to all of the holiness housed in them.

An LDS meeting house just does not fit the needs of the church members for the Temple rites. These are places of worship, but they also are basketball courts and dance floors and are in a sense the centers of the Mormon community for all of its joint activities. The Temple is the Holy place; the others are for meetings. Frequently one sees news stories from here and there of a Mormon Temple dedication. These are written by the unknowing who are impressed by a simple meeting house.

So to solve their problem, the Saints began to build Temples around the world. The first one outside Utah was built at Laie, Hawaii, on the island of Oahu, and dedicated in 1919. The Sandwich Island mission had been opened in the nineteenth century. The next one was at Cardston, Alberta, in 1923. There were large Mormon settlements in the Canadian prairies. In 1927 came the Mesa, Arizona, Temple to serve the descendants of those Mormon colonists in the Arizona desert. It is architecturally interesting that none of these three Temples has a spire or tower.

In 1945, just days after the end of World War II, a Temple was dedicated at Idaho Falls, overlooking the falls of the Snake River and serving the extensive Mormon population of the great irrigated valley of Idaho. The first European Temple was dedicated at Bern, Switzerland, in 1955, followed by the Los Angeles Temple in 1956 and the London Temple in 1958. The Saints opened a Temple in Hamilton, New Zealand, in 1958, and dedicated their most recent Temple in Oakland, California, in 1964. These postwar Temples all have spires. No new Temples are planned for several years.

There are no Temples east of the Rocky Mountains in the United States nor are there any in Latin America. The surge into the Pacific following the Polynesian converts and linking up the transplanted British in New Zealand brought two Temples. There are no Temples in Africa or Asia. Persons converted there must come to another continent to find a place to fulfill their Holy obligations.

Of course, they may accomplish some of these things by mail, such as arranging for the vicarious marriage or baptism of their dead relatives. The baptisms are done in gloriously ornate and symbolic founts supported on the backs of carved oxen, a pattern universally followed in the Temples. Such grandeur is not necessary for the baptism of a living person; this may be done in a fount such as one in the lower floor of the old Tabernacle in the center of Logan, Utah. It was tile-lined, looked highly utilitarian and not in the least bit designed for sacred use. Of course, the attitude of mind of the users lends a dignity to even a muddy creek used for a baptism.

The Genealogical Society is a rapidly rising adjunct of the LDS church. It exists on the need for Mormons to trace back their ancestry in order to be able to have the Temple rites of baptism and vicarious marriage performed for those who have not had it in life. This organization really is not a separate membership society but is an administrative arm of the LDS church. Its headquarters are in the former Montgomery Ward store on Main Street in downtown Salt Lake City, a place occupied in 1961. In addition seventeen branch libraries are maintained around the world for genealogical research. The former store has been filled with rooms, passageways, storage areas, open shelf library stacks, air-conditioned microfilm storage areas, and a large room with 215 microfilm reading machines in it. These cost $450 each. It is a measure of the LDS financial sagacity that the Genealogical Society has a dealership that gives it the wholesale rate.

I came in early that summer morning and was greeted first by Delbert E. Roach, the head librarian. We looked at the card catalogue, which was broken into drawers by geographical location. This is because one here is looking for someone whose name he may not really know when he begins, and for a record that he may not even know exists. All he knows is that his ancestors came from a certain region, and he has from his family lore, or from earlier research, a name to start with. He needs to find that name in these masses of records. Then he must tie it into other names and move back a generation. The card files list poll books, religious court records, wills, church records and official documents from across Europe. The file drawers are labeled with the names of countries, or in England with counties. We looked at a drawer listing documents from Finland. Roach said that in the library stacks were 81,000 volumes, including many, many family histories.

In the next basement room we were among the Recordak microfilm reading machines, which take the rolls of film at the top, and project the records on the ground-glass screen for reading. It was before 10 A.M.; yet the room was half filled. Roach said it would be completely full before long. The students of genealogy poured over their films quietly, using special forms which are standard for this work. One man said he was tracing a family line in Middletown, Connecticut, and that he was an off-duty fireman.

The fireman had found a daughter of his great-great-grandfather who lived in Middletown from 1713 to 1797. He has traced his family back for ten generations to Somerset, England, where they owned a castle and were baronets. He had corresponded, he said, and had received a very nice letter in return from the present holder of the title. This tracing just gave him the trunk of the family tree. He must fill the branches so far as he can locate them. This has come to be a religious duty for Mormons. The argument is that only the descendants will go to the trouble.

There are something under 3 million live Saints today. Yet the vicarious ceremonies have been performed for more than 30 million persons! In 1965, there were 1,246,301 names cleared for performance of the rites, and there were 3,607,962 Temple rites for the dead that year, as against 71,579 for the living.

As many as 1500 people may come during one day to the society's quarters, and the average is 800 a day. They care-

fully fill out the names of their relatives as they discover
them in old books or on microfilmed records. The sheets are
called "family groups." They are turned in with requests
that they be certified by the Genealogical Society. The society does not check behind the research; it merely makes
certain that clerical work is accurate. A sample of one of the
bound family sheets was shown by Roach. It was for a Wil-
son family which lived in Scotland as of 1728. The members
were baptized and the parents sealed "for time and eternity"
in marriage in 1961. These sheets were bound in holders
that filled a series of shelves along one side of a room. Color
codes showed whether the sheets represented families for
whom the Temple rites had been performed, or whether the
"work" still had to be done.

The society also has a great collection of file cards for
individual names, called the Temple Index Bureau. These
fill a large space, rank on rank of cabinets full of more than
30,000,000 cards—one for each person who has ever had
vicarious ceremonies performed in the Temple. By now the
tour was in the hands of Paul Royall, the general secretary
of the Genealogical Society. Did I want to see a card?

Over the years, when I've been offered the opportunity
to have a random name checked in such a compilation, I've
always given my own. Sometimes this raises eyebrows, but
I find the answers interesting. How many people have
been named Wallace Turner? A hell of a lot, I find. Paul
Royall pulled out a thin stack of cards of people with my
name. One of them said Wallace Turner was born in Maine
in 1848, was married in 1872 to Maggie Small, was baptized
June 23, 1961, and had an endowment ceremony in September, 1961, both vicariously. The Wallace Turner born in
Titusville, Florida, in 1921 was not listed in the cards. It is
passing strange—not disturbing, but thought-provoking—
to realize that fifty years from now he might be. The scope
of endeavor of one's descendants is beyond calculation.

The Mormons believe that the soul for whom the vicarious ceremonies were performed will of course approve of them; but if he does not, they hold, he may refuse to accept them when the ultimate Gathering comes in the Celestial Kingdom. Also, they prohibit the performance of vicarious Temple ceremonies except on the request of a descendant of the person for whom they are performed. The exception is given only on the approval of the top officers of the church.

Some interesting exceptions have been made. One church president, Wilford Woodruff, said in 1898 that he had been visited by George Washington and the signers of the Declaration of Independence while in the St. George, Utah, Temple. He arranged for their proxy baptisms. He also baptized fifty other eminent men, including John Wesley, Columbus and every President of the United States to that time—except for three whose names he did not announce publicly. He thought these three might later conduct themselves in such a way as to get the ceremonies done for them, too.

The Mormons have had some real rip-snorting apostasies over the years. Some of these will be explored later as they bear on current conditions. One such was Frank J. Cannon, one of the twenty-one sons of the great nineteenth-century Mormon leader, George Q. Cannon. He was an English convert who was in many ways Brigham Young's successor in direction of the church, although the seniority rules kept him from being president. Frank J. Cannon once told his experiences to Harvey J. O'Higgins, one of the early twentieth-century muckrakers. They produced a vicious attack on the LDS leadership which was published in 1911 as *Under the Prophet in Utah*. This was an account of the church's struggles to accommodate its rulers' commitment to polygamy to the necessity of abandoning the practice.

Frank Cannon claimed that various gentiles friendly to the Saints' cause over the years have been baptized vicariously in the Temple, some even while they were still alive. In the days when polygamy was still in fashion, he asserted, such a series of ceremonies was carried out in behalf of President Theodore Roosevelt. The following paragraph appears in the Cannon-O'Higgins book:

Then—according to the unctuous gossip of the devout— President Roosevelt saw the true answer to his own desire to know what was to become of his mighty personality after this world should have fallen away from him! He saw, in this faith, a possible continuation throughout eternity of the tremendous energies of his being! He was to continue to rule not merely a nation but a world, a system of worlds, a universe of worlds! And it is told—sometimes solemnly, sometimes with a grin—that, in the Temple at Salt Lake, a proxy has stood for him and he has been baptized into the Mormon church; that proxies have stood for members of his family and that they have been sealed to him; and finally that proxies have stood for some of the great queens of the past (who have not already been sealed to Mormon leaders) and that they have been sealed to the President for Eternity!

There is no hint or rumor or suggestion in Salt Lake City today that the Mormon leaders now do such things as those leaders of a half century ago were accused of doing. Nor do I know of any proof that they did what Cannon and O'Higgins accused them of doing. I think, however, that this story permits us to understand two points of value.

First, non-Mormon students of the LDS church history generally would be prepared to accept it tentatively as true, at least in its main outlines, since it falls within the pattern of accepted action in those troubled times.

Second, no one would believe such a story about the church today. It would require a great amount of proof, a vast set of affidavits, and even the findings of a court before it would be accepted. Such action today is outside the high moral standards the church requires its members to follow.

The great surge of interest in the genealogy and vicarious Temple ceremonies for the dead began to build up after World War II, for a reason that is not clear cut. By 1960 the church leaders realized that there was deep interest among the members and in 1961 opened the research facilities described here. Early in 1965 the Genealogical Society produced the "Priesthood Challenge for 1965." The challenge: "Each home is to participate in the three generation family group sheet program." And, of course, the highly organized priesthood quorums—including every active adult male Mormon—would be expected to see that the challenge was met. This means the production by each family of seven of the "family group" forms which list parents, children, and grandparents: a sheet for the immediate family, a set then from both parents which will include their families, their parents' families and their grandparents' families. When the "challenge" was issued, church literature carried a note explaining that the Genealogical Society would alphabetize the family group sheets and microfilm them for future use.

This microfilming of records is a tremendous work, growing in scope continually, operated entirely for the benefit of the ancestor tracing that leads to the vicarious Temple ceremonies. As of July 1, 1965, the microfilm division had a total of 406,682 rolls of microfilm of 100 feet each. There were records from all over the world. Just consider that even from the Bahamas they have 608 rolls containing about 780,000 separate pages of records. The total microfilm load included 579,679,800 pages of documents. There were more than 5 billion names in the files. The Mormons have microfilmed all the pertinent records in Connecticut, Delaware, Maine, Maryland, New Hampshire, North Carolina, Vermont, and Virginia. They are at work in many of the other states. They have almost all of the U.S. census records from 1790 to 1890.

Yet they have just begun.

The church puts about $4 million a year into the Genealogical Society. It has 575 employees and is run by a board which includes two apostles. The microfilm unit sends crews all over the world to locate and photograph records. They sometimes have trouble, as with the Anglican bishops in some parts of England. The bishops occasionally resist the requests for access to church records; yet possession of the English records is a vital necessity for the Genealogical Society since so many Mormons are descendants of the English converts of the early nineteenth century.

The problems are dealt with by the Saints in the way tough problems always are met by intelligent people—they solve them one at a time, and there is no blanket policy except to obtain the records by any honorable means. Many times the microfilm units find it easy to obtain access to records, for they always commit the church to furnish a set of positive film records free to the possessor of the record file. Another set is made for use in the research library in downtown Salt Lake City. The negative microfilms are stored in a great vault system dug out of the rocks of Cottonwood Canyon in the Wasatch Mountains southeast of Salt Lake City. This underground storage system was produced by the church at a cost of $2.5 million. It has six vaults, which each will hold a million rolls of film. As of July 1, 1965, the church had just over 400,000 rolls, not enough to half fill one vault. During 1964, the microfilming units worked in fourteen countries.

Paul Royall said that non-Mormon researchers are welcome. He told the wife of a nationally known figure who had asked for help in finding what had happened to her grandfather who had deserted her grandmother more than 100 years ago. She thought he had gone to Salt Lake City, this lady said. The church researchers found that he had gone to Ogden and were able to tell her what happened to him.

I found Royall to be an interesting example of the devout and highly motivated Mormon. He had served a mission in the southeastern United States as a young elder, and had spent many of his middle years as a radio news broadcaster. He works full time now for the Genealogical Society. His background gave him a skill in speech, and his great and intense devotion to the study of his religion provided him with answers to my questions.

He is thrilled at the growth of his church. He pointed out that the first doubling in size took ninety-one years, the second took thirty-one years, the third eight years and the fourth four years. He said half the membership has come in during David O. McKay's presidency since 1951.

For years, said Royall, he devoted much of his free time to helping with the Temple ceremonies, both the vicarious baptisms and marriages, as well as those for living persons. The Mormons are ever certain; Royall was ever certain. First, they are sure that an answer exists; and then they are certain their religion holds that answer.

As we began to talk, he went to a briefcase and pulled out a zippered case from which he took his well-thumbed collection of sacred works—the Bible, the *Book of Mormon, Doctrine and Covenants,* and the *Pearl of Great Price.* He defended the doctrine of vicarious baptism and marriage. He said that Mormons believe that the dissolution of body and spirit is only temporary. He said, "We believe that in the Spirit World you live exactly as now, that you feel pain and hunger and pleasure and joy and sorrow as now."

Royall personifies the activist attitude of the Mormons. He is a very experienced teacher of doctrine, a positivist on doctrinal matters, a very devout man. He spoke of the president of the LDS church.

"David O. McKay to me is a prophet of God. Several times I have had to change my ideas when I heard what he had to say."

Royall once served on the school board in Salt Lake City. He said he asked President McKay if he should run. He said he was told to run and that he would win. But later, he said, he became much confused by a serious problem on which he was required to vote. He said that again he sought out President McKay and asked which of the unpalatable alternatives he should choose. He was told, "Make up your own mind."

The critics of the LDS church today decry the employment of the great energies of men like Paul Royall in such activities as genealogical research. One of these critics is Ed Moe, a sociologist and community organization specialist. He grew up in a "Josephite" family (the Reorganized LDS), but he admired much about the Utah Saints. However, he said that the great energies of the church today are directed to activities that lack the social and economic benefit of those pushed in the early days by Brigham Young.

"It seems to me that the Mormons get mixed up," he said. "They make the wrong things sacred, and the wrong things are left secular. In the early days, the church devoted its fundamental strength to solving the practical problems of living such as land settlement, irrigation, and building. These things had a sacred nature to them and the things that were ordered done were ordered done in the name of the Lord. All of this gave a strength and vitality to the day-to-day life."

Today, he said, the community suffers because of the emphasis on such things as genealogical research when the time could be better spent trying to work out a means of keeping pollution out of the Great Salt Lake.

"In the last fifty years or so," said Moe, "the church has more and more tried to use its highly structured authority for

purely religious purposes. Sometimes it looks as if they are
in activities just for the sake of activities. Now this means
that things such as the Red Cross drive have trouble. People
seem to spend eighty per cent of their available time on
church projects and have no time for the real problems. This
is because the church no longer recognizes the real problems
as it did in the early days."

This is a common criticism of the LDS church, heard not
only in Salt Lake City, but equally in places like Boise where
many Mormons live.

Moe said that the Great Salt Lake has become the greatest open-ended cesspool in the country. He said many of
the small towns in Utah have water supplies that are outside Federal Housing Administration specifications and
range from questionable to dangerous.

Another problem, Moe said, exists in the basically exclu-
sive-inclusive attitude of a Saint toward anyone else. If
the other person is a member of the church, he is included;
if he is not, he is excluded. The same attitude applies to
organizations so that a Mormon will work his heart out for
the Boys Scouts, which his church dominates in Mormon
areas, but has nothing to do with the Girl Scouts. The Mormons give heavily in money and in free labor for the church
welfare program; but the United Fund drive may have trouble.

One study showed that in many of the Utah towns, the
meeting place for the Mormon men and the non-Mormon
men in the upper levels of community affairs is the Lions
Club luncheon each week, Moe said. The Mormon and
non-Morman elements of a community move in separate
social orbits, intersecting only occasionally at such places
as the Lions Club. This is because life is so highly organized
around the center of things for the Saint—his church.

The young people are tied up in the Mutual Improvement
Association from their early years. There are two branches

of this—the Young Men's and the Young Women's Mutual
Improvement Associations. Offices for both are in Salt Lake
City in the church-owned building which houses the Beehive Bank, which is not owned by the church. Some of the
intricacies of the MIA were explained by Charles E. Mitchener, Jr., assistant secretary of the YMMIA.

The women's organization was put together in 1869 on
Brigham Young's orders, and the men's group was started
in 1875. The boys go into the Boy Scouts, which the YMMIA
has made virtually an adjunct of the LDS church in Mormon areas. The meetings are held in the ward meeting
house and the leader is a Mormon elder. If a boy from a
non-Mormon family wants to be a Scout, he must get along
with the Mormons.

"We make many converts through Scouting," said Mitchener.

The girls go into the Beehive Girls, which is something
like Girl Scouts and Campfire Girls, but is completely the
creature of the LDS church.

All of these programs—just as for the religious instruction programs—are closely controlled from Salt Lake City
through the manuals for the instructors and for the super-
visors and through frequent visits from Utah by authorities,
and to Utah by the local leaders.

Each of the Mormon meeting houses—even in the missions in faraway places—has a space set aside for the physical endeavors that the Saints relish. There is a stage, a basketball court, a baseball diamond, and whatever else the
locality demands for sports and entertainment. The Mormons are among the great group dancers of our age, for the
MIA holds dances in the meeting houses frequently. Once
the space set aside for the activities was called the "recreation hall" but more recently someone has decided that the
"cultural hall" was a better name.

This center of activity serves two purposes for the church.

First, it is a focus of attention for the young members on the religious side of their lives, and secondly, it is a marvelous tool for proselyting. A missionary team in some out-of-the-way spot will attract a boy to the Mormon center by discovering that he likes baseball, or enjoys dancing. When he comes there, he is greeted and gathered up into the group while a gentle pressure is exerted continually on him to think about the religious side of the church that has provided him with these wonderful opportunities for recreation. So long as he keeps up his connection with the church-sponsored activities, so long will the Saints try to persuade him to accept the Restored Gospel of Joseph Smith.

"The Mutual Improvement Programs are very productive for our proselyting programs," said Mitchener.

Some aspects of the 1965 June Conference of the MIA serve to illustrate the aims and atmosphere that surround its activities. The meeting had a theme: "Love Lights the Way in MIA." It had a major speaker from the pinnacle of the church leadership, N. Eldon Tanner, the apostle and second counselor to David O. McKay. Tanner, who was the president of the Trans-Canada Gas Pipeline Company before he went to Salt Lake City on church duty, told his Tabernacle audience:

"We live in a changing world, and it gives us many challenges, which we hope and pray we can meet. You are working under the direction of the priesthood. No other church in the world has the direction of the Lord as we have. There is no one else in the world who understands God like we do.

"This conference makes me think of the hymn 'Behold a royal army . . . victory, victory through Jesus Christ our Lord.' You are this great army. We have 76,000 officers and teachers to guide the 575,000 youth throughout the church world over, and to prepare the 621,000 who participate in dances each year, and the 162,000 in drama and the 76,000 in speech. There is nothing like this organization in the world . . ."

He is absolutely right. There is nothing like it. He also said, "Be sure that you know that God lives and directs his great church, so that you can stimulate the youth of the church today. The Gospel contains all the answers to the questions of life, and we may realize that we are on the way to the Celestial Kingdom while men are trying to land on the moon and communicate with Mars."

The MIA organizations pretty well support themselves, for almost all the work is done by volunteers. Each ward makes a small per capita donation annually for the MIA and of course maintains the facilities which the young people use. Like everything else in the church, the MIA is closely directed from Salt Lake City. It is not firmly required that the program suggestions be followed to the letter, but if they are not, an inquiry probably would be made politely, for the Mormons have learned over the years that deviation from the pattern may indicate an emerging streak of a latent tendency to heresy.

These youth programs of the MIA are marvelously successful, but Mitchener refused to claim that Mormon youngsters are better behaved than those of other backgrounds, or that Utah and Salt Lake City are free of the curse of juvenile delinquency.

"We don't have any corner on good kids," he said. "We have as many problems as anyone."

(In early 1965, the church inaugurated what it called a "home meeting night" program. Everyone in the family was to arrange his time to be at home on an agreed night each week so the members of the family could get to know each other and share problems and pray together. The idea is to maintain the home ties as a means of curbing any tendency in the young toward lawlessness.)

The MIA does not concentrate entirely on the teen-agers.

It has functions for young married persons, and in the summer of 1965 began to emphasize programs designed for married women in the 25 to 35 age group. For the adults, the MIA is a two-edged tool of the church; it has them helping run the programs for the children; it has programs for adults to participate in.

My talk with Mitchener was interrupted by a telephone call, and fragments of his end of it drifted into my mind. He was discussing airplane schedules and reservations for someone at Grosvenor Court and Claridge's in London. As I looked out at the distant and unchanging desert, I realized that a century earlier men had talked together here about making those same missionary trips to England. But the problems of travel and safety were different in those early days.

One is foolish to pick any aspect of the many parts of this remarkable religion and assert that "this is what is its strength." Yet the temptation is strong when one considers the impact on the whole body of the LDS church of the missionary program. The source for the details of this important function was Gordon B. Hinckley, the Apostle. His office is in the third floor of the beautiful church administration building at 47 E. South Temple, a half block from the Temple Square and next door to the Lion House, where Brigham Young kept some of his plural wives.

I waited on the first floor, in the marble-lined lobby, in a brown leather chair much like those in government waiting rooms in Washington. The beautiful carved marble staircase curved upward, and intent people moved back and forth. There was a man at an information desk, a potted plant here and there, and a woman's heels echoed on the marble. It was quiet and sedate and purposeful. As I sat there, the contrast came to me of the hours I'd spent six weeks earlier sitting in the waiting room of a crowded, bustling, lively, disordered office on Auburn Avenue in Atlanta,

Georgia. This was the office of the Southern Christian Leadership Conference, Dr. Martin Luther King's vehicle to fame.

The point, it seemed to me, was that the calm and quiet and good order showed that the Mormons had arrived and enjoyed the benefits of a bureaucracy at the top of their church. Dr. King and his civil rights group still stood on the outside yearning for the accomplishments which would permit them to have the luxury of initiative smothered in procedure.

At the time of our interview, Apostle Hinckley was in his middle fifties, a pleasant and sincere man who was the product of long years in the service of his church. He had been an apostle for four years, but from his twenty-fifth year he had been involved in one full-time church job or another. He had been executive secretary of the General Missionary Committee for seven years, then an assistant apostle and finally an apostle. He served a mission in the early 1930s in Great Britain.

He described the missionary activity as "inherent in our basic philosophy. The Gospel has been restored by divine revelation and we must carry it to men . . . We disseminate the Gospel to the world to further establish the principles set down by the Lord Jesus Christ . . . We work under a program where we expect every member to be qualified to teach the doctrine."

But this training does not wait until just before the mission trip. It is done throughout the formative years, in the MIA and at priesthood meetings. The young men and women—the ratio is about ten men to each woman—are recommended by their bishops, who presumably have talked with them and their families. The families—or some outside sponsor in rare cases—must pay the cost of the missionary's keep, about $100 a month these days.

The bishop forwards a detailed application and recommendation for his choice. It is reviewed by the missionary committee in Salt Lake City. Apostle Hinckley said that the committee accepts every person recommended to it. It then assigns the missionary, and a "letter of call" goes out, instructing the young man—as in one I was shown—to "labor in the Andes mission." This is signed by President McKay.

About 12,000 missionaries are in the field all the time. A mission lasts from twenty-four to thirty months. The church pays each missionary's travel costs to the mission, except for the first $100, and travel costs home. Bed and board must be provided by someone else during the stay.

They come into Salt Lake City from all over the world on Tuesday morning of about twenty-seven weeks every year. The groups range in size from 100 to 300 missionaries. They hear a talk from one of the top leaders of the church, are talked to by Apostle Hinckley about their draft responsibilities, pass through a health examination, hear the rules for missionaries, see the various monuments and Holy places in Salt Lake City, and six days after arrival head out.

"Think of that as preparation for sending a young man to Taiwan!" said Apostle Hinckley.

The answer is, of course, that they have been preparing for this trip since they were children. They have been selected by a bishop who knew them personally, and who was able to make a judgment on whether each one would withstand the physical and spiritual trials of a missionary effort.

One finds these missionaries in strange places, and not all of them go overseas. For example, a Chinese Saint from Hong Kong was assigned to San Francisco's Chinatown. A young man from Vancouver B.C. might be assigned to the southern United States mission.

They take up their mission at about the age when they would be going into the armed services, and this is a problem that the Saints have handled very practically with the assistance of the selective service authorities. Remember that the draft laws permit exemptions for ministers; remember also that every practicing adult male Mormon (except Negroes) is a member of the priesthood of his church, and that the church has no regular ministerial corps. So the LDS church worked it out carefully. For the twenty-four or thirty months of his mission, the young priest is exempted from the draft; when he comes back home he is just as eligible as the next fellow.

While the missionaries are overseas, they will be usually nineteen to twenty-one years old. They will live in quarters they rent, or church quarters for which they pay a fee. Their food will be simple and similar to what is eaten in the locality. They will spend ten to eighteen hours a day on church work, and try to stay out of trouble, while still winning converts to their religion.

Not long ago there was a feature story in the San Francisco *Chronicle* on Mormon missionaries in Uruguay. It reviewed the colorful lives of these young men, and since they were the sources of the information, it was obvious that their religious obligation to spread the Gospel was providing them with the greatest adventure of their lives. But at the bottom, the old nasty question came up again. The last two paragraphs:

> The missionaries, who avoid political topics, reported that one of the most frequent issues they are compelled to discuss is polygamy, once permitted by the religion, though given up under pressure from United States authorities.
>
> The missionaries say that only 3 per cent of the church's membership practiced polygamy at that time, that a man could take on a second wife only with the permission of the first, and that the situation had been encouraged by a shortage of men within the ranks of the religion.

Of course these are the answers provided to these young men from childhood by their religious instructors. But, as

we shall see in a later chapter, they are only partially true—
not even half true.

There is a great residue of good will that accrues to the
United States from the work of these fine young men. There
is no question of this. What they have been doing for generations is comparable to what the Peace Corps has been
doing for a few years. But the foreign countries where they
serve generally win the affections of the young Saints, too.

Apostle Hinckley said that he was in the mill towns of
England as a missionary in the 1930s. He said, "I love the
English. You can never sell the British short in my book."
His son was on a mission to Germany and "he loves the Ger-
mans."

"Salt Lake City is the most cosmopolitan place in the
world because of this missionary program," the apostle asserted. "They go out and live with these people, learn the
language, learn to love the people. What greater thing could
you have than to send out 4000 to 5000 young men every
year to go and lose themselves in the service of others?"

Visitors have wondered how it was that the *Salt Lake Tribune* printed such a great flow of foreign news. On understanding the element of Salt Lake City life that the apostle
described, the answer is plain. A man who did a mission in
Geneva will always have curiosity about things in Geneva
today. The Mormons have been many times where the
action was starting. A footnote to history: The missionaries
left Germany on August 24, 1939, one week before the assault on Poland opened World War II.

The missionaries are well scattered, but they are not everywhere. Many nations have none. There are none in
Black Africa, for reasons that will be explained in a subsequent chapter. There are none behind the Iron Curtain.
The heaviest involvements are in the Pacific and Europe,
but the commitment is growing in South America.

A mission is organized with a mission president and his two counselors. The president has a home furnished for his family. The day I talked to Apostle Hinckley, a group of twenty mission presidents was leaving for duty in various stations. It included lawyers, a merchant, an atomic researcher, an educator, an engineer, an oil company executive, a banker, a real estate developer and a chaplain back from military duty.

There is no question but that the mission maintenance bill is a great drain on the Mormon community. With the cost at about $100 a month per missionary, the families of Mormon country must provide about $1.2 million a month for the support of the 12,000 missionaries in the field. If the numbers of young men seeking a missionary assignment should rise, the cost would be even greater. Economists have commented on this drain.

The first Mormon missionaries went to the British Isles in 1837. This was because they spoke a language understood there. Since then the activity has been self-perpetuating in Europe. The effort in the Pacific grew out of a mission to the Sandwich Islands, and has progressed to the point where now the church is working among the Fiji islanders. It is administering the priesthood to them, even though they are black and generally considered by anthropologists to be Negroid. (The Mormons bar Negroes from the priesthood.)

While the missionary program has been a part of the Saints' religion for almost as long as the church has existed, another great program that has earned favor within the church has grown up within the past generation.

This is the welfare program.

The interview with Bishop Glen Rudd, who is the manager of the welfare plan, was in his office at Welfare Square in Salt Lake City. He is a slender, graying man with thick and well-groomed hair, heavy horn-rimmed glasses that make his face appear heavier than it is. His office opens off the busy room—which looks a little like a clean but uninteresting supermarket—where people were filling their orders for goods that their bishops said they should have. In his office Bishop Rudd was surrounded by remembrances of his youthful mission to New Zealand, including three beautiful paintings of the Maoris, oil on velvet.

Bishop Rudd said, "Now the church doesn't want me to tell you very much about the welfare program. I don't agree with that, but that's the way it is." The only church-published figure was that in 1965 the welfare plan helped 82,315 people. This was but 3.2 per cent of the church membership.

The welfare plan is an outgrowth of two things: First, the Mormons have a strong tradition of sharing to prevent suffering among the poverty-stricken; and second, Heber J. Grant, the LDS president in the 1930s, was an avid opponent of the programs of President Franklin D. Roosevelt. For a long time there was a myth that no Saint ever worked on WPA or took welfare during the great Depression; this of course is nonsense. Today there is a widespread suspicion of error in the Saints' claim to be able to "take care of our own" so that no Mormon need be a public charge. I am convinced that this is true, although it is questionable how long the welfare plan could continue to provide for thousands of persons if a depression of the magnitude of that of the 1930s came again. This is a point where much anti-LDS sentiment focuses. These critics of the church insist the welfare program really does not "take care of their own" but actually falls far short.

The welfare organization is set up in such a way as to provide little—if any—drain on the general church revenues which come almost entirely from tithing. Each stake—and there are 400 or more stakes as this is written—has a project for the welfare program. Some of them own farms; others have factories; others have canneries. Each is provided with a quota for its production for a season. The stake president, his counselors and the bishops of the wards in the stake then must rustle up the volunteer workers and provide the materials to meet the quota.

As Bishop Rudd talked, one of his assistants came in to tell him that 30,000 cans of peas were processed the night before in the cannery adjacent to the Welfare Square storehouse. All labor was donated by a stake 20 miles away.

The welfare organization is controlled by the Council of the Twelve Apostles which created the General Church Welfare Committee which at that time had about twenty members. The chairman was the presiding bishop, John H. Vandenberg. Bishop Rudd had been in the program from its inception and was well able to make clear the use of wards, stakes and their officers to fulfill the goals set by the church-wide welfare committee.

The welfare program is set up in regions, which are clusters of stakes. There are eighty of these, each with a chairman who consolidates information and reports to Salt Lake City. For example, there is a region for New Zealand, another for England, four near Los Angeles, one in Hawaii.

One of the quarterly conferences which each stake holds is devoted to welfare programs. Another is for missionary activity, and a third is for home teaching. Bishop Rudd explained that the quarterly conferences make it possible to "check constantly to keep from diluting the doctrine as happened after Christ died."

Each ward bishop estimates annual welfare commodity requirements. These are totaled and the figures work their way up to the General Church Welfare Committee which divides the work assignments with the knowledge of what each region can do best. As a bookkeeping measure, a dollar value is assigned to all of this, as the estimates move up and the assignments come back down. However, this dollar value figure has only a cousinly connection with reality. The welfare program pays cash for its supplies only for such things as razor blades, light bulbs and shoes.

Using the dollar figures for convenience, the welfare committee will give an assignment to a stake. The per capita contribution for all church members for welfare for a year may be set at $2.10, as it appears to have been in 1965, and the stake is told to produce so much goods—which are specified. A stake in the southwest part of Salt Lake City, for example, was told to produce 125,000 pounds of milk, 5423 dozen eggs, 2500 pounds of pork, 1832 pounds of chickens. An arbitrary value of about $11,000 was assigned to this.

The older stakes have some project such as a farm or a factory. Bishop Rudd said that his home stake was made up of about 5500 people, and that for years its families paid $10 or $20 a year each until it now owns a $150,000 farm. But the general welfare committee assigns the use to which the farm is put.

When a Mormon family is in need, that need is discovered quickly through the visiting system of the priesthood quorums. They are obligated to make contact with each family within their assigned area within a relatively short period. At the quorum meeting that week, the visiting priests who have found a family in need will report that fact. The head of the Women's Relief Society will be dispatched by the bishop to visit the home and report to him. Then an order will be drawn on the welfare system storehouse for the food and clothing and supplies that the family may need. If the family needs money, the bishop has a fund to provide that in limited amounts. The money comes from contributions in lieu of two meals the Saints are supposed to skip each month on Sacrament Sunday. No set contribution is demanded; the individual family works out what it thinks would be the proper amount. One Saint told me his family gave $8.80 a month, which probably is in the high range.

The needy family will take the bishop's order to the store-house, such as the one outside Bishop Rudd's office at Welfare Square. There the order can be filled, and the baskets are checked, but no money ever changes hands. The bishop's order is surrendered in lieu of cash. A broad range of food and clothing and household supplies is available, 92 per cent of it produced by the Saints themselves. Where brand names are used, the Mormon-produced things are branded "Deseret."

Here are some of the materials: Peanut butter from Houston; tuna from San Diego; tomatoes from Utah; macaroni from Utah; raisins from Fresno; prunes from Santa Rosa, California; soap from Utah; gelatine from Kansas City; toothpaste and shaving cream from Chicago; orange juice from Los Angeles; grapefuit juice from Phoenix and Mesa; Utah and Idaho sugar for which the welfare plan has traded sugar beets contributed from its farms.

No one receiving public welfare can get help from the Mormon church, Bishop Rudd assured me. But another bishop said this was only the ideal, that in practice there is a joint support of some persons by both public and religious agencies.

In an adjoining room the garments produced by the Women's Relief Society hung on racks, ready for distribution. An effort is made to avoid the "institutional" look in clothing from the Welfare Plan. Shoes are purchased from manufacturing companies; the Women's Relief Society does not have patterns furnished to it.

As Bishop Rudd showed me around the cannery next door, the afternoon shift from some stake was appearing to take the peas brought in from the fields that day. Here were the Mormon women of today—strong, reliant on themselves and their religion, dressed in the common-sense denim slacks and shirts for their job. They were there as a religious duty, and they looked ready to perform it.

Down in the basement, Bishop Rudd introduced a crippled girl in a wheelchair and a boy who had trouble articulating his words. The boy had been rescued from a home for the retarded and put into the egg candling room where he met the girl, said the Bishop. Now they are married.

The Saints are extremely proud of their welfare program. They have managed to get it on the Gray Line Bus tour of Salt Lake City so that thousands of persons a year tour the Welfare Square operation.

Their program has enjoyed great success in the upsweep of the economy since it was founded. It also has the benefit of inheriting an organization based on the philosophy of the upward reach, of striving and thrusting always forward. There are no great minority groups attached to the Mormon kite, as with the general culture of the United States today. The church is able to find jobs for anyone who is at all employable. It is able to take the time—through the volunteer counseling of its priesthood quorums—to help its "hard luck" members to pull up and out of trouble.

The church is able to exert the strongest of sanctions against people who refuse to follow the rules for self-help that are given to them—it can disown them, although I have never heard of its doing that to someone who was poor. Again, in discussing various phases of Mormon life, one hears phrases like "people need an opportunity to work." Failure to understand that some people do not find work uplifting seems to be a Mormon trait.

The Relief Society of the Church of Jesus Christ of Latter-day Saints is for the women of the church, commonly called the Women's Relief Society. Its international affairs are conducted from an office building behind the Hotel Utah on the old tithing office property. This was established in 1842 at Nauvoo by the Prophet Joseph to look after the needs of the poor and to "assist by correcting the morals and strengthening the virtues of the community," as a church publication describes the reasons. There were eighteen members on March 17, 1842, when it was organized; now there are more than 250,000. For the organization's 123rd annual conference in the Salt Lake City Tabernacle in 1965, over 10,000 attended from all over the world.

The Relief Society grew strong in Utah, and in 1880 came under the control of a general board. The president in those days was Eliza R. Snow, who was one of the plural wives taken by the Prophet. They were married by Brigham Young on June 29, 1842. After Joseph was murdered, Eliza became a wife of Brigham Young. Her brother, Lorenzo Snow, was the fifth LDS president, serving from 1898 to 1901. The Relief Society organization reaches into all parts of the LDS structure, paralleling the priesthood quorums which the men attend. The women have programs that vary somewhat depending on their locality and interests. In Salt Lake City, for example, in the early 1960s they spent several years in a comprehensive English literature study conducted by Mormon elders who were on the faculty of the University of Utah. The Society publishes its own magazine.

The Deseret Sunday School Union is another valuable tool of the church. This grew up in haphazard fashion at first, but by the 1860s, the organizational genius of George Q. Cannon, the important leader of the late nineteenth century, saw the opportunity. In 1866, the magazine, *Juvenile Instructor*, began to appear. A church publication says:

> It contains uniform lessons for each department of the Sunday Schools. . . . As an organization, auxiliary to the priesthood, the ultimate aim of the Sunday Schools is to teach the principles of the Gospel and to stimulate the pupils to render willing obedience thereto. More specifically, the Sunday School aims so to equip its members that they will be able not only to work out their own salvation through the application of, and obedience to, the principles of the Gospel

which they have been taught, but also to prepare themselves for service in the priesthood, in the mission fields, and in the organizations at home, through which opportunities are afforded them to render service to others.

U.S. Senator Wallace F. Bennett, elected in 1950 and re-elected in 1956 and 1962, has been a member of the Sunday School General Board since 1935, and treasurer since 1938. LDS President David O. McKay was the chief operating officer of the Sunday School for many years when he was a young man.

As one looks at these broad outlines of the organizational structure of the LDS church, it becomes clear that all the parts fit together, that every member has a place. The key to it all is the strong emotional commitment that one must give to the Restored Gospel. Not believing this, the sacrifices involved would be meaningless and soon would stop. If there is no opportunity for exaltation in the Celestial Kingdom by good works on earth in the Mortal Existence, then why put up with all of these other things?

But if the doctrine is true, then no sacrifice is too great.

IV

"One Tenth of Their Interest Annually"

THE FINANCIAL foundation of the Church of Jesus Christ of Latter-day Saints is a revelation Joseph Smith received on July 8, 1838, on the Missouri frontier where he had led his people. The Prophet's attempts to set in motion the United Order of Enoch had failed, even though he created it in the terms set down in an earlier revelation. This was a plan for a religious cooperative, which usually have had very bad luck. When the United Order caused arguments, a new way had to be found, so prayers had been offered: "O, Lord, show unto thy servants how much thou requirest of the properties of thy people for a tithing."

The Prophet said this was the Divine answer to his prayer:

Verily, thus saith the Lord, I require all their surplus property to be put into the hands of the bishop of my church in Zion.

For the building of mine house, and for the laying of the foundation of Zion and for the priesthood, and for the debts of the Presidency of my Church.

And this shall be the beginning of the tithing of my people.

And after that, those who have thus been tithed shall pay one-tenth of all their interest annually; and this shall be a standing law unto them forever, for my holy priesthood, saith the Lord.

Verily I say unto you, it shall come to pass that all those

who gather unto the land of Zion shall be tithed of their surplus properties and shall observe this law, or they shall not be found worthy to abide among you.

And I say unto you, if my people observe not this law, to keep it holy, and by this law sanctify the land of Zion unto me, that my statutes and my judgments may be kept thereon, that it may be most holy, behold, verily I say unto you, it shall not be a land of Zion unto you.

And this shall be an ensample unto all the stakes of Zion. Even so. Amen.

Faithful Mormons today accept that as a statement of Divine purpose delivered through their Prophet Joseph. They give up more than $100 million a year in tithes in support of this belief. The money is collected by their bishops. Receipts are given and records kept of who did and didn't tithe. The money is sent directly to Salt Lake City to the high officers of the church. This forwarding of the tithes is in obedience to a short revelation Joseph Smith recorded on July 18, 1838. This one directed what should happen to the money collected under the tithing revelation which was then just ten days old. The new one said:

Verily, thus saith the Lord, the time is now come, that it shall be disposed of by a council, comprised of the First Presidency of my Church, and of the bishop and his council, and by my high council; and by mine own voice unto them, saith the Lord. Even so. Amen.

In those days almost everyone who was involved in the tithing revelation was near at hand, for the church consisted of only a few hundred families. But today, with Mormons scattered around the world, the same organizational pattern is followed. The millions of dollars are distributed according to decisions reached by a group made up of the Mormon president and his advisors in the First Presidency; the presiding bishop and his two advisors; and the Council of the Twelve Apostles.

They give no accounting; no Mormon would dream of demanding one. It is popularly supposed—by many Mormons as well as by Gentiles—that these men at the top of the church have used the money to create a fat portfolio which gives the Saints control over a broad range of businesses.

This is not true. The church owns a few companies, and has small holdings in a few more. The management of the church's money is not the chief task these religious leaders set out for themselves. They consider that their lives are lived in the further spread of the Restored Gospel.

Often it is said that the church leaders are "set apart" to devote their lives to the church's business. They get no salary, inquirers are told, but individual payments are given to them to enable them to live, and these payments will vary since some of the apostles created wealth for themselves before they were "set apart" while others did not.

However, another view of this statement of income has been given by Jerald and Sandra Tanner, the Mormon apostates, in their attack on the LDS church, *Mormonism, Shadow or Reality.*

Insurance companies in Utah are required to submit a report showing the salaries that their officials receive. The general public are allowed to examine this report which is kept at the State Capitol Building. The Mormon Church owns the Beneficial Life Insurance Company, and many of the General Authorities of the Mormon Church are on the board of directors. We have copied some of the salaries received by leaders of the Mormon Church for the year 1963. They are as follows:

David O. McKay, president of the church $13,400
Hugh B. Brown, member of First Presidency 9,200
Henry D. Moyle, member of First Presidency 6,750
Nathan Tanner, member of First Presidency 1,700
Joseph Fielding Smith, Apostle 6,200

Henry D. Moyle died during the year, and Nathan Tanner moved into the First Presidency. This is probably the reason that Henry D. Moyle's salary was not as high as it was in 1962 (in 1962 it was $9,200) and also why Nathan Tanner received only $1,700. . . . To our knowledge, there is no way to find out how much the church authorities are being paid by the other companies owned by the church.

In all particulars, it is difficult to discuss the financial status of the LDS church. Precise information is lacking. The church has a policy of secrecy on financial matters that makes it difficult to check the accuracy of reports picked up from non-church sources.

One of the best of these sources is Dr. Leonard Arrington, the economic historian who is a professor at Utah State University at Logan. Another source is the fragments published infrequently by the church. There are also knowledgeable Mormon and non-Mormon sources—who demand anonymity. These sources enable us to make a set of assumptions about LDS church finances:

The church income runs about $100 million to $125 million, and by far the greatest part of it is from tithes.

The church does not have the great set of investments which have been attributed to it by folk lore in the Mountain West.

After David O. McKay became LDS president in 1951, the church went into a period of rapid expansion which consumed much of the financial fat stored during the presidency of Heber J. Grant from 1918 to 1945.

Two projects take the lion's share of the tithing money. These are the missionary program and the growth of the various phases of the LDS educational program.

The Mormons as individuals have earned a reputation for financial sagacity, but their leaders are just as capable of fumbling and error as are those of any other large organization.

As the examination of the Mormons progresses, one gradually becomes aware that history has provided something unusual in this study. Biologists have a normal group that is uninvolved in the changed environment. This is the control group. But these are not to be found usually in history. However in the separate Reorganized Church of Jesus Christ of Latter Day Saints, we have a religious institution that in many ways parallels the LDS church headquartered in Salt Lake City. When we compare them, the differences in their development become even more startling; the differences of the Mormons from the rest of American society become more readily recognized.

One example of this is in the theological basis of tithing and its eventual pattern in the two groups. Both accept the divinity of the revelation on tithing, just as they share many other fundamentals. But the Utah Mormons have interpreted the revelation to mean that a faithful member would give a flat 10 per cent of his income "off the top." The Reorganized Mormons interpret it to mean that a member should give 10 per cent of what he has left after he has paid his normal expenses of living. This is a highly significant difference in interpretation of a document fundamental to both groups. The difference has given one church—the Utah Mormons—a great fund of money with which to push church development and expansion. The other church has remained smaller.

The Reorganized Church also lacks the compulsion for secrecy which has gripped the Utah church for many years. The Reorganized Church publishes its income and some of its expenditures. In 1964, total income was $3.5 million from about 190,000 members. The Utah Mormons, with ten times as many members, had thirty times the income—if the minimum estimate we use is correct.

From the earliest days, the Utah Mormons have been harried by their leaders for the collection of the tithes, except perhaps in cooperative enterprises in the remote valleys. In those places the priesthood controlled everything so that the church was fed from the common loaf. Even today, the pressure is strong on the Saints to produce their gifts for the church. No one but the Bishop knows if a family tithes the full 10 per cent; but the bishopric is an office that is held by different men during the years that a family will live in a neighborhood, so the moral pressure of peer opinion grows. A family may be permitted to give less than the full tithe and yet maintain good standing; but the requirement is poverty and what Mormon wants to plead that excuse?—Remember also that the bishop passes on applications for admittance to the Temple. If a father has not been tithing, yet his son hopes to be married in a Temple ceremony, will the bishop issue a "Recommend" that will pass the father inside to witness the ceremony?

The type of pressure on Mormons to tithe probably was clearly shown for outsiders in a speech to the faculty of Brigham Young University on September 25, 1957, by Ernest Wilkinson, the president of the school. Here is a section of the speech as it was quoted by the Tanners in their anti-Mormon book, *Mormonism, Shadow or Reality:*

When I am called upon this year to pass on proposed promotions in academic rank for members of the faculty, I hope I do not have to refuse any on the ground that the nominee does not adhere in practice to one of the qualifications approved by the faculty of this institution for advancement in academic rank, namely: "Adherence to the principles and teachings of the Gospel as taught by the Church of Jesus Christ of Latter-day Saints," one of which is the payment of tithing. And I trust that such payment will be voluntary, for we do not want any person on this faculty to share his income with the Lord because of any coercion or compulsion. Should there be any member of the faculty who does not voluntarily desire to pay his tithing, the honorable and manly thing for that person to do is to resign his position. We shall be strong as individuals and collectively as a faculty only to the extent we exercise our free agency by freely choosing to obey the commandments and revelations of the Lord.

Wilkinson would argue in justification of this threat to punish those who didn't tithe. One justification would be the fact that the entire Brigham Young University is supported by the tithes given up by the faithful, whether or not they can afford it, whether or not they would rather spend the money for something else. He would expect the intellectual elite of the church—the faculty at B.Y.U.—to pay its share as well. Those who would be tempted to shade a little off the Lord's 10 per cent would be sharing a problem that confronts so many of the Saints: How to stay right with the church, yet enjoy some of what modern civilization offers in the market place?

Most Mormons try hard to pay the tithe and somehow fill the gap in income that paying it leaves. They are a devout people, and their religion demands so much else of them that the sacrifice of the tithe can be carried without flinching.

The economic impact of paying is community-wide. Its meaning can be illustrated by one example given to me by a highly reliable source in Salt Lake City. He spoke of a small Mormon settlement with which he was acquainted. He said that of the two score families, seven were on relief and three or four tithed only occasionally, leaving about twenty-nine or thirty families to carry the load. Yet the tithing income to the general authorities in Salt Lake City from this village was about $9000 a year.

This is very important money. It is about all that the relatively poor people of that little settlement could afford for outside investment. When they surrendered this for the good of their souls, it meant that an equivalent amount of work was not going to be done somewhere in the social-economic structure of their village. It meant that they could not invest in new machines, new homes, or even in stock ownership. Such figures must be multiplied many times, and such examples repeated over and over as the church each year amasses its millions and millions.

What happens to all of this money? Only a dim picture filters through to the outside world of the decision-making process. Even the network of pipelines through which the money goes out is not well understood except in the top reaches of the LDS Establishment. Generally, the decisions are made in the form of recommendations by committees which report to the Council of the Twelve Apostles and to the First Presidency. Sometimes, these committees are made up of the council and the presidency, operating under one title; then this same group sits as the Council on the Disposition of Tithes and passes on its earlier recommendation. Such is the case when the church education program is considered.

No one outside the top administrative levels of the church can say in detail where the money goes. Broadly, it is possible to designate the main areas in which it is spent, and to estimate the sums spent in each area. For example, the missionary program took about $17 million in 1964 and the education program took about $25 million. It costs something to operate the bureaucracy in Salt Lake City, but not so much as might be expected, since so much work is done for nothing, and much of the rest is done at prices far below the going rate for the talent involved. Remember that almost every Mormon religious job and administrative job at the low levels is filled by a volunteer who supports himself doing something else.

There is no shortage of typists and file clerks to work in the church offices. In the higher level jobs, a subsistence salary is paid when a man wanted for a specific job lacks the financial resources to support himself while giving full time to the church. At the top, where the apostles and others are "set apart" for their church assignment, they leave the work-a-day world and the church undertakes to support them and their families—perhaps, as we have seen, by putting them on the payroll of a church-owned company. LDS President McKay has lived for years in an apartment in the church-owned Hotel Utah. The apartment above him was held on a long lease by Marriner S. Eccles, former chairman of the Federal Reserve System and head of the First Security Corporation of Salt Lake City. Eccles was born into a Mormon family at Ogden. He served his mission in Scotland, but has not been active as a churchman.

Much of the tithing money goes into financing new meeting houses and Temples, and also into real estate purchases and developments in Salt Lake City. The church has used various devices to hold its property titles. Early plats of Salt Lake City give the impression that the city was owned by Brigham Young, for each of the church-owned lots was held in his name. However, this was as the trustee-in-trust for the church—a device blown out of the water in the great struggles with the federal government in the 1880s.

Today, there is a variety of ownership structures. Most of them are meaningless unless one is a title surveyor. The main properties are held by the Corporation of the President, such as the property which is essential to the operation of the church—the Temple Square, for example, or the block which holds Hotel Utah, the church administration building and Brigham Young's former homes.

There are many other church-owned properties in downtown Salt Lake City. By one reliable estimate, the church owns thirty acres of downtown property. Periodically, a struggle can be seen by which the Saints seek to recover a bit of land alienated from their control. The Zions Securities Corporation, a wholly owned subsidiary of the church, takes the lead in these operations. Spokesmen for the church always point out that Zions Securities pays taxes on what it earns.

In addition to the Hotel Utah, the church owns the Hotel Temple Square and the Hotel Utah Motor Lodge. Not long ago it turned the New Ute Hotel into a hostelry for missionaries. It owns the new Kennecott Building on the site of a bank which the church once owned and then merged into a bigger banking system in which the church sold its interest. Thus the Saints lost control of the property where their bank had stood. It is widely believed in Salt Lake City that the Kennecott Building was constructed to regain possession of the land.

In addition to the network of chapels, office buildings, and other real estate holdings which are the dominant realty interest of Salt Lake City, the Saints also have a set of business holdings that are essential to supplemental programs of the church. These include a newspaper, the *Deseret News*, which fills the afternoon market in Salt Lake City; KSL radio and KSL-TV, both wholly owned by the church and both affiliated with the Columbia Broadcasting System; and interests in KBOI-TV in Boise, KID in Idaho Falls, and KIRO radio and KIRO-TV in Seattle.

The *Deseret News* is the mouthpiece of the church. The editor of the editorial page is William Smart, my friend for many years. He is the Bishop of his ward. He is a graduate of Reed College, the ultra-liberal arts school in Portland, Oregon, and was ready for admission to Harvard Graduate School in the late 1940s when he was offered a job on the newspaper published by his family's church. He told me he was very happy with his decision. As a man born into the LDS church, as a fervent follower of his religion, and as a man of excellent education Bishop Smart is well equipped to discover, understand and explain the answers that the

Restored Gospel offers to the problems of the times. On moral questions, the *Deseret News* speaks with the church's voice. The Saints respond.

As in everything else connected with the Mormon church, the ultimate authority rests with the President, and his counselors, the First Presidency. Nathan Eldon Tanner, the second counselor in the First Presidency, oversees the *Deseret News*. The Council of the Twelve is represented by Apostles Gordon B. Hinckley and Thomas S. Monson. At one time, Apostle Mark E. Petersen was chairman of the board of the *News* but he was "excused," i.e., removed, when he went to Europe on a mission. In that same set of assignments, President McKay also sent another conservative apostle, Ezra Taft Benson, to Europe. Both since have been brought back to Salt Lake City. Apostle Petersen's removal from the board of the *News* ended a life-long connection with the paper. He began as carrier boy, moved through the chairs to become editor and general manager before being "set apart" as an apostle in 1944.

The addition of Apostle Hinckley and Counselor Tanner from the First Presidency came in response to the requests of executives of the *News* who wanted closer ties with the center of power of the church. With these two, they have it so long as David O. McKay is president, for Tanner will continue as a counselor. Apostle Monson, born in 1927, is the youngest member of the Council of Twelve. He was manager of the Deseret News Press, the church's commercial printing operation, when he was made an apostle in 1963.

The editorial board of the *Deseret News* meets every week. Apostle Hinckley sits on that board. If the employees of the *News* are in deep disagreement with some expression of view put forward by the apostle, who presumably sits there to speak for the church leadership, they may walk up the street and talk to the First Presidency or other apostles. Such a thing would be unusual; but it is not unthinkable.

There is little likelihood of a sanction being exerted against the complaining employees, either. No observer is likely to advance the argument that the LDS church is a democracy; but neither is it directed by cruel, power-mad men. It is a world of great talkers, of great arguers, and they respect a point of view. One must believe the Restored Gospel as interpreted in Temple Square, but he is reasonably free beyond that.

However, it is plain that the *Deseret News* is the organ of the LDS leadership, and will enunciate whatever that leadership decrees.

It is through the *Deseret News* that the LDS church holds 300,000 shares of stock in the Times Mirror Corporation, publisher of the *Los Angeles Times,* one of the nation's most important newspapers and by far the best published in the West. There are about 5,500,000 shares of common stock so that the church's ownership amounts to about 5.5 per cent. This is the next largest bloc to the 49.9 per cent controlled by the Chandler family which directs Times Mirror Corporation. The Mormon ownership traces back to the purchase by the *Times* and the *News* of the Hawley Pulp and Paper Company at Oregon City, Oregon, after World War II. This venerable paper plant was renamed Publishers' Paper, built up, and has become a major source of newsprint. Early in 1965 Times Mirror Corporation exchanged the large block of its stock for the 32.3 per cent of Publishers' Paper owned by the *News.* This made the LDS church an imporant stockholder in the *Los Angeles Times.* In early 1966, the stock was worth approximately $18,675,000.

The control and use of the radio and television holdings to advance the church's religious views is not obvious, because the Saints want to conform to the Federal Communications Commission's rules on operation. Yet, there is no doubt that the church control of those broadcast channels causes them to carry programs that otherwise would not be broadcast. As an example, the Tabernacle Choir, a CBS radio staple for about four decades, now appears on television in four markets every Sunday. These, of course, are the four stations that the church owns. At the same time, these stations are generous in their time for other religious groups, more generous than the usual broadcaster.

The church also owns the Deseret Bookstores which provide an outlet for the various publications of the church, as well as for commercially printed books of other publishers. However, no book which has an anti-Mormon cast is sold there, nor are any permitted which have a nature judged to be immoral by the store's management.

In the late summer of 1965, the church's communications network was in the news in a different way. President François Duvalier, the dictator of Haiti, complained to the United States against what he said were worldwide broadcasts shortwaved from New York denouncing his government. He wanted them stopped. The programs were carried on Radio New York Worldwide (WRUL) and who do you think owns that? The Saints.

The announcers spoke the Haitian patois, Creole, and gave Papa Doc unshirted hell, but their scripts were prepared by the United Haitienne Internationale, an exile group, not by the U.S. government and certainly not by the Saints. WRUL was paid $2,362.50 a month by a group headed by Dr. Paul Magloire, a former Haitian president. Ralf Brent, president of WRUL, said it was purely a commercial deal. The Mormons took over the station in 1962. Five transmitters carry mostly commercial messages, but the church got the property because it also can use it for carrying LDS programs around the world. After all, the system ties a Mormon in Australia closer to Salt Lake City than his Catholic neighbor is tied to Rome. The best estimates are that WRUL loses money every year which the church makes up.

A church-backed building program around the fringes of

Temple Square in the 1960s has aroused the animosities of many of the longtime residents of Salt Lake City—not all of them Gentiles, either. Some of this feeling comes from the outrage any old-timer feels when the scene around him changes. But beyond this is the feeling that the church is putting up buildings that are going to hide its architectural jewel, the old Temple, with its strange design that someone called "remembered Gothic." Thomas F. O'Dea, the Catholic scholar who became an authority on the Mormons, said: "What the Rockefellers did for the Catholics in New York in overshadowing St. Patrick's, the Mormons are doing for themselves in Salt Lake City."

A Mormon critic of the church building policy added: "And St. Pat's is not the Vatican. This Temple is the center of the Mormon world and these people are acting like they want to hide it."

A little of the building has been in Temple Square itself. An annex was built onto the Temple, but this does not seriously detract from the old building, since the annex was constructed with gray rock from the same quarry that produced the stone for the Temple almost a century ago.

The greatest anguish came in 1963 with the announcement of plans for a twenty-five-story office building that would rise on half of the old Tithing block, completely overshadowing the Temple, the Hotel Utah, the Greek columns of the administration building, the Lion House, the Beehive House and everything else in Salt Lake City except the Wasatch Mountains. This would house church offices, it was explained, but critics pointed out that half of that end of town was office buildings owned by the church and that these now would be empty.

Outwardly, it appeared the protests had made no difference. The building was started. The great underground garage has been completed. It includes the foundations for the twenty-five-story building. But as this is written, the plans for the building itself seem to have been shoved into a drawer somewhere. The roof of the garage is being covered with dirt for lawn, and the bare metal of the steel supports for the walls of the building are being treated against corrosion, since they stick up about three feet above the concrete of the garage roof. The plans are at a standstill.

But in typical Mormon fashion, the top leaders of the church speak of a "progression of plans for the building. The work is moving forward." Hugh B. Brown, the first counselor to President McKay, insisted that the office building was being constructed according to plan.

While the office building is still in the future, the nineteen-story Kennecott Building was opened in 1965, built by the church to be filled with offices of the copper mining company. It stands across from the administration building. But this practice of surrounding the Temple with towers goes back to the construction of the Hotel Utah, which has towered over the Temple for many years. This is unpleasing particularly at night when a garish neon sign on the hotel roof clashes with the floodlights on the spires of the Temple.

However, one must agree that these are the properties of the Mormons and theirs is the right to surround them with whatever they want.

The Mormon real estate holdings in Salt Lake City are fairly well understood, but much mythology exists about the extent of their stock holdings. For example, it is widely believed that the church owns a great block of the Union Pacific Railroad. This is untrue. The supposition arises from the fact that a high official of the church for many years held a seat on the board of directors of the UP, and because the railroad was built across Utah with Mormon labor.

The leading expert on Mormon business life, Professor Arrington, says that the church owns no UP stock. Intead, it appears, the railroad has for many years had a Mormon leader on its board for the public relations value. Professor

Arrington also has traced the church interest in the UP that derived from Mormon workmen building its Utah route. He said that Brigham Young signed contracts obligating his church members to do the grading, tunneling and bridging for the UP in their state. They fulfilled the contracts. Then, when the road went bankrupt as soon as it was opened because of the great manipulations during construction days, the Mormons did not get paid. Brigham took partial payment in rails and rolling stock which he used to build a railroad from Ogden to Salt Lake City. He sold that one and used the money to build more railroads, taking the steel to more Mormon areas.

However, the church does have stock holdings. It is impossible to pinpoint information on all of these. The most one can do is discover some church interest and list it. For example, the beet sugar business: The church owns about 60 per cent of Utah and Idaho Sugar Company; it once had a position in Amalgamated Sugar, but traded this away to get out of Amalgamated which was dominated by Marriner S. Eccles. This withdrawal from Amalgamated came under the administration of President Heber J. Grant, who generally is considered in business circles in Utah and by historians to have been oriented toward conservative business practices. The church owned about 15 per cent of Amalgamated and traded it for a block of U. & I. owned by Floyd Odlum, the investor and business manager. Odlum sold his Amalgamated, but the church kept its U. & I. so that today it dominates the beet sugar company.

The Mormons own the Beneficial Life Insurance Company. Its sign flashes from atop the church-owned Union Pacific Building, asking of the night Is YOUR LIFE INSURANCE BENEFICIAL? The church also has the Home Fire Insurance Company.

The developmental nature of these enterprises is plain. The Saints needed insurance. They needed a fair market for their sugar beets. They also in the beginning needed a store where they could buy without making the Gentile rich.

Zion's Cooperative Mercantile Institution (ZCMI) goes back to the foundations of the religious colony in the desert. Today, it is one of the most progressive department stores in Salt Lake City and its flirtation with cooperative movements and its position as the closely controlled official store for the church are far behind it. The church owns about a third of the stock, which is enough for control. But the management is not controlled by the church in the same sense that it controls, say, the *Deseret News*.

In 1952 the church took an interesting step to assure the *News* of a clear field in the afternoon newspaper market in Salt Lake City. It bought out the competing *Telegram* which had been operated by the morning *Salt Lake Tribune,* owned by generations of Catholics and once viciously anti-Mormon. It is widely accepted in Salt Lake City that the *Deseret News* had been losing heavily, so that the price of $2 million paid for the *Telegram* was considered to be a bargain by the church leaders. Soon after this purchase, the *Tribune* and the *Deseret News* formed a joint printing, circulation and advertising solicitation company—the Newspaper Agency Corporation—which leaves the *News* free to follow its editorial courses, which generally are politically independent except where an issue or candidate is seen to be injurious to the purposes or doctrines of the LDS church.

At one time the church owned about two-thirds of the stock of the Hotel Utah. This other stock was called in and bought up a year or so before the hotel corporation borrowed $4 million from Salt Lake banks in the 1960s for a modernization program. When these church corporations borrow money, never does the church guarantee repayment. Nor does the loan have any religious property behind it. All that guarantees repayment is the secular-use property involved.

Over the years, the Saints have acquired huge ranch properties, some of which are operated as a part of the welfare program, some of which are not. The Canadian ranches include about 80,000 acres near Cardston, Alberta, where thousands of head of feeding cattle are kept. The proceeds go toward costs of new chapels and other building programs in Canada. Originally, the ranches were bought because tithing money from the thousands of Canadian Saints could not be taken out of Canada. The investment was a good one and has increased the value of the formerly blocked currency. Title is held by the Corporation of the Presiding Bishop in Salt Lake City.

The Deseret Farms in Florida were bought in 1950. This amounted to about 220,000 acres of swampland. The land was drained. The insect pests were destroyed. About 30,-000 head of cattle were put for feeding. This was integrated with a feed lot operation in Albany, Georgia. Heavy borrowing had to be done to finance this. The borrowing amounted to about $25 million. A part of the property was sold and the loan was down to about $18 million in late 1965.

One picks up information about the Mormon's finances and business activities in strange places. Once in an airport in Grand Rapids, Michigan, a specialist in animal diseases told me that the Mormons had done poorly at first on the feed lot operation until they concentrated on raising the quality of stock they brought to it. Then they began to make money rapidly, he said.

In 1965 Hugh B. Brown, the first counselor, was the highest ranking church official available for interview, with President McKay in decline as he passed his ninety-second birthday. President Brown, who holds that title as a member of the First Presidency, made the point emphatically that borrowing to improve the properties of the church was not in any way connected with the religious activities or with the tithes. He said also that the church buildings must be completely paid for before they are dedicated.

This is in the LDS tradition that abhors debt as somehow placing the debtor in the hands of the lender. Joseph Smith had trouble with debts in the early church. Brigham Young disliked debt, and indoctrinated his followers with his feeling. However, the demands of modern capitalism for credit financing have created patterns of business life that Brigham could never have understood. So the Saints drift into credit relationships in their business dealings, while avoiding them in building houses of worship. They have been successful in their use of credit. The money brorrowed for the Florida farms development was used to increase the value of the swamp from $3 to $100 an acre.

As Mormons increase in number and their geographic distribution widens, the new chapels and ward houses and Temples being built around the world have provided a great drain on the income from tithing. These buildings cost from a few thousand dollars to the $7 million for the Oakland Temple opened in 1964. The general authorities at Salt Lake City attempt to get a local congregation to build its own chapel—ward houses they are called in many Mormon areas —but will make contributions that are a gauge of the necessity, according to the General Authorities, for having the church built.

The top contribution from Salt Lake City is 70 per cent of the cost. This is for a new chapel in a new area where the church is attempting to expand its membership to a sustaining level. The local members—who may be just a handful— must provide the additional 30 per cent, and they cannot mortgage the chapel building, as other churches are accustomed to doing. The members must raise the money to pay off the building before they can have it dedicated and begin using it. And they must raise this money while still paying

their tithes, their various assessments, supporting missionaries, and so forth.

The numbers of buildings the Saints have financed in the
past few years is not published. But there must be many, as
the church has forged new chains around the world. The
cost must be in the millions, and this building program, together with one at Brigham Young University, has caused a
minor retrenchment at the top levels.

"As of this year, we are on a pay-as-you-go program in all
things," said Nathan Eldon Tanner, the second counselor
to President McKay and a leading financial voice in church
affairs. That was in 1965.

My interview with him was not by appointment. I stopped
by his office hopefully. These top officials of the LDS church
are like executives of a big business or high officials of government in the demands on their time. The General Authorities are required to travel almost every weekend to visit
some stake conference, for each stake holds four conferences a year. Members hope to have an apostle attend each
conference. In addition to this travel, each man has specific
duties he is charged with in the religious and non-religious
commitments of the church.

As one enters the lovely church Administration Building, President Tanner's office is on the left, President
Brown's office on the right. I asked to see President Tanner,
and a pleasant woman suggested that I wait, that he was
now giving an apostolic blessing to a young man.

The Saints attach special significance to these blessings.
One of the General Authorities may deliver them, and they
are today a sort of discussion in idealistic terms of the future
that could come for the person receiving the blessing, if only
he makes use of his talents and adheres closely to the rules
of life set down in his religious books. To me it is very remarkable to think of Nathan Eldon Tanner, once a promi-

nent political leader in Canada, once a major figure in the natural gas business, now in effect the manager of the financing of the LDS church, taking his time to talk to a young man, lay his hand on the boy's head, and give him a blessing.

While I was outside, noting the attractive decor of the office, the gold carpet, the comfortable furniture, this ceremony was going on inside. After a few minutes, a family group, accompanied by what appeared to be a church functionary, came out. The subject of the blessing was a teenaged boy on crutches, one leg amputated. The man and wife I took to be the parents looked comforted, and the boy looked buoyed up by the words of the apostle.

President Tanner showed me into his office. He indicated a red leather-covered chair at his right, behind the line of his desk, situated so that he thus shares his office with the occupant of that chair. The desk is not between them to prevent the feeling of welcome and the flow of communication.

Nothing much productive or new to me developed from the short talk, for President Tanner was very able to deal pleasantly and noncommittally with my questions. As I left, he went with me. He was going next door to the Hotel Utah for a private luncheon meeting. We walked together for about 200 feet. He was stopped by about a half dozen people for greetings or hurried words. But he managed to ask me to describe him as a political conservative in what I wrote about him. He said also that he was the president of the Trans-Canada Gas Pipeline Company before being called to Salt Lake City in the late 1950s to be "set apart" as an apostle. He was an important figure in the Social Credit government of Alberta in those years in Canada. He hoped that I would not call the Social Credit party "socialist."

"It was perhaps the most conservative government in Canada," he said.

President Tanner is an enigma to many in Salt Lake City.

He is not one of them, but is an outsider. The same may be said of his cousin, President Brown, who was born in Salt Lake City, but lived much of his life in Canada.

However, Tanner's lineage goes back to the early days of the church. John Tanner in 1835 helped prevent the foreclosures of mortgages on the Temple at Kirtland, Ohio, and Thomas Tanner was captain of the cannon in the small party of pioneers who were led to the Great Salt Lake in 1847.

Where Hugh B. Brown has been in Salt Lake City long enough to be recognized as a liberal Democrat—liberal, that is, by standards of the Council of the Twelve Apostles—N. Eldon Tanner has not become known. He is looked upon as the successor of the late Henry D. Moyle as the financial advisor of the First Presidency, and thus becomes a very important figure. So the financial interests of the West look curiously at this tall, rugged man from Canada.

In a brief conversation, he indicated a conservative financial outlook that may mean the church is now through with the open-handed spending that has liquidated much of its investments. The money went into a widespread system of seminaries around high schools and institutes around colleges. These buildings are used to bridge the critical period of life when young Mormons must make the transition from the blind faith of their childhood to the reasoned acceptance of the faith the church hopes they will achieve. The seminaries are used for released-time instruction of Mormon high school students. The institutes are social and religious centers for Mormons in college.

There are more than 2000 seminaries in forty-two states, and others in Mexico and Canada. Upward of 100,000 students go to classes in them. There are 185 institutes of religion, mostly built within the past two decades. These are connected with colleges and universities, and operate adjacent to a campus. About half the Mormons in colleges where institutes are located take advantage of them by attending functions or religious classes; about 85 per cent of the Mormon high school students attend the seminaries.

Both institutions are supported as a part of the Mormon educational system which takes about 25 per cent of the tithing income of the LDS church. This would be upward of $25 million. The Mormons have a special commitment to education, they will tell you. This is traced to a revelation given through the Prophet Joseph at Kirtland, Ohio, on May 6, 1833, when the church was but three years old. This revelation confirms some of the vision of St. John, and then makes this assertion:

"The glory of God is intelligence, or, in other words, light and truth."

The Saints cherish this statement. They repeat it often. They spend heavily to bring "light and truth" to their children. They do not run a parochial school system, although at one time the church operated Latter-day Saints High School in Salt Lake City (George Romney, alumnus). They have concentrated on a church-supported college system and the system of seminaries and institutes.

The flowering of this has been Brigham Young University at Provo, south of Salt Lake City. Even this blossom has not bloomed until the last 15 years, when great sums were poured into development of the school. My best estimate is that the church has invested at least $60 million in B.Y.U. in that period. None of this has come from federal or state subsidy. It has all come from tithing income, or from sale of investments. I suspect that the sale of control of Zion's First National Bank was to get $10 million to spend at Brigham Young University. Sale of the bank ended the practice of having a church-controlled bank in Utah.

But Brigham Young University had to be supported, for this is the major LDS effort in education. This effort has been mounted under the leadership of Ernest L. Wilkinson, a man of deeply conservative political views. His office is on the third floor of Abraham O. Smoot Administration Building on the campus, where his desk stands in front of a stunning and inspirational picture of sunshine slanting through trees to the floor of a forest glade. His office is decorated in a bright modern style. He rises, paces, talks, stops to stare unblinkingly, and then resumes the pacing and talking—a successful trial lawyer who now works on an assignment for his church. He addressed himself to the question: Who was Abraham O. Smoot?

"He was the founder of the Utah Stake at Provo, the second stake outside Salt Lake City. He didn't want to come down here. He was mayor of Salt Lake City and told President Young that finally he'd managed to live in a big house and was comfortable and was making up for those years of trouble and he didn't want to come down here.

"President Young told him 'Brother Smoot, you can either go to Provo or go to hell!' "

Wilkinson's face broke into a sardonic grin. One could sense that he liked that way of doing business. One accepted orders and upheld his religious and community obligations, as did that Mormon leader of long ago. The grin faded and he continued to explain about Smoot. The pioneer Mormon founded Brigham Young Academy in 1875 after a brief note was sent down by the church president instructing him to open the place. Smoot kept at the building of Brigham Young Academy even though Young died not long after the founding. Much of the Smoot family resources went into the school. When Smoot died in 1896, said Wilkinson, the estate barely covered the debts of $30,000 largely incurred in behalf of the school. Reed Smoot, his son, was made an apostle soon after his father's death. Reed Smoot became one of the important Mormon political leaders in the first third of the twentieth century.

By the mid-1960s the school founded by the elder Smoot

is a magnificent plant, situated on a natural terrace to the northeast of the city of Provo. Its site affords a view to the west, toward the desert and mountain-shadowed sunsets that are a part of the Utah Mormon environment. From the east, the ever-present Wasatch Range hovers over the campus. This school exploded in growth after 1950. Two circumstances contributed to the growth. David O. McKay, who became president in 1951, was an educator by background and supported the growth of B.Y.U. When Wilkinson became head of the church school system in 1951, the reins were in the hands of a man of determined aims, a skilful operator in any arena and a very knowledgeable operator in his church circles. Wilkinson wanted the university to be the biggest and best if he were to be associated with it; President McKay gave him help from the top.

A remarkable place has resulted. In 1951 it had 5429 students; in 1965 it had 18,731. More than eighty major buildings were put up in that time. The church will not say how much it put into capital expenditure on the campus, but the best estimate is about $60 million.

It was all done out of income and money on hand. No mortgages exist. It is all paid for. No money came from the federal government. The church paid it all, except for some gifts from church members; one building was paid for mostly with student fees.

The church makes a concession in tuition to its members, charging them $320 a year in 1965 while Gentiles pay $430. About 93 per cent of the students are LDS members, but Wilkinson still can brag that the level of non-Mormon enrollment has doubled in his years. It was 3.5 per cent in 1951.

Why does the LDS church refuse to take federal money for its school expansion? The answer is Wilkinson's. It reflects his philosophies:

1. The school is greatly concerned over the increasing national debt. Wilkinson said, "We now owe $328 billion and when we add all the deferred claims our debt exceeds $1 trillion. The Saints do not want to expand that debt."

2. The church believes in separation of church and state. Its members do not believe this separation exists when the government supports educational institutions operated by churches such as B.Y.U. Wilkinson said that he believes that "if there is to be separation, we cannot accept federal aid."

3. The church leadership believes it is impossible to accept federal aid without also accepting some degree of federal control.

Wilkinson said that in the early 1960s, B.Y.U. could have had $4.5 million from the federal government for building construction. But the money was turned down. He granted, in response to a question, that the school allows its faculty to apply for federal grants for specific research programs. But the school governs the proposals advanced and refuses faculty members permission to make those that Wilkinson and others believe would only result in waste of federal money.

In 1964, Wilkinson left the university presidency to run for senator against the incumbent Democrat, Frank E. Moss. Senator Moss was re-elected and President Wilkinson returned to his home and duties as president of the university. He thoroughly enjoys those duties and showed this enjoyment as he conducted a tour of the place. He knows the history of every building, how much it cost, the place it holds in the school's scheme of operation, the problems that were involved in getting it built. He knows every foot of the campus.

"This was all full of trees when I came here," he said, "old trees that somebody had planted. You can't imagine what trouble I had with the botany department when I had them cut down to give us room for the new buildings."

Wilkinson also is very much the head man of the school, and he has very strong opinions on how it should operate. These are followed.

"Our primary emphasis is on undergraduate education," he said. "We conceive this to be a faculty of teachers, not researchers, and we must have teachers here. We encourage them to publish, but we insist that this must not be at the expense of their classes. No 'publish or perish' rule exists here."

B.Y.U. offers doctorates in twenty fields, but Wilkinson insists that the emphasis is on undergraduate education. He said the aim is to maintain a small campus feeling to the school, but of course this has become little more than an aim, for certainly it is not a reality. There is housing for about 5000 students on the campus, and another 2500 commute from their homes in the Provo area, but 9000 live in apartments, rooming houses and so forth in Provo. Housing the B.Y.U. students may well be the biggest business in town.

No one is permitted to forget that B.Y.U. is a school maintained for the education of Mormons. True, there are nonmembers enrolled, but the emphasis is on educating the children of the church people whose tithes have built this marvelous, modern, lovely campus. The buildings are named for church leaders. There is resentment among some of the faculty that the student union building is named for Ernest L. Wilkinson. Some feel that the name is an attempt at self-aggrandizement. Others argue that most of the cost was from student fees and the place should not be named for someone connected with the university administration.

But to walk through the building with the short but wiry and energetic Wilkinson is to acquire the feeling that naming the building for him was no mistake. This is a place where he feels complete, perhaps one of the few where that feeling comes to him, for the Mormon trait of insatiable ambition for ever-greater accomplishment is as great in Ernest L. Wilkinson as it has ever been in any of his co-religionists. He enjoys walking through the other buildings, and feels a strong sense of personal achievement—a feeling he has earned—in the creation of this school. But when he walks into the student building and unfolds to a visitor its wonders and unique attributes, he radiates pride of achievement. Why not name it for him? There really is no reason, save the one of personality. A man like Wilkinson— driving, pushing, hurrying—can arouse resentments in people who would rather move more slowly and not so far.

He was proud of the library, too, for it was build at a cost he found lower than any other new library of equal facilities. And the science buildings, and the multi-purpose classrooms, and the dormitories . . . all of these thrilled him, and he knew a story about the construction of every one of them.

Take the women's dormitories. The Saints emphasize self-reliance and the value of personal effort. So these dormitories are built with suites for the housing of the women students. Each suite has four bedrooms, each for two girls, and a common study room, and a common kitchen. The school "suggests" that each girl cook and do the housework for a week, rotating these chores. President Wilkinson said he was advised against this plan by people at other schools who told him that the girls would refuse to live in the dormitories, that they would much prefer to eat in cafeterias. He insisted that the kitchens be included. They have been a great success, he said.

One need only understand that every Sunday the university becomes one big meeting chapel to have impressed on his memory that this is a church school. Wilkinson managed to get the General Authorities to dip into the tithing money to pay a quarter of the cost of the student center. He argued that it really was a meeting house, a chapel, because it is used by so many students for LDS church services every Sunday.

Sixty different wards—congregations—are organized among the students. Everyone goes to church on Sunday. There are ten stakes on the campus—the entire church had only 400 stakes in 1965. All of these ward and stake organizations mean hundreds of jobs for bishops, stake presidents, high counselors and so forth among the students and faculty. This great attention to religion at B.Y.U. goes back to the orders that Brigham Young gave. He said that the school was "not to teach even the alphabet or the multiplication tables without the spirit of God." He gave the order to Dr. Karl G. Maeser, a German, when he sent him to Provo to open the academy.

(The dictatorial church president also sent an order to the long-suffering Abraham O. Smoot who was told that Maeser was to open the school—and that Smoot was to find the money to pay for it.)

The Saints believe in B.Y.U. Students come there from Mormon homes all over the world—thirty-five nations in 1965. They represented 347 of the 400 stakes that year. A part of the idea, of course, is that B.Y.U. will provide a higher education that is compatible with the Restored Gospel.

The members have a financial stake in the school, too. Three-fourths of the cost of a student's education is paid by the tithes collected from Saints. The school has announced this figure in its literature; but a request to translate the figure into dollars of LDS subsidy each year was rebuffed. Once again, in tracing the LDS church's financial affairs, we are reduced to dead reckoning.

A Mormon student pays $320 a year tuition. The church says this is but a quarter of the cost of his instruction. So the cost per student must be $1280 a year. For the 18,000 students which B.Y.U. President Wilkinson says are enrolled, this would be a budget of $23 million. The LDS church's contribution would be about $17.7 million. This is a very imprecise figure, and my intuition tells me it is high. But in the absence of a solid statement of subsidy costs from church authorities, it is as close as one can arrive with data available.

In addition to his stewardship of B.Y.U. for many years, Wilkinson for a long time was the chancellor of the LDS educational system which includes Ricks College at Rexburg, Idaho, a small school; the LDS business college in Salt Lake City; a high school at Colonia Juarez, the former polygamist colony where George Romney and many other prominent church members were born; twelve schools in the Pacific Islands; and the Church College of Hawaii. When he quit both jobs to run for the Senate in 1964, Wilkinson could have been out of it all after building the schools. But the church leaders asked him to come back to B.Y.U., while turning the other schools over to another man.

Now he presides happily over his university, showing it off to visitors, leading them at a rapid walk from the statue of Brigham Young overlooking the quadrangle toward the library, to the classrooms and to the student quarters. The statue, by the way, was by Mahonri Young, the grandson of Brigham. He lived and worked in Boston for many years before his death, and his works also include the monument to the miracle of the gulls that stands in Temple Square.

In addition to its heavy expenditure for missions and education, the LDS church has a great commitment to a hospital program established after World War II. The church is involved in about a dozen and a half hospitals, of which three are community owned and the rest church owned. These are mostly in Utah, with a few in Idaho and one in Wyoming. Each hospital is separately incorporated and is managed by local civic and church leaders, with the church leaders of course the dominant figures on the boards. The chairman of the board in each instance is a member of the presiding bishopric. The general church in Salt Lake City has matched contributions of local congregations to build the hospitals, but each hospital is expected to be financially sound on its own account. Again, an outsider has no way of getting the financial data.

The major discovery for me in a long examination of the scattered and largely hidden financial data of the LDS church was a negative one: The LDS church is not run by financial masters who have constructed a great theocratic-financial octopus. It is a financial system based on the great devotion of the faithful around the world who will deprive themselves of great pleasures and possessions during what they think of as "this mortal existence" in order that they may enjoy greater exaltation in the Celestial Kingdom that the Prophet Joseph and his successors have told them comes next.

The "great financial empire" of the LDS church would begin to fall on its face within thirty days if the tithing income were cut off.

Great mistakes are made sometimes in the financial management, but these usually are concealed in the inner councils of the church. Some are just too big to be hidden. Who, for example, can say what the worth of the church would be today if it had from earliest times exploited the mineral wealth of the deserts and mountains where it was located? But Brigham Young thought mining was a very unreligious way of life. The Mormons have never lived down the fact that Joseph Smith as a young man worked as a "treasure digger."

It was one thing for Mormons to work in the diggings around Sutter's Mill in the California gold rush and bring their money home. It was another for them to be free to rush off their farms in the difficult life of the irrigated valleys of Utah to go and dig holes in the ground.

The old mansions built by the mining millionaires line E. South Temple Street in Salt Lake City, monuments to President Young's prejudice. That attitude of his enabled the Gentiles to come to Salt Lake City and take possession of a part of the commercial life of the city through wealth they won in mining ventures. The *Salt Lake Tribune* was founded by Catholics who made their money in mining and used it to fight the LDS church successfully and bitterly for years. There are other examples.

Sometimes these mistakes of the church financial management are explained as actions required for religious reasons. This was said when the church sold its 60 per cent control of a great banking system a few years ago. Yet, the church had been in banking for generations until someone decided that this new and powerful bank should be sold at bargain prices.

Another example was the decision of Heber J. Grant to put all the church's sugar interests in one pot—to sell out of Amalgamated Sugar and acquire more interest in Utah and Idaho Sugar. This was a glaring mistake. Amalgamated became immensely valuable, its stock shooting up, while U. & I. has done little. It is said in Salt Lake City that this decision was made because Marriner S. Eccles would not allow President Grant to dominate Amalgamated.

However, no one should mistake the underlying truth that in Salt Lake City one must get along with the LDS church in order to be reasonably successful in big enterprise. It is unquestionably true that the major corporations doing business in Utah always have an eye cocked and an ear tuned for messages from the First Presidency. After all, even Lyndon B. Johnson asks the advice of David O. McKay.

Business life in Salt Lake City always considers the Saints. This is their town, regardless of who is in the majority in it, they or the Gentiles. Strings of family relationships play a great role in business dealings everywhere, and perhaps no-

where to the degree that they do in Salt Lake City. There
are prominent men in the capital of the Saints who were
born into the LDS church but have not set foot inside one of
its chapels for decades. Yet, they daily deal in the currency
of being Mormons. They would never withdraw from the
church, for to do so would be disastrous to their business
operations. It would make them seem to be apostates in the
eyes of their colleagues, although their attitude toward the
church would not be really one whit different because they
asked to have their names taken off its enrollment records.

One of the anonymous sources to which I went for information on the LDS church's economics was a businessman
who has been very successful with the Mormons, although
not one of them. He is a member of a pioneer Utah family
which has never been Mormon.

He said his Mormon friends really were easy to do business with. One just must never insult them, he said. One
must always be mindful of their pride of religion and background. One must maintain a position that permits him to
be independent of the church financially, for the Mormons
have a tendency to respect a strong position, while they will
quickly destroy and consume a weak one.

But one must never forget, he said, that the church exists
and that it provides a line of communication and help for its
members that their opponents in the business transaction
do not have.

When all of these things have been said; when the position of the church against credit and in favor of careful financial management has been enunciated from the top; when
the glorious achievements in philanthropy, education and
health care of the Saints have been set forth—

After all of these, there still remains a computation printed
in the *Salt Lake Tribune* in May, 1965. Utah's bankruptcy
rate jumped in a year by 38 per cent, while the national increase was only 10 per cent. The bankruptcy proceedings

in Utah wiped out debts of about $10 million that year. There was one bankruptcy for every 714 persons, compared to one nationally for every 1100 persons. Almost all of these were filed for individuals who were overly extended in installment buying.

Finally, one of the financial experts I talked with said that he sees the Mormon country as a debtor area, kept that way by the heavy financial demands of the church on its people. He said that he believes this to be a reason why so much of the productive business enterprise of Utah is owned elsewhere. The Saints, he said, have not had enough left after making their church contributions to be able to invest in these businesses.

What are some of those annual contributions, as we can piece them together? We can take only a few steps, and then the darkness of closed books blinds our eyes.

Tithes, $100 million
Maintenance of 12,000 missionaries, $14 million
Local contribution to church buildings?
Contributions to ward and stake operating costs?
Welfare plan?
Education costs?
Hospital costs?

In the end it becomes clear that no outsider can know the cost. Perhaps the 2.5 million Mormons pour as much as $250 million a year into their various religious purposes. It could be even more.

One Mormon in an important administrative job said that one year he kept track of the demands on his money. He found that if he had met all of them, it would have amounted to 35 per cent of his income for the church and its related activities.

Another man of equal stature in the same field said he could not imagine such a figure would be accurate. He doubted if it could be much over 15 per cent. Certainly, he said, no higher than 20 per cent.

"Unless," he qualified, "they were building some new meeting houses in his ward. He would be expected to contribute heavily."

Yet a different Mormon told of borrowing $500 which it took him a long time to repay. This was the amount he was told to contribute to a new church building. It was proper for him to borrow his contribution but improper for the LDS ward to borrow.

He since has quit going to church.

V

Divisive Forces at Work

THE RICH CURTAINS of Mormon life give the outward appearance of great solidarity and unity of purpose, but among the millions listed as members of the LDS church a number of contradictory forces are at work.

In the source springs of the religious-economic-social system that the Saints have established there are answers for almost everything. These answers require the acceptance of certain premises on no more evidence than faith. There are those who sometimes question, who no longer are able to believe. There are those who accept the doctrine, but disclaim certain of the social manifestations of Mormonism. And still others believe the doctrine too well to suit the leaders of the LDS church. They are excommunicated and called "fundamentalists."

To put it another way:

The faithful of the church are the centrists, those who swerve neither to the left nor the right, but follow the doctrine as it is interpreted by the General Authorities. These stay on the theological and sociological highways that the leaders have constructed since the church was founded in 1830.

The apostates fall off both to the right and the left. The rightists take the view that the church today has drifted away from the purity of the Restored Gospel and that only

in their lives and practices is that pure truth of salvation and
ultimate exaltation found among the various *Book of Mormon* followers today. The drifters to the left have stopped
believing. Sometimes this is a complete loss of Christian
faith. These have left then the Judeo-Christian philosophy
of social order and they are lonely in Mormon country.
Sometimes the loss of faith applies only to the aspects of
doctrine deriving from Joseph Smith and his successors; in
such cases the ex-Saint may become a Protestant, or even a
Catholic, for he still accepts the proposition of the divinity
of Christ and other Christian doctrines.

Almost every religion has had its apostasies, and the great
faith required of a Saint has caused the Mormons to have at
least their share. It is not our purpose here to pursue those
of the dead past, except where they have influenced the
church as it exists today. But the drifting away of members
today is worth examination. No one can say how great is this
drift; but it is substantial, although probably not in any sense
dangerous to the survival of the LDS church.

An outsider can see but one great black cloud over the
LDS church. This is the problem of its peculiar, theologi-
cally based discrimination against the Negro, a subject
that will be treated at length. For many years the church
has managed to ignore this situation, for the Negro had
many problems in many places, and his resentment of the
Saints' exclusion of him on racial grounds had to take its
place in a set of priorities. However, in the 1960s, this irritation has worked itself up higher on the list, and Negro organizations have shown signs of readiness to attack the
Saints.

But there are many other little gray clouds that bring trouble to the Mormons and diminish their vigor. For example,
the Saints in 1965 were claiming just under 2.5 million members. When one asks if these are all really members, or if
there are many inactives on the rolls, one gets no straight

answers. The reason is not a desire to deceive. The church does not actually know how many of these millions have drifted away.

There are so many things required to be a Mormon. One woman, the wife of a devout man in whose religious activities she shared and gloried, said that "this is a hard religion to live." That it is. Many give up the fight but do not ask to have their names expunged from the rolls of their ward.

An entire way of life is set out for the Mormon in his religious study. To reduce this to a few pages is almost impossible. He works all his life to understand the nuances of doctrine. But it is possible to pick out the elements of the LDS religious practice that cause the most trouble to the Saints in these times.

First, here are the Articles of Faith for the Saints:

1. We believe in God, the Eternal Father, and in His Son, Jesus Christ, and in the Holy Ghost.

2. We believe that men will be punished for their own sins, and not for Adam's transgression.

3. We believe that through the atonement of Christ, all mankind may be saved, by obedience to the laws and ordinances of the Gospel.

4. We believe that the first principles and ordinances of the Gospel are: first, Faith in the Lord Jesus Christ; second, Repentance; third, Baptism by immersion for the remission of sins; fourth, Laying on of hands for the gift of the Holy Ghost.

5. We believe that a man must be called of God, by prophecy, and by the laying on of hands, by those who are in authority, to preach the Gospel and administer in the ordinances thereof.

6. We believe in the same organization that existed in the Primitive Church, viz.: apostles, prophets, pastors, teachers, evangelists, etc.

7. We believe in the gift of tongues, prophecy, revelation, visions, healing, interpretation of tongues, etc.

8. We believe the Bible to be the word of God as far as it is translated correctly; we also believe the *Book of Mormon* to be the word of God.

9. We believe all that God has revealed, all that He does now reveal, and we believe that He will yet reveal many great and important things pertaining to the Kingdom of God.

10. We believe in the literal gathering of Israel and in the restoration of the Ten Tribes; that Zion will be built upon this (the American) continent; that Christ will reign personally upon the earth; and, that the earth will be renewed and receive its paradisaical glory.

11. We claim the privilege of worshiping Almighty God according to the dictates of our own conscience, and allow all men the same privilege, let them worship how, where, or what they may.

12. We believe in being subject to kings, presidents, rulers, and magistrates, in obeying, honoring and sustaining the law.

13. We believe in being honest, true, chaste, benevolent, virtuous, and in doing good to all men; indeed, we may say that we follow the admonition of Paul—We believe all things, we hope all things, we have endured many things, and hope to be able to endure all things. If there is anything virtuous, lovely, or of good report or praiseworthy, we seek after these things.

That was the total condensed statement of faith produced by Joseph Smith in Nauvoo, Illinois, not long before he was murdered. There is nothing difficult in these concepts for a religiously minded person. Nor does the set of beliefs include much of what we are examining as Mormonism. There is nothing about tithing, nor about vicarious baptism, nor missionary journeys to the ends of the earth, nor abstinence from tobacco and liquor. Nothing here obligates one to spend four nights a week in church work, nor to go without pay to work in a pea cannery, nor to spend his days digging up the names of his ancestors.

A non-Mormon Christian begins to have trouble in the center of the list—such as the second clause of No. 8 identifying the *Book of Mormon* as the word of God. But all these matters set out questions of faith, and are not difficult to live with, particularly if one has been born a Mormon and has grown up in the church.

People do drift away from the church. They become alienated. Yet they will still consider themselves Mormons and will identify their religion as "LDS" when filling in the blanks in a census of some sort. One can state the reasons generally for this drift; but the people who admit they have drifted away state them better. First, the reasons. Then the statements of those who have drifted away.

1. The Word of Wisdom: This is the revelation that the church holds forbids tobacco, coffee, tea and alcohol. If one is to be an active Mormon, one must follow the Word of Wisdom.

2. Tithing: In a time when the economic order is based almost entirely on exchanges of money for the necessities of life and the possibility of tithing in corn or wheat or wool or cheese does not exist, the sacrifice is almost too much for many persons. The most reliable estimate I heard of the degree of tithing in the church was that it was done by about one family in four.

3. Activity: Some persons just refuse, after a time, to keep on the high plane of activity that the LDS church has organized for its members. They will not go out night after night to meetings concerned only with religion.

4. Education: There is great irony in the fact that as the Mormons strive for ever greater education for their young people, this very exposure to arguments in science, history and philosophy tends to alienate the young. The growth of the church university, the creation of the seminaries and institutes, the emphasis on activity for the young in connection with the church—all of these are the means by which

the Saints attempt to meet the challenges offered to their doctrine in the very educational uplift that they want for their children.

5. Doctrine: The emphasis on study of LDS doctrine results in raising questions among some as to the purity of that doctrine as it is preached today. Certainly, there are vast differences that exist between the church of 1830 and of today.

So, many different stories are told of the drift away from the church. One man described the way he took his family out of the LDS establishment. This is a family of eight, carried on the lists still and a part of the totals which the Saints announce each April. But actually, these people no longer are members, and probably never will be members again. Their story is multiplied many times; how many only the top authorities of the church could establish. The knowledge exists in the priesthood quorums that call on the homes in each ward at short intervals. These men know who is faithful and who has lost his faith. They could tell the General Authorities immediately what the effective strength is, how many yet stand in the Legions of the Lord. They could deliver the information with all the precision of a first sergeant making his morning report.

But what good would this information be? And what would be the effect of receiving it? Would it not give the appearance that the Saints were losing ground? And would it not have the effect of shutting off those drifters from return to the church, the course that the devout men at the top hope sincerely will come about?

The man who talked of his drift away must have been in his forties. But he looked less than thirty. He had six children, the oldest past twenty, and a wife who had followed him through all the events he told about. His skin was brown from the sun, his body well-muscled from his active life, and his manners were considerate. He told me that he was not active in the church until after he went into military service in World War II, taking his books with him. He began to read the *Book of Mormon* and *Doctrine and Covenants* and the *Pearl of Great Price*.

"I became convinced of the truth of the Prophet's work," he said.

Then he got up and got us both a glass of beer. This simple act is as clear a renunciation of modern doctrine as a Mormon could give. It is a direct contravention of the Word of Wisdom and is much opposed by the church. Yet, history shows Mormon students that the Prophet Joseph drank wine in his cell the night before he was killed.

When the former Mormon was out of the room, his wife said that her father was a bishop and that her upbringing had been very devout. She became silent when her husband came back.

He said that when he came home from the war he assumed his place in the priesthood quorums, and was asked if he would conduct religious classes for some of the young boys— the deacons of twelve to fourteen years of age, and the teachers of fourteen to sixteen years. He plunged into this with all his enthusiasm and resolve. He tithed faithfully, and took his family to church. He attended all the meetings. He taught classes in the Mutual Improvement Association, as well as the doctrinal classes. He was gone from home three or four nights every week, and his Sundays were given over completely to the church activities. In the free time he had left, he began to study ever more deeply the foundations of his religion.

This completely sincere man said that he felt it was not proper for him just to teach from the manuals that were provided to him from Salt Lake City. He had a deep sense of responsibility, he explained, and this led him to the conclusion that he should thoroughly understand what he was telling the boys in the Aaronic priesthood. This is why he studied. This is what led to his alienation from the church.

By about 1949 he had come to the conclusion that there were three serious deviations of doctrine between that preached by Joseph Smith and that followed in the modern church. He decided that these were:

1. Plural marriage (polygamy) plainly was the intent of God.

2. God meant for the Saints to live together in a communal society called the United Order of Enoch.

3. The present structure of the priesthood and control of the church was entirely wrong, for the patriarch—now largely a ceremonial office—actually should be the head of the church.

"I began to have doubts about the correctness and righteousness of the present church," he said, sipping his beer. He also was disturbed that "people don't care about these things but just are willing to go along wherever the General Authorities take them."

These three points arrived at by the young church worker were among the most serious doubts that a Saint can have under the church as it is now organized. Remember that before one goes into the Temple, he must agree that he has no connection with any underground movements. He must say that he does not question the supremacy of the General Authorities. Posing these questions is out of order. It is dangerous for a Mormon even to think them.

But it is much more dangerous for them to be raised in instructional classes for young deacons and teachers, which is what this man did next. Accounts of his actions began to circulate, and soon he was contacted by about a half dozen different fundamentalist groups which gave him further information on matters where he found himself in conflict with the General Authorities. At about this time he read Fawn M. Brodie's biography of the Prophet Joseph, *No Man*

Knows My History, and accepted it as a generally reliable account.

"It didn't offend me at all," he said. "But it caused me to be more disturbed by the church attempt to dress up the Prophet's life and that of the other early leaders."

Then he began to question the real open-heartedness of his co-religionists. He was—and is—an idealistic man and was offended by the unwillingness of his friends to make sacrifices to help those who were outside the church.

"When you honestly think in your heart that you're a chosen people, there's something wrong with you," he said. "That attitude doesn't bring people together. It divides them."

This reflected dissatisfaction with Mormon official decision at the edges of doctrine in that area where faith shades into pragmatism, where the decision to help or not help is based on whether the help will be a benefit to the church, or just to the needy person who is helped. An example is the general rule that help from the LDS welfare plan goes only to members, except in those cases of wide disaster where the Saints make large and generous gifts. But a poor non-LDS family in Logan had best look elsewhere than the bishop's storehouse for help.

The dissatisfaction of the church leaders with this idealistic young Saint showed up one day when a stake president visited one of his classes and raised questions because the church-provided instructional manuals were not being used. Instead, discussions were in terms of the source documents. The former instructor who told this story of his apostasy said he explained to the stake president that the class had indicated a wish to be taught fundamentals of LDS philosophy.

At the next leadership meeting the stake president complained and denounced unnamed teachers who placed their own interpretations of philosophy and church history ahead of the carefully prepared and approved materials in the manuals from Salt Lake City. After the meeting the instructor—who was by then the president of his quorum of the priesthood—spoke sharply with the stake president, who denied that he had anyone in mind as the target of his criticism. Again the instructor explained that he was trying to make his students fully aware of all there was to know about their religion. He disliked being criticized for this devotion to his teaching assignment. The stake president tried to calm the young man.

This was not the end of it, of course. From that time forward the classes taught by this Saint were attended by church officials who stopped his discussions when he veered into areas that were considered closed by the church leadership.

One of the questions he wanted to raise concerned the insistence on certain rites being performed only in the Temples. He said his research proved to him that the Temples were not required for any ceremonies. He said he believed that the requirement for their use was only a device to enforce control of the believers by the men who controlled access to the Temples.

"They make you believe that you have to get into the Temple to be able to achieve exaltation," he said, "and if you don't do what they say, they won't let you in the Temple, because they control the Temple. My research showed me that there is no doctrine that requires a Temple for the ceremonies."

After continuing his classes under such close supervision he became convinced that he should quit, since his conscience would not allow him to meet the requirement that he teach only what was provided in the manuals. He continued to go to church and to tithe and to take his family to church. He was toying around with the various fundamentalist Mormon groups that exist in Utah outside the established church, but he found that none of these met his understanding of doctrine.

By then he had been in contact with many different non-church groups, including some who practice polygamy. Certainly he was not practicing polygamy. A grand jury investigation of these groups was in progress. An anonymous caller told one of the executives of the company where this man worked that "you people had better get rid of him before he involves you in some polygamy thing." Nothing came of this. The breaking away from the church came on a much smaller matter.

"One Sunday," he recalled, "we had a family reunion in the afternoon, and when we went to church I told the whole family that we would leave at one o'clock to go to this. My boy was not there when we were ready, and then I saw him coming. He was crying, and as he started to tell me about it, here came his deacon's class advisor to try to drag him back physically. His group had a 100 per cent attendance record and this fellow wanted to maintain that no matter what. It set me to thinking."

The family group went to the reunion. Not long after, the bishop of their ward called the husband and wife in for a talk. He asked them what they had been doing? What had they been believing? Whom had they been seeing? They refused to answer the questions and stopped going to church.

The formerly devout priest of the LDS church reflected on his experiences with dissent.

"You can talk about all kinds of things, but the one question you'd better answer right is this: Do you sustain the powers of the General Authorities of the church?"

Since leaving the church both he and his wife have found that their friends of past years no longer are available to them. It is a strange feeling of being shut out. Those who once were socially close are not chilly or unkind; they just are not the same as before.

"We don't have anything to talk about," he said. "Before we did the same things at church, we believed the same things, we had the same problems and the same sort of lives. We don't belong to that life any more and we don't have much to talk to them about."

His wife once enjoyed the Women's Relief Society, and saw her friends there, but this no longer is open for her. He once spent his nights and weekends on church work, but this is gone. The going has left an emptiness in their lives. He thought about this:

"Every phase of your existence is provided for in the LDS church. They want to direct every activity in every phase of your life."

Many months later, over lunch at Fisherman's Wharf in San Francisco, I heard another chapter of this family's disaffection with the LDS church. It was told by a Gentile friend who knew the family in Salt Lake City.

He said a devout Mormon who knew him as well as the family one day approached him with this story:

"You're pretty close to them and I wanted you to know that he and his wife took a young unmarried woman camping with them lately. I just wanted you to know."

My luncheon companion said he was puzzled at first by the intensity of his informant's attitude, then caught the drift. He said he asked:

"Are you trying to tell me that you believe he is a polygamist and that this young woman is his plural wife?"

The Mormon was quoted as saying:

"I didn't tell you that. I just told you what I know. Just the facts. I thought you should know them. Everybody who has anything to do with him should know them."

My luncheon companion said he challenged the "facts"

and his Mormon acquaintance admitted he was passing on what he had been told. The Mormon was dressed down, and promised to himself ask the former Mormon about the story of the camping trip.

"But he didn't ask," said my companion. "I asked my friend later and he told me he had heard the story and that it was a part of the campaign they were running to isolate him from all of his friends."

Among the intellectuals, the rate of falling away in spirit if not in body is fairly high. A well-educated and accomplished man in Salt Lake City told his experience. He said he grew up as a Mormon, and his relationship to his faith was shaped by the war.

"I grew up in a little village, and there was not a non-Mormon among the 120 people there. I never really thought seriously about it until I was wounded in combat and then I began to ask the big questions about life. I began to doubt. I went to Brigham Young University for graduate work, and the air of piety there was very thick."

He drifted away. But his name still is on the rolls. He talked about the LDS church as a social institution, a force in life.

"People are given security on a broad basis. The non-thinking Mormon is socially at home. He is made into an activist of the first order. He burns up energy among people who make him feel at home. As long as you can keep from thinking critically about it on an intellectual level, it is one of the most effective social systems I've ever studied. They have made very efficient use of Madison Avenue techniques over here at the church. They also are a marvel of centralization and communications so that it frightens me."

He didn't look frightened. I asked how it was that so many Mormon intellectuals manage to keep their faith. His quick answer was profound.

"When evidence comes in on truth or falsity of doctrine and history, you shuck the evidence and continue to believe, no matter what."

He thought for a few moments, then—in a typical Mormon thought pattern—reached back into his family history to prove a point against the church. He told of a relative who was employed by Brigham Young. He said the relative began to doubt his religion because he was badly cheated by President Young who would pay him less than a job was worth and charge various costs against him so that after nine years' work, he owed President Young $500.

In effect, this man was marooned in the desert where his faith had led him, at the mercy of a strong-minded and determined business-religious-political leader in whose integrity and honor he had begun to have doubts. His descendant told how it was resolved:

"He had a serious illness, which today we would recognize as a mental breakdown brought on by the pressures against his peace of mind, and he resolved never again to doubt if only he could get well. This removed his anxieties and he got well and never again did he doubt."

A friend in Salt Lake City first raised the question of large numbers of intellectual Mormons having drifted away from the church. He said that he had not attended since 1950 and never intended to go again. He was born into a Mormon family and was listed on the rolls. His ward and stake still send him meeting notices. He has not asked for excommunication because of consideration of his devout mother's feelings. Still another man, a high government official in Washington, gave this same reason for not breaking the tie. It is commonly the explanation in such instances.

But a highly successful businessman said he did not intend to ask for excommunication because the act had no meaning to him. He said he had no more emotional interest in the church, that he had written off his years of devoted effort to it, and never intended to go back except occasionally to watch. If his name were taken off the rolls, he said, he wouldn't care; but he doesn't intend to ask for excommunication. Like everyone who has been near it and has been able to maintain a critical eye, this man was fascinated by the church's inner structure.

"The nerve center of the church's strength is full activity for everyone in it," he said. "There is universal participation. They go to all lengths to see that everybody has something to do. This cuts off their independent thinking, don't you see? The minute you have to stand before a group and assume a position, you have shut off your independent thinking. That position is now your position and you're stuck with it."

He talked for a few minutes of other things, and then came back to the subject.

"The Mormon church has exploited this mass participation and cessation of independent thought. Every time someone begins to drift, you hear them talking about it. How many times have I heard them say: 'We must get him active.' They believe that if they can get someone involved, they can hold him."

He also commented on the creation of the feeling that the church provides the answer to the human need for progression, for new, exciting vistas and hope for betterment.

"Every Mormon who went to church Sunday is struggling for upward reach," he said.

When it was suggested that the church was in a crisis, that it was losing valuable members and that internal strains were dangerous, he looked out the window of his lovely paneled office at the summer sunshine on the street and pondered. Then he turned to resist the suggestion.

"The church is not in a crisis on any front. It has perfected institutional controls until there is no crisis possible anywhere except perhaps in the race question."

As an example of the institutional controls, he said that the church now habitually inquires into the private beliefs of its members in order to identify and isolate heretics. He said this has the effect of ferreting out and isolating the liberal voices who would bring change—and of course it also isolates the conservative voices who would return to the past.

"The ward is so well organized and disciplined that the bishop knows where everyone stands. Formerly, when the teachers made their home visits, their question was 'Are you all well?' This has been changed to help the bishop find out who is slipping. It is suggested that the mother often is the strong personality who can give the answers, so they are directed to ask her about the faith of her family. (If they find some person who is beginning to drift, they move in on him.) They go at it like a life insurance salesman. They know everything they can discover about the person involved. They know what he says to others, they know the confidences he makes to the family. They move in on him."

This man was disturbed by the practices he described, for as one who has drifted away from his family's religion, he feels that the Saints are being somehow unscrupulous, underhanded and devious in dealing with the problem of apostasy through these organizational tools. And this in spite of the fact that, as he knows well, the men who do these things are completely convinced that they do them in the best interests—totally unselfishly—of the person to whom all of this mechanism is directed. He feels the method is unscrupulous.

Remember that their doctrine was shaped at the hands of Brigham Young, who preached such things as Blood Atonement—that it was better that a man be killed than that he be permitted to sin against God and his fellow Saints. Just spying on a fellow to try to shape the successful arguments to lead him back into the church is pretty tame stuff by comparison.

The LDS membership figures—even though they certainly must include some large numbers of people who really should not be counted—show a constant growth that proves the contention that the church is so strong now as to overcome any crisis that it meets. In the quarter century since 1940, the growth has been upward every year, as these figures show:

As of December 31 for each year:

1940	862,664	1953	1,246,362
1941	892,060	1954	1,302,248
1942	917,715	1955	1,357,274
1943	937,050	1956	1,416,731
1944	954,004	1957	1,488,314
1945	979,454	1958	1,555,799
1946	996,905	1959	1,616,088
1947	1,016,170	1960	1,693,180
1948	1,041,970	1961	1,823,661
1949	1,072,671	1962	1,965,786
1950	1,111,314	1963	2,117,451
1951	1,147,157	1964	2,234,916
1952	1,189,053	1965	2,395,932

Dr. Thomas F. O'Dea, a sociologist at Columbia University, who wrote a major study called *The Mormons* when he taught at the University of Utah, insists that the church is in the midst of a crisis. O'Dea grew up as a Catholic and spent many years in Mormon country. He is fond of Mormons. Like many others who have studied the Saints, he is fascinated by the intricacies of the doctrine, and of the interplay between doctrine, necessity, and practice. He said that "Mormonism is in a sleeping crisis."

"It is a strange crisis, one not easily noticed; a lotus-eating crisis, a sleeping crisis, an unrecognized crisis of prosperity and acceptance. It has met all its crises of adversity. But can it survive its own success?"

O'Dea said that today the church has become very middle class and anxious for respectability. Those aspects of its former practice which work against acceptance are ruthlessly rooted out, such as the lingering taint of polygamy. He said church policy increasingly has been accommodationist, that the old-time socio-economic experiments now are not allowed.

As a scholar who himself was the product of a strongly felt and inclusive religious group, O'Dea was well able to understand the problem of withdrawal that is created for many who lose faith in the LDS doctrine. He said being a Mormon is like having a second nationality. The Mormons of the Rocky Mountain West are almost like a nation. Their organization has its traditions of settlement, in the Perpetual Emigration Company, and government, in the organization of the church paralleling the organization of the territory of Deseret in the early days. Some of this feeling of quasi-nationality was what led Richard Burton, the explorer, to make his prediction that one day the Mormons would exist as a separate nation in the desert.

"There is a common tradition of suffering and achievement," said O'Dea. "Even for those who no longer believe, the very area evokes a loyalty and bond of history with those who are still devout. The story of settlement, the story of the church, and the family story are a single narrative for many."

Small wonder, then, that a relatively small number ask to have their names removed from the rolls in a formal excommunication. When they do, of course, this signals a great and violent personal apostasy.

Some of these have had tremendous impact on the church in years past. Some of the top leaders have been cast out. But in keeping with Dr. O'Dea's theory of the sleeping crisis, one of the most influential apostates of the 1960s has been a young machinist, who with his wife, left the church and now makes a living printing books and documents which contradict official Mormon pronouncements.

His name is Jerald Tanner. His wife, Sandra, is a great-great-granddaughter of Brigham Young. She said, "this doesn't mean much. There are probably 5000 of us around Salt Lake City." They lived in the summer of 1965 in an old house at 1350 S. West Temple Street in a section which is being overrun gradually by other things, such as the ballpark across the street where the Salt Lake City professional team plays. Tanner was a dark-haired man then in his late twenties and she looked to be about the same age. There were three children, ranging from about eighteen months to about seven years. He and Nathan Eldon Tanner, the high LDS official, are both descended, he thought, from John Tanner, the man who helped Joseph Smith in the 1830s. Both the young man and his wife grew up in the LDS church. He drifted away first and she followed.

That day an apostasy was in the making. A young man visiting Tanner was reading one of the Tanner books. In an agitated voice he exclaimed:

"That does it! That's all! I can still get out of it and I will!"

Something in the book had convinced him that one of the minor church officials had misled him about existence of a microfilm copy of a document. When his emotions had quieted, he explained that he had been converted to Mormonism in order to marry a devout Mormon girl. She had insisted that he become a Saint, and that he promise to work in the church as a condition of marriage, for the doctrine holds that she can progress in exaltation only as the wife of her husband, whose good works in the priesthood win a higher place for him and thus for her. There is a double-barreled effect to this doctrine: It gives a devout Mormon man a head start in courtship among Mormon girls; and it causes Mormon wives to urge their husbands to ever greater activity in church work.

But for this young convert standing in Jerald Tanner's house, it seemed to be all finished. He explained his way out of the marriage.

"I can get out of it still because it wasn't consummated," he said as he left the house.

After he was gone, the three of us sat in the high-ceilinged living room of the old house and discussed the general question of how one feels on leaving the company of the Saints.

"It was a long time before I could admit I didn't believe the *Book of Mormon*," said Sandra Tanner, dandling Brigham Young's great-great-great-grandchild on her knee. "It was weeks after that before I could say it out loud."

"They absorb your whole life in church activities," said Jerald Tanner. "We always thought and were told again and again that we had the only true church, that everybody else was in a state of apostasy."

The Tanners operate as the Modern Microfilm Company. They specialize in copying books and documents that are out of print, or have been suppressed in one way or another, but that bear on the history and doctrine of the LDS church. When I talked with them, they had thirty-one titles for sale. the best seller was *Mormonism—Shadow or Reality?* prepared by them jointly. They had sold about 3000 copies. It was priced at $5 for a single copy, down to $3 in lots.

The Tanners have republished some of the most violent attacks made on the church during its existence. For example, they have reprinted the statements of three of the witnesses to the *Book of Mormon* attacking the LDS church; they have printed *The Confessions of John D. Lee*, written in 1880 before he was shot on the site of the Mountain Meadows massacre; and they have brought out *Brigham's Destroying Angel* by Bill Hickman who claimed he killed people on the orders of LDS President Young. They even have uncovered and reprinted *View of the Hebrews* by Ethan Smith, a book published in 1825 which has great importance to students of Mormon history. Some anti-Mormon writers have urged that it was from this book that Joseph Smith acquired the ideas for the narrative of the *Book of Mormon.*

Near the end of their book attacking the LDS church and denouncing its doctrines the Tanners have signed individual statements setting out their religious experience. Jerald Tanner wrote that he was born and reared in the Mormon church, but that he was nineteen years old before he heard the Word of Christ preached.

"I remember being told that a certain man who was excommunicated from the church was possessed with the devil," he wrote. "I can remember walking past this man's house and being afraid of him because I firmly believed that he was possessed of the devil. I believed that a person would almost have to be possessed of the devil to leave the 'true church.' So strong was my conviction that I was greatly shocked to hear a boy in Sunday School say that he didn't know for certain that the church was true. I felt it was strange, indeed, for a person to be a member of the Mormon Church and yet not know it was true . . .

"When I was about eighteen years old I had to face reality. I can remember that the first time I saw David Whitmer's pamphlet, "An Address to All Believers in Christ," I threw it down in disgust. After throwing it down I began to think maybe that wasn't the right way to face the problem. If David Whitmer was wrong in his criticism of Joseph Smith, surely I could prove him wrong. So I picked up the pamphlet and read it through. I found that I could not prove David Whitmer wrong, and that the revelations Joseph Smith gave had been changed. I later went to Independence, Missouri, and saw a copy of the original *Book of Commandments*, which confirmed David Whitmer's statement that the revelations had been changed.

"Since that time I have found more and more proof that the church in which I was raised is in error. The most important thing that I found, however, was not that the Church was in error, but that I myself was in error. I found that I was a sinner in need of a Savior . . ."

This is a remarkable statement, telling much about the young man who made it as well as giving his views on the religion he is trying to undermine. He considers himself a Protestant, a believer in Christ and in the doctrines of eternal salvation preached by Protestants. However, he now refuses to accept any of the doctrine that belongs exclusively to the LDS church.

Jerald Tanner very nearly joined the Reorganized LDS church, but decided against it when he made up his mind that he did not believe that Joseph Smith was a true prophet.

Sandra Tanner's statement shows that she had doubts about her religion, but was generally able to contain them —until "I met Jerald and we began studying the Bible and Mormonism together. As we studied I began to see the contradictions between the Bible and the teachings of the Mormon church."

As a child she had been taught to admire her ancestor, Brigham Young. This was the point at which Jerald Tanner made his attack on her faith. He did it in Brigham's own words.

"Then Jerald had me read some of Brigham Young's sermons in the *Journal of Discourses* on Blood Atonement," Mrs. Tanner wrote. "I was shocked! I knew what Brigham Young was saying was wrong but I couldn't reconcile these sermons with the things I had always been taught concerning him. I knew these were not the words of a Prophet of God.

"As I studied I not only found errors in Mormonism, I also began to comprehend there was something wrong in my own life. As I studied God's word I realized I was a sinful hypocrite."

That day as she talked in the living room of the old house across from the ballpark in Salt Lake City, she remembered her first meeting with Jerald Tanner. She was visiting her grandmother.

"I fell in love with him," she said quite simply and without embarrassment. Then she used a typical Mormon analogy to explain what she thinks their present life purpose to be. "What we do is more of a mission, you might say."

When we begin to inquire we find that we are held in bondage to some degree by our origins. Those who were Mormons and are not now followers of the doctrines of the LDS church yet are Mormons in some ways. The Tanners' statements and procedural methods show their origins.

For example: Their letters from two apostles. The Mormons have a strong tradition of persecution, and this tends to give them courage in adverse circumstances, but it also tends to make them accept persecution almost with pleasure for the illogical feeling that being persecuted shows they were right. This seems to me to be the explanation of the Tanners' use of two letters they received from LDS apostles complaining of the use by the young couple of documents from Mormon sources. The letters really have no special significance beyond showing that the apostles—Mark E. Petersen and LeGrand Richards—are deeply offended by the Tanners. Yet they are reproduced over and over.

There also is the demonstration by the Tanners that an apostate from the Mormon church generally takes with him their techniques of indefatigable research and argument that he was taught while in the church's embrace. The Tanners' masterwork, *Mormonism—Shadow or Reality?* is an intricate weaving of arguments from many sources against the fundamental precept of the Saints' doctrine—that Joseph Smith, Jr., was a prophet of God and that his production of the *Book of Mormon*, the revelations set down in *Doctrine and Covenants*, and further writings in the *Pearl of Great Price* represented the fruits of divine inspiration.

The tone of the book is carried in the chapter titles, such as:

"Changing the Revelations"
"False Prophesy"
"Plural Marriage"
"Avenging Blood at Mountain Meadows"
"Mormonism and Money"

The book has about 400 typewritten pages, and must run close to 200,000 words. It is not set in type and printed, but it is produced by photographing typewritten pages which are printed in an offset process.

The technique followed throughout is to quote from Mormon sources extensively to place the church in a bad light in view of its currently successful drive for widespread acceptance. The chapter titled "The Virgin Birth" serves as well as any to show this. The aim is to outrage the feelings of those religious believers who subscribe to the doctrine of the Virgin Birth. This is done by quoting from about a half dozen Mormon sources and tying the quotations together with short transitional sentences.

Brigham Young is quoted: "Jesus Christ was not begotten by the Holy Ghost" and it is explained by the Tanners that this conflicts with the Bible and the *Book of Mormon*. Joseph Fielding Smith, now the president of the Council of Twelve Apostles, is quoted thus:

"The birth of the Savior was a natural occurrence unattended with any degree of mysticism, and the Father God was the literal parent of Jesus in the flesh as well as in the spirit."

In another quote, the Apostle Smith is set down thus: "Christ was begotten of God. He was not born without the aid of man, and that man was God!"

Then the Tanners reached back to Orson Pratt, an apostle who wrote in the days of polygamy. From his work, *The Seer*, they took this paragraph:

> The fleshly body of Jesus required a mother as well as a father. Therefore, the father and mother of Jesus, according to the flesh, must have been associated together in the capacity of husband and wife; hence the Virgin Mary must have been, for the time being, the lawful wife of God the Father; we use the term lawful wife, because it would be blasphemous in the highest degree to say that he overshadowed her or begat a Savior unlawfully. . . . He had a lawful right to overshadow the Virgin Mary in the capacity of a husband and begat a son, although she was espoused to another; for the law which he gave to govern men and women was not intended to govern himself, or to prescribe rules for his own conduct. It was also lawful in him after having thus dealt with Mary, to give her to Joseph her espoused husband. Whether God the Father gave Mary to Joseph for time only or for time and eternity, we are not informed. Inasmuch as God was the first husband to her, it may be that he only gave her to be the wife of Joseph while in the mortal state, and that he intended after the resurrection to take her as his wife in eternity.

Then the argument comes back to quote Brigham Young that "the birth of the Savior was as natural as are the births of our children; it was the result of natural action. He partook of flesh and blood—was begotten of his Father, as we were of our fathers."

The final quotation was from another of President

Young's sermons, this one in 1852, and by the standards of taste that prevail among Mormons in Salt Lake City today, this is just as raw and crude and offensive as any act of bad taste could be. This is the quotation wherein President Young even relates one of his own *bon mots*:

> I have given you a few leading items upon this subject, but a great deal more remains to be told. Now remember from this time forth, and forever, that Jesus Christ was not begotten by the Holy Ghost. I will repeat a little anecdote. I was in conversation with a certain learned professor upon the subject, when I replied, to this idea—"if the Son was be- gotten by the Holy Ghost, it would be very dangerous to baptize and confirm females, and give the Holy Ghost to them, lest he should beget children to be palmed upon the elders by the People, bringing the elders into great diffi- culties."

With the Tanners the church today finds itself faced by its own techniques of argument and its own words turned back against it to create doubts and uneasiness among some members. The campaign is effective, too, and of this there is no doubt. Once I was in a discussion of some as- pects of the life of the Saints with a highly placed young man whose own faith was beyond question. Jerald Tanner's name came into the conversation, and this man's face dark- ened. He astounded me by this unexplained remark:

"Yes, I know of him. My wife is in his clutches—intellec- tually speaking, of course."

This was strange language to describe Jerald Tanner. Sandra Tanner still could remember that when she was to be married to Jerald, the ceremony was to be in her home. Many LDS families stayed away from the reception because she had married an apostate. She still remembered that in her circle a girl friend was being married on that same week- end in a ceremony in the Los Angeles Temple. All of the girlish talk was about the other girl's marriage plans, while Sandra's were ignored.

A modern apostasy can be understood through the story of the Tanner couple. The fact that today they can live comfortably in Salt Lake City, relatively unmolested by the LDS church (beyond a letter or so from anguished apostles) demonstrates as much as anything could the way the church has changed. In the old days, those who disagreed had better be able to defend themselves.

But through this example of drifting away we also see a truth about the strength of Mormonism. It is, as Dr. O'Dea said, a second nationality for those born into it. They may leave the church—as an immigrant leaves Europe to settle in the United States—but they have ties with the church and share a common history, common values and common thought and speech patterns with those they left behind in the great congregation of the Saints.

When we consider these apostasies, we must remember that many, many more people remain solidly in the church than have drifted away. For every bitter apostate, there is a happy and emotionally composed Saint—perhaps hundreds of them—charging around on the Lord's business as his church defines it.

Many of them can be found any day one wants to look. One who comes to mind is J. D. Williams, a dedicated Mormon. He is a professor of political science at the University of Utah. He is a lean, handsome, intense intellectual of under forty. As a political liberal he abhors the church's attitude on Negroes. He holds a bachelor of arts degree from Stanford University, a doctor of philosophy degree from Harvard University. This is a man with a keen mind. He was asked:

"Would I be right in thinking of you as a devout Mormon?"

"You bet."

Williams has been a bishop of his ward (which annoyed some of the high church officials who find his liberal views offensive). He now is a high counselor of his stake, one of the important jobs in the church organization. In order to understand him and gain the full flavor of his views, one must understand where we talked. We sat in an alcove on one of the upper floors of the LDS hospital in Salt Lake City. Outside the rail his father paced, distraught and fearful. In a room nearby his mother was near death from a heart attack.

Williams said the LDS church provided him with many comforts for his emotional well-being. He said he was tied emotionally to the doctrine of free agency, the doctrine of continual acquisition of knowledge, and the doctrine of continual opportunity for progression.

"I love the doctrine that every soul has worth in the eyes of God," he said. He indicated his father pacing a few feet away from us and spoke of the comfort they both could feel from the doctrine of sealing of families and marriages for eternity.

"That is of much comfort to him at this moment," Williams said.

Professor Williams represents the sort of Mormon whose intellect and education allow him to believe the doctrine devoutly, but keep him from accepting the policies built up by the lesser figures of the church over the years. Sometimes, these men have become powerful figures who managed to bring some change into the church. At other times they have been cast out as their opponents gain ascendancy.

He was critical of the policy of secrecy attached to the church archives. This prevents historians from examining source documents. No one but a church official has access to them, although the library is a treasure house of answers to questions that have had to be answered by guesses.

"I would open it all up and be sure the truth could be known," said Williams. "Sure, some would take advantage of us and use the materials in there to hurt us. But after a while the truth would become plain. I think the truth cannot hurt us."

Just as Williams can be considered as a revealing example of a devout, but yet critical Mormon intellectual, Senator Wallace F. Bennett, the conservative Republican from Salt Lake City, can be considered as an interesting example of devotion and conformance.

Senator Bennett was elected in 1950, and re-elected in 1956 and 1962. He is on the finance committee and the joint committee on atomic energy of the United States Senate. He was president of the National Association of Manufacturers before going to the Senate. He ran his family's paint and glass company in Salt Lake City. Since 1935 he has been a member of the Deseret Sunday School General Board.

In 1958 Senator Bennett wrote a book published by the Deseret News Press and sold in the Deseret Bookstores, a combination that stamps it clearly as approved by church authorities. This book is *Why I Am a Mormon*. For 271 pages the Senator reviewed church history, doctrine and organization. Then he gave his answer:

I am a Mormon because I was born of Mormon parents into a Mormon home.

I have remained a Mormon because I have found spiritual, intellectual, and social satisfaction in my membership.

These answers might be reason enough. But there are more. I am a Mormon because all that I have learned in the Church and all that I have experienced because of it have brought the unshakeable assurance that this plan and program are of God. Through my membership and participation in the church's program, my family and I have been protected, healed, and blessed. In seeking to live by its principles, we have been given faith in their divinity. For us, it is the true church of Christ, and we are humbly proud to be called Mormons.

But even though the fundamental LDS doctrines satisfy the spiritual needs of such different men as Senator Bennett and Professor Williams, there are many others born into the church who became apostates.

Those we have examined in this chapter are of the left, of the people who wanted to leave not only the LDS church, but the *Book of Mormon*. Those on the outside tend to think of Joseph Smith and the *Book of Mormon* and the present Church of Jesus Christ of Latter-day Saints as being all one package. This is not exactly true.

What of those for whom the present LDS church is a liberalized—and therefore corrupted—version of Joseph Smith's Restored Gospel? In the early days, Mormon leaders spoke of the Catholic Church as "the whore of Babylon." There are those today who call themselves Saints who describe the present LDS church by that name.

Who are those people? What do they believe? How can one be so "fundamentalist" that he no longer can fit into what is a highly conservative religious organization?

VI

Origins and Importance
of Polygamy

OF ALL THE theological structures raised by Joseph Smith, the Prophet, and his successors, none stood so tall, none cast such a dark and thick shadow, none caused such trouble and heartache as the one erected on a revelation he dictated on July 12, 1843, to his clerk, William Clayton. It ordered the Saints into polygamy.

The LDS church became powerful and vigorous; this revelation almost destroyed it. This revelation was responsible for the creation of the Reorganized LDS church—as a haven for those, including the Prophet's widow, Emma—who denounced the plural marriage doctrine. It was responsible for bitter disputes with the United States government, for delaying Utah's admission as a state for many years, for imprisonment of the leadership of the Saints, for murders, for insurrection, for passage of federal laws which almost destroyed the LDS church financially.

Almost without exception, today's leadership of the church is descended from polygamists. Seven of the nine LDS presidents have been polygamists. Yet polygamy is outlawed by the Saints, and if one of them is found "living the doctrine," as they call it, he is excommunicated. The church is ruthless in its attempts to stamp out polygamy. But this discipline inhibits only LDS church members not "true believers" outside the church.

The most reliable authority in Utah on modern polygamy practice said that as many as 30,000 men, women and children are living in polygamous marriages in the 1960s.

Where does this drive for plural marriage come from? How did it originate? Why is it a part of Mormonism? The devout Mormon will answer these questions simply: It all came from God who told the Prophet just what is set out in the revelation. The Gentile students of Mormon history have other suggestions. One of them is that the practice was introduced into Nauvoo, Illinois, under the guidance of a rogue named John C. Bennett who was a great "womanizer" and led the Prophet into his evil ways, then persuaded Joseph to give theological basis to the practice through a revelation. This is one of those recurring questions about the Saints' religious belief which the non-Mormon need not decide. The actions were taken, and they set up reverberating reactions. Those are what interest us here.

A wealth of material exists on the history of the plural marriage revelation. One begins to feel that a lot of it has been carefully edited, and that perhaps a lot of it was produced out of whole cloth. The passions were high among those supporting and resisting the doctrine. One document of great fascination is the affidavit sworn February 16, 1874, by William Clayton, the clerk who took down the Prophet's dictation of the revelation. He was describing events of more than three decades earlier. Well down in his narrative, he reached the crucial day:

> One day in the month of February, 1843, date not remembered, the Prophet invited me to walk with him. During our walk, he said he had learned that there was a sister back in England, to whom I was very much attached. I replied there was, but nothing further than an attachment such as a brother and sister in the Church might rightfully entertain for each other. He then said "Why don't you send for her?" I replied, "In the first place, I have no authority to send for

her, and if I had, I have not the means to pay expenses."
To this he answered, "I give you the authority to send for
her, and I will furnish you with the means," which he did.
This was the first time the Prophet Joseph talked with me
on the subject of plural marriage. He informed me that the
doctrine and principle was right in the sight of our Heavenly
Father, and that it was a doctrine which pertained to celestial
order and glory. After giving me lengthy instructions and
informations concerning the doctrine of celestial or plural
marriage, he concluded his remarks by the words, "It is your
privilege to have all the wives you want." After this introduction our conversations on the subject of plural marriage
were very frequent, and he appeared to take particular
pains to inform and instruct me in respect to the principle.
He also informed me that he had other wives *living* besides
his first wife Emma, and in particular gave me to understand
that Eliza R. Snow, Louisa Beman, Desdemona W. Fullmer
and others were his lawful wives in the sight of Heaven.

On the 27th of April, 1843, the Prophet Joseph Smith married to me Margaret Moon, for time and eternity, at the residence of Elder Heber C. Kimball; and on the 22d of July,
1843, he married to me, according to the order of the Church,
my first wife Ruth.

On the 1st day of May, 1843, I officiated in the office of
an Elder by marrying Lucy Walker to the Prophet Joseph
Smith, at his own residence.

During this period the Prophet Joseph took several other
wives. Amongst the number I well remember Eliza Partridge, Emily Partridge, Sarah Ann Whitney, Helen Kimball
and Flora Woodworth. These all, he acknowledged to me,
were his lawful, wedded wives, according to the celestial
order. His wife Emma was cognizant of the fact of some, if
not all, of these being his wives, and she generally treated
them very kindly.

On the morning of the 12th of July, 1843, Joseph and Hyrum Smith came into the office in the upper story of the
"brick store" on the bank of the Mississippi River. They were
talking on the subject of plural marriage. Hyrum said to

Joseph, "If you will write the revelation on celestial marriage, I will take and read it to Emma, and I believe I can convince her of its truth, and you will hereafter have peace." Joseph smiled and remarked, "You do not know Emma as well as I do." Hyrum repeated his opinion and further remarked, "The doctrine is so plain, I can convince any reasonable man or woman of its truth, purity and heavenly origin," or words to their effect. Joseph then said, "Well, I will write the revelation and we will see." He then requested me to get paper and prepare to write. Hyrum very urgently requested Joseph to write the revelation by means of the Urim and Thummim, but Joseph, in reply, said he did not need to, for he knew the revelation perfectly from beginning to end.

Joseph and Hyrum then sat down and Joseph commenced to dictate the revelation on celestial marriage, and I wrote it, sentence by sentence, as he dictated. After the whole was written, Joseph asked me to read it through, slowly and carefully, which I did, and he pronounced it correct. He then remarked that there was much more that he could write, on the same subject, but what was written was sufficient for the present.

Hyrum then took the revelation to read to Emma. Joseph remained with me in the office until Hyrum returned. When he came back, Joseph asked him how he had succeeded. Hyrum replied that he had never received a more severe talking to in his life, that Emma was very bitter and full of resentment and anger.

Joseph quietly remarked, "I told you you did not know Emma as well as I did." Joseph then put the revelation in his pocket and they both left the office.

The revelation was read to several of the authorities during the day. Towards evening Bishop Newel K. Whitney asked Joseph if he had any objection to his taking a copy of the revelation; Joseph replied that he had not, and handed it to him. It was carefully copied the following day by Joseph C. Kingsbury. Two or three days after the revelation was written Joseph related to me and several others that Emma had so teased, and urgently entreated him for the privilege of destroying it, that he became so weary of her teasing, and to get rid of her annoyance, he told her she might destroy it and she had done so, but he had consented to her wish in this matter to pacify her, realizing that he knew the revelation perfectly, and could rewrite it at any time if necessary.

The copy made by Joseph C. Kingsbury is a true and correct copy of the original in every respect. The copy was carefully preserved by Bishop Whitney, and but few knew of its existence until the temporary location of the Camps of Israel at Winter Quarters, on the Missouri River, in 1846.

After the revelation on celestial marriage was written Joseph continued his instructions, privately, on the doctrine, to myself and others, and during the last year of his life we were scarcely ever together, alone, but he was talking on the subject, and explaining that doctrine and principles connected with it. He appeared to enjoy great liberty and freedom in his teachings, and also to find great relief in having a few to whom he could unbosom his feelings on that great and glorious subject.

From him I learned that the doctrine of plural and celestial marriage is the most holy and important doctrine ever revealed to man on the earth, and that without obedience to that principle no man can ever attain to the fulness of exaltation in celestial glory.

This affidavit of William Clayton is a most remarkable document. It demonstrates in almost every incident a facet of the character of the earliest First Family of the Saints. Here is Emma—angry, hurt, her self-confidence shattered that the Prophet would want other women, believing she could turn back the tide by merely destroying the written copy of the revelation. And Joseph—fascinated with the doctrine, yet compelled to keep it concealed from all but a select few who were in his immediate circle of confidence. And Hyrum—following faithfully his brother, the Prophet, and anxious to solve the vexing problem of an unhappy home life. The awarding of a plural wife to William Clayton within two months of telling him of the doctrine is revealing, too.

As is plain from reading the Clayton affidavit, Joseph had been spreading the plural marriage doctrine carefully for a long time before he talked with his clerk about it in February, 1843. Some affidavits collected by the Utah Mormons place his revelation on the subject as early as 1831, but other sources indicated he began the practice in 1841 on April 5 with his marriage to Louisa Beaman. (Clayton spelled her name Beman.) As Clayton made clear, the practice of plural marriage was carried on frequently in the high levels of the church long before the revelation was set down formally in July, 1843.

The doctrine fitted into the patriarchal theories Joseph had followed in organizing the church. By 1843, the church had settled into the pattern of a nomadic tribe or a feudal system—a system wherein the Prophet stood at the pinnacle, supported by his apostles and other high officials who in turn were supported down the line to the men who made up the quorums of the priesthoods. Yet, unlike the old Hebrew patriarchs, Joseph and his Mormons had only one wife apiece. Thus the revelation begins—in language quoted in an earlier chapter—as an answer to Joseph's question of justification of the wives and concubines of old. Here too he outlines the doctrine of celestial marriage:

Therefore, if a man marry him a wife in the world, and he marry her not by men nor by my word, and he covenant with her so long as he is in the world and she with him, their covenant and marriage are not of force when they are dead, and when they are out of the world; therefore, they are not bound by the law when they are out of the world.

Therefore, when they are out of the world they neither marry nor are given in marriage; but are appointed angels in heaven; which angels are ministering servants, to minister for those who are worthy of a far more, an exceeding, and an eternal weight of glory.

For these angels did not abide my law; therefore, they cannot be enlarged, but remain separately and singly, without exaltation, in their saved condition, to all eternity; and from henceforth are not gods, but are angels of God forever and ever.

The Prophet is saying that God has revealed to him that if people want to have marriages in the spirit world which Mormons believe is the life after death, they must engage these marriage partners during mortal existence. The marriages must be through rules set down by this revelation. Otherwise, these persons will be just servants in the afterlife.

Then the revelation sets out just how to achieve the desired result:

And again, verily I say unto you, if a man marry a wife by my word, which is my law, and by the new and everlasting covenant, and it is sealed unto them by the Holy Spirit of promise, by him who is anointed, unto whom I have appointed this power and the keys of this priesthood; and it shall be said unto them—Ye shall come forth in the first resurrection; and if it be after the first resurrection, in the next resurrection; and shall inherit thrones, kingdoms, principalities, and powers, dominions, all heights and depths— then shall it be written in the Lamb's Book of Life, that he shall commit no murder whereby to shed innocent blood, and if ye abide in my covenant, and commit no murder whereby to shed innocent blood, it shall be done unto them in all things whatsoever my servant hath put upon them, in time, and through all eternity; and shall be of full force when they are out of the world; and they shall pass by the angels, and the gods, which are set there, to their exaltation and glory in all things, as hath been sealed upon their heads, which glory shall be a fullness and a continuation of the seeds forever and ever.

All of this sets up the Mormon belief in the eternity of marriage performed in the Temple, although the Prophet said nothing about Temples in recounting his revelation. It was at this point in time that he was working out his Temple rites; up to the move to Nauvoo, the Temple rites had not been known to the Saints.

The revelation moved on through discussions of the various old Hebrew patriarchs who had wives and concubines —Abraham, David, Isaac and Jacob were named. What they did was good because God told them to do it, the Prophet explained. He was working his way near to the passages that would command the Saints to begin plural marriage. But first, one other matter must be dealt with:

Verily, I say unto you: A commandment I give unto mine handmaid, Emma Smith, your wife, whom I have given unto you, that she stay herself and partake not of that which I commanded you to offer unto her; for I did it, saith the Lord, to prove you all, as I did Abraham, and that I might require an offering at your hand, by covenant and sacrifice.

And let mine handmaid, Emma Smith, receive all those that have been given unto my servant Joseph, and who are virtuous and pure before me; and those who are not pure, and have said they were pure, shall be destroyed, saith the Lord God.

For I am the Lord thy God, and ye shall obey my voice; and I give unto my servant Joseph that he shall be made ruler over many things; for he hath been faithful over a few things, and from hence forth I will strengthen him.

And I command mine handmaid, Emma Smith, to abide and cleave unto my servant Joseph and to none else. But if she will not abide this commandment she shall be destroyed, saith the Lord; for I am the Lord thy God, and will destroy her if she abide not my law.

Imagine the scene when Hyrum read her those passages! Toward the end of the revelation, Joseph turned to the

plural marriage doctrine itself, the subject which had fascinated him for years and which was to be the reef that almost
wrecked his church.

And again, as pertaining to the law of the priesthood—if
any man espouse a virgin, and desire to espouse another,
and the first give her consent, and if he espouse the second,
and they are virgins, and have vowed to no other man, then
is he justified; he cannot commit adultery for they are given
unto him; for he cannot commit adultery with that that be-
longeth unto him and to no one else.

And if he have ten virgins given unto him by this law, he
cannot commit adultery, for they belong to him, and they are
given unto him; therefore is he justified.

But if one or either of the ten virgins, after she is espoused,
shall be with another man, she has committed adultery, and
shall be destroyed; for they are given unto him to multiply
and replenish the earth, according to my commandment, and
to fulfil the promise which was given by my Father before
the foundation of the world, and for their exaltation in the
eternal worlds, that they may bear the souls of men; for
herein is the work of my Father continued, that he may be
glorified.

And again, verily, verily, I say unto you, if any man have a
wife, who holds the keys of this power, and he teaches unto
her the law of my priesthood, as pertaining to these things,
then shall she believe and administer unto him, or she shall
be destroyed, saith the Lord your God; I will destroy her;
for I will magnify my name upon all those who receive and
abide in my law.

Therefore, it shall be lawful in me, if she receive not this
law, for him to receive all things whatsoever I, the Lord his
God, will give unto him because she did not believe and
administer unto him according to my word; and she then
becomes the transgressor; and he is exempt from the law of
Sarah, who administered unto Abraham according to the law
which I commanded Abraham to take Hagar to wife.

And now, as pertaining to this law, verily, verily, I say unto you, I will reveal more unto you, hereafter; therefore, let this suffice for the present. Behold, I am Alpha and Omega. Amen.

But there is no record that Joseph ever revealed more on the plural marriage doctrine. Less than a year later he was dead. What the Saints might have made of this practice under Joseph's leadership we shall never know. But this one revelation had immense impact on the church. Actually, two doctrines were set out in it. For half a century or more the plural marriage doctrine dominated the church. But the other one was of equal importance in the long run. The possibility that a man would have his earthly wife with him in the Celestial Paradise opened up stunning and beautiful hope for a people hard-pressed by the life their religion and the times required of them. This doctrine still is cherished.

But at the time, the minority who favored the doctrine of plural marriage seized upon the opportunity to improve the bare outlines given in the revelation. To read the speeches and sermons and written arguments produced by LDS leaders in the nineteenth century in Utah is to discover that Mormonism of the leaders of that day was strongly tied to—if not dominated by—a doctrine of patriarchal sexuality.

Some of the nineteenth-century Mormon leaders in Utah even argued that Jesus Christ was married—not just once, but to a plurality of wives who followed him about. Orson Hyde, one of the first apostles of the church, argued that "Jesus Christ was married at Cana of Galilee, that Mary, Martha and others were his wives, and that he begat children."

That story is told in the second chapter of the Gospel According to St. John. It is as follows in the King James Translation:

And the third day there was a marriage in Cana of Galilee; and the mother of Jesus was there:

And both Jesus was called, and his disciples, to the marriage.

And when they wanted wine, the mother of Jesus saith unto him, They have no wine.

Jesus saith unto her, Woman, what have I to do with thee? mine hour is not yet come.

His mother saith unto the servants, Whatsoever he saith unto you, do it.

And there were set there six waterpots of stone, after the manner of the purifying of the Jews, containing two or three firkins apiece.

Jesus saith unto them, Fill the waterpots with water. And they filled them up to the brim.

And he saith unto them, Draw out now, and bear unto the governor of the feast. And they bare it.

When the ruler of the feast had tasted the water that was made wine, and knew not whence it was: (but the servants which drew the water knew;) the governor of the feast called the bridegroom,

And saith unto him, Every man at the beginning doth set forth good wine; and when men have well drunk, then that which is worse: but thou hast kept the good wine until now.

This beginning of miracles did Jesus in Cana of Galilee, and manifested forth his glory; and his disciples believed on him.

Apostle Hyde told the Saints that the bridegroom was Christ. At another time he told them, "I will venture to say that if Jesus Christ were now to pass through the most pious countries in Christendom with a train of women, such as used to follow him, fondling about him, combing his hair, anointing him with precious ointment, washing his feet with tears, and wiping them with the hair of their heads and unmarried, or even married, he would be mobbed, tarred and feathered, and rode, not on an ass, but on a rail."

You don't hear that kind of talk in Salt Lake City today. The modern Mormons do not believe in plural marriage. They have succeeded in their minds and in their theology in sifting the celestial marriage doctrine of sealing for time and eternity from the polygamy doctrine set out in the same revelation. These reflections of early doctrine are something today's Saints would just as soon the rest of us left buried. But understanding that doctrine and the atmosphere which it produced enables us to understand what the LDS people are in the last half of the twentieth century.

While those early leaders might rise in meetings and thunder their devotion to all of the doctrine enunciated through the Prophet Joseph, there is indication that they were still a shade nervous about the plural marriage system, however much they were plunging into it with as many wives as they could persuade and support.

In the early days of the church there were many injunctions against polygamy. In fact, in the first edition of *Doctrine and Covenants*, printed in 1835, there was a section of four paragraphs headed "Marriage." This set out the church's view on marriage and even included the questions that should be asked by the officiating church official of the couple to be married. They were asked:

"You both mutually agree to be each other's companion, husband and wife, observing the legal rights belonging to this condition, that is, *keeping yourselves wholly for each other, and from all others,* during your lives."

Nor is this commitment to monogamy all that occurs in that short statement. The last paragraph contains this sentence:

"Inasmuch as this church of Christ has been reproached with the crime of fornication, and polygamy; we declare that we believe that one man should have one wife; and one woman but one husband, except in case of death, when either is at liberty to marry again."

(This is still printed as Section III in the version of *Doctrine and Covenants* published by the Reorganized LDS church which, however, carefully describes it only as a statement of church position on marriage, not a revelation. The Reorganized LDS church has never accepted the later revelation of 1843 and so has never had polygamy or celestial marriage.)

It is fair for the Mormons to answer questions about this early prohibition against plural marriage by pointing out that the Prophet's revelation was not recorded until eight years after that edition of *Doctrine and Covenants* was issued. But there also are answers required beyond that.

The section committing the Saints to monogamy continued to appear in *Doctrine and Covenants*, edition after edition, while the leaders married more and more wives, until 1876. At that time an edition appeared which removed the monogamy statement and for the first time included the 1843 doctrine of celestial and plural marriage. By that time children born under the plural marriage system were close to thirty years old, and were themselves living in plural marriage. The polygamy revelation was an integral part of Mormon life for more than thirty years before it was ever printed in the sacred works. Why did the Mormons wait? I don't know. Why, having waited, did they finally put the revelation in the book? One can guess.

By 1876, the great struggle over polygamy had been joined with the United States government. The Mormons' first line of defense was to claim the freedom of worship protection of the Constitution. If they wanted to do this, they had to get the revelation that ordered polygamy into print in their sacred works.

For all those years until necessity decided the matter for them, the LDS leaders had been hesitant over just what to do with the revelation on marriage. When the first party arrived at the site of Salt Lake City on July 25, 1847, Brigham

Young and many of the other leaders already were living in polygamy. However, the rank and file still were unaware of the theological basis for this mode of life. Certainly, the members could see strange carryings-on, but this was a patriarchal religion and so much was taken for faith that accepting these things without too many questions was not much problem. Gradually, of course, the rank and file learned of the plural marriage system and probably heard of the existence of the revelation. It was not a stunning surprise when at a conference on August 28-29, 1852, the nine-year-old revelation was read in public for the first time. The Saints then had been five years in the wilderness redoubt.

Brigham Young and Orson Pratt, one of the first twelve apostles selected by the Prophet Joseph, stood before the church leaders and about 2000 Saints to formally unveil the doctrine. Said Apostle Pratt: "It is well known to the congregation before me that the Latter-day Saints have embraced the doctrine of a plurality of wives as a part of their religious faith."

At that time the Mormons had successfully transplanted their religious and sociological institutions to the desert. Their proposed state of Deseret, which they had actually organized in 1849, still might become a reality. Internal pressures must have been strong for public recognition of the plural marriage doctrine. Or else the leaders may have considered themselves and their people beyond reach of the United States government. One who had traveled it on foot, on horse and in an oxen-powered wagon train would know well just how far they were isolated from the rest of the American people. Or it may have been that they considered they were too strong to be hurt. Remember that Richard F. Burton, the world traveler, thought they might become an independent nation. The Saints were colonizing in Arizona and Nevada and California and Idaho. They were constructing a supply route to the Pacific in Southern California and soon might be able to abandon the old crossing from Gulf ports or the Eastern seaboard.

Whatever the reason for unveiling the polygamy doctrine, it was a miscalculation. Within five years the United States government had dispatched troops to take possession of the territory, and Brigham Young was deposed as governor of Deseret by a Gentile. This conflict, in which there were no pitched battles between the troops and the Saints, has been known as the Mormon War. Salt Lake City was evacuated, except for a small group left behind to burn it down if the troops tried to take possession. But the army built a camp in the desert and the Saints returned to sell supplies to the army and turn the episode into an economic shot in the arm for the Mormons.

A great many things went into the federal decision to move in on the Mormons, but one of these things was widespread criticism of the practice of polygamy. Once the army was there, and Gentile federal officials appeared, the contest over the plural wife doctrine was soon well joined. In 1862, ten years after the formal announcement and reading of the revelation, the first federal law was passed that punished "polygamy in the territories." Not until 1879 was a test case ruled upon by the United States Supreme Court, which brushed aside the claim that the Mormons could practice their plural marriage doctrine under constitutional guarantees of religious freedom. Printing the revelation had done no good.

"Suppose," said the United States Supreme Court in a devastating rhetorical question, "one believed that human sacrifices were a necessary part of religious worship, would it be seriously contended that the civil government under which he lived could not interfere to prevent a sacrifice?"

By 1879 Brigham Young was dead. The Council of Twelve Apostles ran the church. The next year, John Taylor became president. As a young man he had gone to jail in Carthage and was wounded in the gunfight where Joseph and Hyrum Smith were killed. Taylor had a deep resolve never to go to jail again.

But the Gentile law enforcement officers were mounting terrible pressure. Church leaders, who had watched Nevada be carved as a state in 1864 out of their proposed State of Deseret, wanted statehood, for then state law enforcement officers would be responsible for enforcing such laws as a Mormon legislature might pass against plural marriage.

The federals recognized this, too, and were opposed to statehood. For a time, because they could not get access to church marriage records, the federal appointees were hampered in their prosecutions for bigamy under the 1862 act, for to prove bigamy one must prove a multiplicity of marriages. However, in 1882 a new federal statute provided punishment for living in lewd cohabitation. Mormon leaders began to go to jail in bunches. By June, 1887, almost 200 Mormon men were in jail for lewd cohabitation. By then John Taylor, the third LDS president, was dead. He had spent almost his entire time in office in flight under an assumed name. And in that year the federal government struck another hammer blow at the doctrine of plural marriage.

The Edmunds-Tucker Act dissolved the Corporation of the Church of Jesus Christ of Latter-day Saints and took some other anti-Mormon actions of less magnitude. The dissolution of the church corporation shook the Saints badly, for it had the effect of destroying their joint holding company, the LDS church, as an economic institution. They took various moves to circumvent the act, and were moderately successful, but the pressure was becoming unbear-

able. The new law cost them more than $1 million—in 1890
dollars, too. They had to have statehood.

A story of the negotiations on statehood is told in biased
but still fascinating detail in the book written by Harvey J.
O'Higgins, one of the early twentieth-century muckrakers.
It is the story told by Frank J. Cannon, one of the first
United States senators for Utah, and is called *Under the
Prophet in Utah.*

Frank J. Cannon was a son of Apostle George Q. Cannon,
the powerful and important LDS leader from the time of
Brigham Young's death until into the twentieth century.
The apostle had twenty other sons, but Frank was his political operator. Frank Cannon is presented as a semi-apos-
tate even in those years, working in behalf of his people more
than in behalf of their religious belief. The book tells of his
negotiations through various national figures for a solution
that would end the federal pressure. He had a long interview with President Grover Cleveland. He also describes
a visit to his father in prison on the edge of Salt Lake City
where the old man was serving time on conviction of lewd
cohabitation. Frequently in the book Frank Cannon and
Harvey O'Higgins show contempt for religious Mormonism,
and just as frequently are overcome with respect for the
deep faith of the Mormons. Here, where they describe the
attitude of polygamous Mormons toward their marriages,
is a typical passage:

> I do not wish to idealize the polygamous relation—but in
> monogamy a man is not persecuted for his marriage, and
> sometimes he does not appreciate the tie. In Polygamy, the
> men and women alike had been compelled to suffer on its
> account by the grim trials of the life itself and by the hatred
> of all civilization arrayed against it. They had grown to
> value their marriage system by what it had cost them. They
> had been driven by the contempt of the world to argue for

its sanctity, to live up to their declarations, and to raise it in
their esteem to what it professed to be, the celestial order
that prevailed in the Heavens!

President Wilford Woodruff was the leader of the church
by then. In the summer of 1890 he showed Frank Cannon a
paper and asked if Cannon thought this would end the problems with the United States government. This was one of
the historic documents of the church. It has come to be
known as "The Manifesto."

It was made public on September 24, 1890. It is a most
curious document as it appears at the very end of *Doctrine
and Covenants*. The other parts of that religious book are
presented in Biblical style with numbered verses and dou-
ble-columned pages. The language of the other sections
also is usually Biblical—one skeptic called it "Reformed
King James English." These other sections usually end with
"amen" or some other religious closing words.

However, The Manifesto is printed in a different type-
face. It is set in wider lines of type. It has no number, but
it is headed "Official Declaration." The printed signature
of President Woodruff follows the text. This is the language:

> To Whom it may Concern:
> Press dispatches having been sent for political purposes,
> from Salt Lake City, which have been widely published, to
> the effect that the Utah Commission, in their recent report
> to the Secretary of the Interior, allege that plural marriages
> are still being solemnized and that forty or more such mar-
> riages have been contracted in Utah since last June or dur-
> ing the past year, also that in public discourses the leaders
> of the Church have taught, encouraged and urged the con-
> tinuances of the practice of polygamy . . .
> I, therefore, as President of the Church of Jesus Christ of
> Latter-day Saints, do hereby, in the most solemn manner,
> declare that these charges are false. We are not teaching
> polygamy or plural marriage, nor permitting any person to

enter into its practice, and I deny that either forty or any other number of plural marriages have during that period been solemnized in our Temples or in any other place in the Territory.

One case has been reported, in which the parties allege that the marriage was performed in the Endowment House, in Salt Lake City in the Spring of 1889, but I have not been able to learn who performed the ceremony; whatever was done in this matter was without my knowledge. In consequence of this alleged occurrence the Endowment House was, by my instructions, taken down without delay.

Inasmuch as laws have been enacted by Congress forbidding plural marriages, which laws have been pronounced constitutional by the court of last resort, I hereby declare my intention to submit to those laws, and to use my influence with the members of the Church over which I preside to have them do likewise.

There is nothing in my teachings to the Church or in those of my associates, during the time specified, which can be reasonably construed to inculcate or encourage polygamy; and when any Elder of the Church has used language which appeared to convey any such teaching, he has been promptly reproved. And I now publicly declare that my advice to the Latter-day Saints is to refrain from contracting any marriage forbidden by the law of the land.

This is rather strange language. Was it a revelation? Was it merely advice? Did it mean that the Mormons were giving up plural marriage?

About a year later in a sermon at Logan, Utah, President Woodruff said that his Manifesto was the result of a revelation. He said he has asked God in prayer for guidance.

"The Lord showed me by vision and revelation exactly what would take place if we did not stop this practice," he said on November 1, 1891. ". . . All the ordinances (religious rites) would be stopped throughout the land of Zion. Confusion would reign throughout Israel and many men would be made prisoners. This trouble would have come upon the whole church and we should have been compelled to stop the practice. Now, the question is, whether it should be stopped in this manner, or in the way the Lord has manifested to us, and leave our prophets and Apostles and fathers free men, and the Temples in the hands of the people so that the dead may be redeemed."

The sermon also had passages that indicated President Woodruff felt the criticism of those diehards who would have had the church destroyed rather than surrender. But he insisted that "the God of Heaven commanded me to do what I did." He stated it very simply:

"I went before the Lord, and I wrote what the Lord told me to write."

At the end he delivered the typical Mormon patriarchal admonition:

"I want the Latter-day Saints to stop murmuring and complaining at the Providence of God."

Thus, it becomes clear, The Manifesto was a revelation. But it did not mean that the Mormons were giving up plural marriage. They were only promising to give up performing plural marriage ceremonies in Salt Lake City and Utah and in the United States.

The Apostle Abraham Cannon, the brother of Frank and the son of George Q. Cannon, entered into a plural marriage in a ceremony performed at sea off Catalina Island well after the issuance of The Manifesto. Frank Cannon said he was horrified at what he thought was a betrayal of his promises to federal officials. He blamed Joseph F. Smith, who was to become the church president within a few years. Frank Cannon said that Joseph F. Smith persuaded President Woodruff to approve the marriage, then performed it himself.

Abraham Cannon and this plural wife, Lillian Hamlin, had a daughter, Maharba, I was told. When the apostle died, not long after the marriage, they went to the Mormon colony at Colonia Juarez, Mexico. In Salt Lake City I talked to a man who was Maharba's playmate when they were children there. This is Stanley S. Ivins, one of the great authorities on Mormon polygamy. His father was Anthony W. Ivins, who was an apostle and was first counselor to President Heber J. Grant.

Anthony Ivins was an elder in the church in the mid-1890s when he was called in and told to go to Mexico to be president of the stake there. He was told that he was to have authority to perform plural marriages for those who were sent to him for that purpose. He would be able to identify them from the letters of introduction they would present, he was told.

After Anthony Ivins died in 1934 at eighty-two years of age, his family found the records of these marriages among his papers. They were turned over to the LDS church. More than fifty polygamous marriages were easily identifiable, beginning in June, 1897, when three men from Utah were married at Juárez, just across from El Paso. They had crossed over into Mexico just for the marriage ceremony, then went back into the United States. However, Ivins refused to perform marriages for the regular population of the Mormon colonies because the men lacked the letters from Salt Lake City which he considered to be his authority for the ceremony. However, by 1898 polygamous marriages were being performed routinely in Mexico by other Mormon leaders.

Stanley S. Ivins, the authority on polygamy, said that by 1890 the main body of the Mormons had willingly given up plural marriage. He said it was a practice that was never widely favored, anyway, and that the increases in the rate of plural marriage were connected with increased prosecution of the Mormons. He believed many such unions were made out of a feeling of resistance to outside pressure. They were a restatement of faith under pressure of persecution.

Stanley Ivins said that the relatively small percentage of men who took plural wives took just one or two. He said that at the very highest rate of plural marriage, which was in the late 1850s, no more than 20 per cent of Mormon men were living with more than one wife. Of 1784 such cases that he studied, 66.3 per cent married only one extra wife; 21.2 per cent married two extra wives; and 6.7 per cent had as many as three extra wives. Thus fewer than 6 per cent had more than four wives.

"The typical polygamist, far from being the insatiable male of popular fable, was a dispassionate fellow, content to call a halt after marrying the one extra wife required to assure him of his chance at salvation," Stanley S. Ivins wrote in the *Western Humanities Review* in 1956.

Another false conception was that polygamists were bearded patriarchs who continued marrying young girls as long as they were able to hobble about. [Ivins said.] It is true that Brigham Young took a young wife when he was 67 years old and a few others followed his example, but such marriages were not much more common with the Mormons than among other groups. Of 1,229 polygamists, more than 10 per cent married their last wives while still in their 20s, and more than half of them before arriving at the still lusty age of 40 years. Not one in five took a wife after reaching his 50th year. The average age at which the group ceased marrying was 40 years.

He also drew a statistical portrait:

The composite polygamist was first married at the age of 23 to a girl of 20. Thirteen years later he took a plural wife, choosing a 22 year old girl. The chances were two to one that, having demonstrated his acceptance of the principle of plurality, he was finished with marrying. If, however, he took a third wife, he waited four years, then selected another

girl of 22. The odds were now three to one against his taking a fourth wife, but if he did so, he waited another four
years, and once more chose a 22 year old girl, although he
had now reached the ripe age of 44. In case he decided to
add a fifth wife, he waited only two years, and this time the
lady of his choice was 21 years old. This was the end of his
marrying, unless he belonged to a three per cent minority.

Ivins, in his examination of all available records on Mor-
mon polygamy, found that men often married sisters. The
Prophet Joseph married three sets of sisters. Among Heber
C. Kimball's forty-five wives were four sets of sisters. John
D. Lee, the man executed for the Mountain Meadow Mas-
sacre, married three sisters, and then their mother.

The thread of sexuality always ran through the theological coating that the LDS leaders put on their polygamy.
The plural wives of the Prophet generally became the wives
of one of the other Mormon leaders after his murder, and
Lucy Walker became the wife of Heber C. Kimball. It was
she who was married to the Prophet by the clerk who copied the revelation as Joseph dictated. She was one day past
seventeen when she married Joseph; he was nearly thirty-
eight. She and Apostle Kimball had nine children. In later
years Kimball said:

> I would not be afraid to promise a man who is 60 years of
> age, if he will take the counsel of Brother Brigham and his
> brethren, that he will renew his age. I have noticed that a
> man who has but one wife, and is inclined to that doctrine,
> soon begins to wither and dry up, while a man who goes
> into plurality looks fresh, young and sprightly. Why is this?
> Because God loves that man, and because he honors His
> work and word. Some of you may not believe this; but I
> not only believe it—I know it. For a man of God to be con-
> fined to one woman is small business; for it is as much as we
> can do now to keep up under the burdens we have to carry;

and I do not know what we should do if we had only one wife apiece.

The Mormon leaders in those days of polygamy expected their practice would produce a great many children. Once the church newspaper, the *Millennial Star*, calculated that a man with 40 wives might have 3,508,441 descendants by the time he was 78. It did not work that way in practice. Apostle Kimball with 45 wives had only 68 children and Brigham Young had only 56. John D. Lee, with 18 wives, had 65 children.

Stanley Ivins found that the rank and file did better. He studied 1651 families. There were ten or more children in four out of five families. Half had 15 or more children and a fourth had 20 or more. There were 88 families that had 30 or more children, 19 that had 40 or more, and seven that had 50 or more. When one six-wife elder had been dead 55 years, he had 1900 descendants.

Ivins even calculated that the wives of polygamists bore fewer children on the average than the wives of monogamist Mormons. The polygamists' wives had 5.9 children on the average; the monogamists' wives had an average of 8 children.

But they did not give up the practice until absolutely driven to surrender. Once statehood was achieved in 1896 and the marriage laws no longer were subject to federal oversight, the top leaders of the church began to drift back to polygamy, Frank Cannon charged in his account of those years. He insisted that Joseph F. Smith, LDS president from 1901 to 1918, had twelve children born to plural wives after The Manifesto was issued.

Frank Cannon was present when President Woodruff announced The Manifesto to the apostles. He told them that The Manifesto meant an end to further plural marriages; and he said it meant an end to living in plural marriages already entered into. Cannon and O'Higgins described the scene:

> I saw their faces flush and then slowly pale again—and the storm broke. One after another they rose and protested hoarsely, in the voice of tears, that they were willing to suffer "persecution unto death" rather than to violate the covenants which they had made "in holy places" with the women who had trusted them. One after another they offered themselves for any sacrifice but this betrayal of the women and children to whom they owed an everlasting faith. And a manlier lot of men never spoke in a manlier way. Not a petty word was uttered. Their thought was not for themselves. Their grief was not selfish. Their protests had a dignity in pathos that shook me in spite of myself.

Frank Cannon described how they argued there on the day the bill came due for Joseph's revelation of a half century earlier. One by one they spoke, but one was left, the nephew of the Prophet, the son of Hyrum who died also at Carthage jail, the man who would soon be the president of the church. Cannon's account:

> Joseph F. Smith was one of the last to speak. With a face like wax, his hands outstretched, in an intensity of passion that seemed as if it must sweep the assembly, he declared that he had covenanted, at the altar of God's house, in the presence of his Father, to cherish the wives and children whom the Lord had given him. They were more to him than life. They were dearer to him than happiness. He would rather choose to stand, with them, alone—persecuted—proscribed—outlawed—to wait until God in His anger should break the nation with His avenging stroke. But—
> He dropped his arms. He seemed to shrink in his commanding stature like a man stricken with a paralysis of despair. The tears came to the pained constriction of his eyelids.
> "I have never disobeyed a revelation from God," he said. "I cannot—I dare not—now."

He announced—with his head up, though his body swayed —that he would accept and abide by the revelation. When he sank in his chair and covered his face with his hands, there was a gasp of sympathy and relief, as if we had been hearing the pain of a man in agony . . . I knew then as I know now, that he and those others were at this moment sincere. I knew that they had relinquished what was more dear to them than the breath of life. I knew the appalling significance, to them, of the promise which they were making to the nation. And in all the degraded after-years, when so many of them were guilty of breach of covenant and base violation of trust, I tried never to forget that in the hour of their greatest trial, they had sacrificed themselves for their people; they had suffered for the happiness of others . . .

This was the real tragedy, the actual trap for the polygamists—the time when they would have to give it all up, when they would either give up their families or suffer jail and persecution and cause the destruction of the carefully built religious, economic and social system called Mormonism.

They were able to make the transition back into monogamy for succeeding generations and yet to maintain their own plural marriages. When the shock had passed, they found ways of adapting to the new situation. Today there is little tendency to deny that the church leaders tried every way they could to circumvent the implied provisions of The Manifesto that they give up living with their plural families. Some continued to live with their wives; some just supported plural families; a very few wives were abandoned.

After 1896, they seemed to think that having won statehood and control of their courts, they no longer could be punished as they had been during the territorial days. The first shadow on the horizon came when Brigham H. Roberts, an important church leader, was elected to congress in 1898—and was refused his seat because he was a polygamist.

In 1900 Reed Smoot, the vigorous son of Abraham O. Smoot who was President Young's viceroy in Provo, was selected as an apostle. In 1901, Joseph F. Smith became LDS president, and in 1903 the legislature of Utah selected the Apostle Smoot as United States senator. Immediately the anti-Mormon group, led by Protestant ministers, demanded that Smoot not be seated. The Senate committee on privileges and elections held hearings for two years, then—in a divided report—recommended that Apostle Smoot be barred from his seat. The Senate voted to seat him and Senator Smoot served until his defeat in 1932. He was a conservative Republican.

But in the hearings by the Senate committee, as well as in the very action itself, things occurred which shook the resolve of the high leaders of the church. President Joseph F. Smith, was forced to testify and to admit that polygamy was still being followed among Mormons. He estimated that 4000 families were even then living in polygamy in Utah. It is widely accepted among historians that the Smoot case was the real death knell of church-condoned polygamy. If the Mormons had lost a duly elected United States senator over that issue—and Senator Smoot was no polygamist himself—what then of their hopes of freedom with statehood? Could statehood have been taken away from them?

Senator Smoot was very close to President Smith and insisted in his dealings with the First Presidency that the active polygamists among his fellow apostles—John W. Taylor and Matthias Cowley—be either required to stop promoting plural marriage, or be dismissed from their position. They were dismissed in 1905.

As time passed, the church's position toward the polygamists hardened. The pressures eased, also, as the population in which polygamy had been strongest began to grow older and to die. Eventually, in the administration of President Heber J. Grant, the church began the practice of ex-

communication for any members found practicing polygamy.

Today the LDS church would be shattered if polygamy
were demanded of its members. Wives of many Mormons
told me when polygamy was under discussion, "I couldn't
take it. I'd leave the church." It was one thing to impose
this on the small, hard-core group that was in Salt Lake City
in 1852; it would be another to try to impose it today on the
2.5 million listed as members.

But that does not mean polygamy has disappeared. It
thrives.

—— VII ——

Polygamy Today—
Rejected by Saints

HE WAS a handsome, proud man who from his second sentence in our conversation identified himself as a polygamist.
Inasmuch as he talked freely that night, and because he
said things that could bring him again to trouble, there is
no reason to remember his name. Call him Harold. He—
and the others like him—constitute a small discordance in
the Mormon communities of the Mountain West, for they
exist wherever the LDS church has been strong. Probably
some of them exist quietly and secretly within the body of
the church itself. But when they are found out, they are
excommunicated.

How many of these people are there? No one can say for
certain, for their style of life does not lend itself to a census
taker. All of these marriages are between people who believe they are following the Word of God as set down in the
revelation recorded by the Prophet Joseph in 1843. The
best way to attempt to understand them is to listen to the
man who talked that night, the man who described himself
proudly as a polygamist.

Harold was then in his early sixties, and his body was
thickening at the waist and his hair lightening. He still was
an impressive male figure with a gift for talk which he sometimes had to restrain in the name of good manners. He wore
a blue shirt, dark trousers, no tie, and his hair was neat, his

mustache trimmed. I saw him six hours after I let it be
known that I wanted to talk to a polygamist. When the talk
began, his son came in and sat listening. The son was twenty-one years old, quiet, a very muscular young man, tanned
and with his dark brown hair sun-streaked from outdoor
work. He was Little Harold and before the evening was out
he brought in his baby son, Harold III.

A relative, a man of about fifty years, probably also a polygamist, came and went throughout the long talk, but took
no part in it. A wife sat outside the conversation in an adjoining room, listening, and gracefully entering into the talk
to help Harold remember dates and names and places. He
needed her help, for example, in counting up how many
children he had fathered.

So we began.

Harold was born in Berne, Idaho, a Mormon settlement
named for the Swiss city. His grandparents came over from
Switzerland after their conversion by missionaries, bring-
ing his father with them. They went to Salt Lake City in
either 1863 or 1867 (Harold was unsure), and Brigham sent
them to Idaho. The grandfather was a polygamist, as was
the father, who had two wives. Each wife bore eleven children. There were fifteen boys and seven girls. Harold was
the fourteenth son and the twentieth child. His mother died
when he was four and his father when he was twelve. An
older brother was a soldier in World War I and died of Spanish influenza in San Antonio, leaving an army insurance
policy to the boy and a sister.

"I got about $28 a month and it was enough to let me
be a missionary," he said. He went to Switzerland on his
eighteenth birthday in 1922, and came back in the spring of
1925 after thirty months. While in Switzerland he was
slightly acquainted with David O. McKay who then was
president of the European mission. Harold has a picture of
himself and others with McKay. After his mission he

worked in a wholesale hardware. His first marriage was on March 31, 1927, in the Temple at Salt Lake City. This wife, whom we will call Alice, was married to him legally. She bore eight of his children. Her family had practiced polygamy.

"When I went to her father to ask him for her," Harold remembered, "he told me I could have her if I'd promise him to go into plural marriage as soon as I could find someone. We talked it over and we decided that my next wife would be her sister."

We will call this second wife Bernice. She really was a half sister to Alice in the polygamous household of their father.

By this time Harold had moved to Boise where he became active in the LDS church. As a city fireman, he had considerable free time to travel through Idaho to speak on church matters. Harold was very devoted to his religion.

His second marriage plans presented a problem. No ordinary Mormon priest would perform the ceremony, because of the church prohibition of plural marriage. Nor indeed would such a man have been acceptable to Alice, Bernice and Harold. They believed that a priest must have special authority to perform plural marriages. Harold told of casting about to find a man with this authority. His story was full of allegory and accounts of troubled dreams and ended with a shadowy account of success.

But he would not say who performed the plural marriage.

Harold believes that the special authority to perform plural marriages traces back to an event that occurred in a rural farmhouse in Utah in the 1880s. LDS President John Taylor, a dedicated polygamist, was in hiding there from the officers who ran the anti-polygamy campaign that led to the issuance of The Manifesto.

Various polygamous groups trace their plural marriage authority to different events. Harold traced his to what he believes happened when President Taylor was there in hiding. The LDS leader is said to have been visited at night by Christ, God, Joseph and Hyrum Smith. With these four, he is believed to have given the authority and duty to a small group of Mormon priests to keep the doctrine of plural marriage alive on earth until Christ returns in the millennium.

The place where Harold and his co-religionists believe this to have occurred is the old Woolley house in Centerville, Utah, north of Salt Lake City.

The address of the old home was 244 South 400 West, Centerville. Looking for this place later, I drove down a dirt lane to a dusty yard and a tumbled-down old house that seemed to be held up by the stucco on its outer walls. There were big trees, a barn out back, bits of farm equipment, and a rotating line of children waiting to ride a patient horse with a big brand burned on its hip. There were peace and contentment and the satisfactions of rural childhood.

A woman came into the yard. She and her husband had leased the farm thirteen years before and lived there while he worked with a highway maintenance crew. She was the mother of several of the boys who waited to ride the horse and of the baby girl who was too small for the horse but just the right size for the joys of dirt-digging at the base of a tree.

The family were Saints, the mother said. She was accustomed by then to the frequent visits of the fundamentalist sect members, but was not exactly clear about what was supposed to have happened in the house. Nor did she believe that Christ and the Prophet Joseph appeared there in 1886.

"I wouldn't be a polygamist at all," she said.

The polygamist visits will end sometime soon, for she said the house was to be pulled down to make way for a suburban development. But from events that they believed occurred in that house, Harold and Bernice felt they had

Heavenly sanctification of their polygamous marriage, performed July 3, 1931, in Boise. The date was established by the wife who sat in the next room. Harold was unable for certain to remember which year it was, although he remembered it was just at the start of the Independence Day holiday. Bernice bore six children.

Although by this time LDS President Heber J. Grant had begun the crack-down on polygamists, Harold continued his activity in the established LDS church in Idaho, living with the half sisters who were his wives. Everyone seemed to be happy, as he remembered it. The women were companionable, and seemed to work out things between them so that he had no conflicts to settle. He knew he was violating the stated church doctrine in having a plural wife; but he also believed that the revelation in *Doctrine and Covenants* ordered him to have plural wives. So he went ahead.

One day Harold's stake President called him in for a talk. He met the stake counselor coming out. The counselor happened to be a public prosecutor. Inside the stake president's office, Harold was told: "I don't know what you're doing and I don't want to know. But I heard you're planning to go to Salt Lake City for a vacation, and if I were you I wouldn't come back."

Harold pressed for an explanation and was told: "The counselor is planning to charge you with polygamy and put you in prison."

Harold said he asked for and got a Temple Recommend from the stake president. This would enable him to shift his LDS membership to a stake and ward in Salt Lake City. But from that time forward he was all through with the LDS church. He did not transfer to a new ward. He felt this would cause him more trouble.

He moved quickly to Salt Lake City, taking his legal wife, Alice, with him, but allowing Bernice to buy her own ticket and travel alone on the train so that he could as nearly as possible avoid violating the federal Mann Act that.forbids interstate transportation for immoral purposes.

In Salt Lake City he found work at different jobs. He also found a new wife—call her Carla. They were married on Christmas Day, 1933. Carla bore ten children. It was she who sat in the next room during the interview and helped Harold remember dates and numbers.

On July 16, 1934, Harold was married to a fourth wife. Call her Della. She gave him five children before she died in April, 1947. His last marriage was on March 4, 1961, to a woman who has had no children. This may not be a marriage of sexual partners, but only a sealing in the religious sense, in order to give the women an anchor for the celestial kingdom.

In 1938, Harold bought an acreage far south of Salt Lake City and began to build a house for his rapidly growing family which then included four wives and a dozen or so children. It was in the living room of this house that he talked that night. Now the city has caught up with Harold. New housing developments surround his enclave.

But many worse things have happened to Harold in those years than having the Saints move close to him, looking down their noses at his attempts to follow the directions of a book that he and they hold to be the Holy Writ.

In 1941 his first wife, Alice, moved out and sued him for divorce. Then in short order her half sister, Bernice, moved out. They took some of his children with them.

"That was the bad part of it," he said. "They took some of the kids away and turned them against me. Why, here a year or so ago one daughter told me she was so glad she came to see me because she now loved me and she used to be afraid of me. Now, I ask you, who turned her against me?"

Before they left, he had taken a job as fire inspector at Hill

Field, a military aviation installation at Ogden. He drove back and forth about forty miles each way. He said, "I had four wives and about twenty-six kids at home, and I could support them that way." He continued the job, however, when the defection of Alice and Bernice cut the size of the household.

Disaster came on a cold day in March, 1944. There were sixteen inches of new snow, but Harold went through it to the firehouse. A polygamist neighbor usually went with him, but stayed at home that day. About mid-day, one of this man's wives called Harold and told him:

"They've taken Joe away."

At first Harold thought she meant his friend had gone to the hospital, but she explained that the police had arrested him. Soon after that call, three deputies arrested Harold at the firehouse. He paused in his narrative, and told a story that was as typically Mormon in its emphasis and interpretation as is the story told by Joseph Fielding Smith of the miracle of the gulls. Harold said:

"There was this little lawyer who was telling them he wanted to handle my case, he was going to give that polygamist Harold what for. He was really going to prosecute me. So he had a little wreck with his car and hurt his leg a little, and somebody said it was a shame his leg was hurt just a little. I said 'If God wants his leg to be hurt more than a little, it will be.' Well, sir, in a few days' time he was dead. I guess those three deputies that arrested me are dead, too."

He looked at me knowingly to emphasize his point: God looks out for those who follow His word.

In all, fifteen members of fundamentalist Mormon sects were arrested and charged with unlawful cohabitation and conspiracy. Further, some wives were arrested, including Harold's first wife, Alice, who had been gone from his side for three years. This reminded him of something about that marriage:

"When I married her and Bernice, everything was just fine. The old man—their father—thought I was just great. But when I married Carla, they all got mad at me."

He entered a plea of not guilty to the charge—"In my book it wasn't unlawful cohabitation. In the sight of God we were married." Bailed out, he worked to support his family. Attorneys advised the polygamists to stipulate some facts rather than have long trials.

"Why," said Harold, "I didn't know what that meant. It meant that we admitted everything they wanted and they just found us guilty without any trial and we got five years. We got stipulated right into jail."

(Without agreeing with Harold's implied charge that he was railroaded, it is possible for us to examine the question in the context of the time and place. Certainly, the LDS church would not have wanted a trial in open court in which the names of the oldtime church leaders would have been dragged out, attached to their statements in support of polygamy. Nor would the church have wanted any extensive examination of its position on Section 132 of *Doctrine and Covenants* at the hands of lawyers unfriendly to its aims. How much more convenient it was to stipulate the facts that Harold lived in the marital relationship with more than one wife at a time in violation of the law. Then they could tuck him quietly away in jail.)

For the first nine months the prisoners were kept at the old Utah prison at the Sugar House district in the south end of Salt Lake City, a few miles from Harold's home. His family had to go on relief. After those nine months, the polygamists were moved to the then new prison at Point-of-the-Mountain, halfway to Provo. They first were given the opportunity to trade their principles for their freedom, a device that has been used in theological disputes throughout history.

Harold went to the other room and brought back a

printed form, folded and worn but unsigned. It committed the signer to refrain from advocating, teaching, or countenancing the practice of plural marriage, and extracted his promise not to solemnize plural marriages.

"I just looked at them and told them no honest man would sign a document like that," Harold said, echoing the sentiments of religious martyrs through the ages. "I brought these children into the world and I'm proud of it. I thank God I never signed it."

His voice rose in passion as he said this.

Eleven of the fifteen signed and got out of jail. The other four—including the stepfather of Carla, Harold's third wife, refused to sign. In the spring of 1947 Della, wife number four, was killed accidentally. Suddenly Harold was removed from the ranks of the practicing polygamists. He had only one wife, since two had left him and one had been killed. Bernice, his second wife to whom he was married in a Mormon ceremony, not legally, tried to sue him for divorce while he was in jail. The suit was dismissed on the grounds that no marriage ever existed.

Yet he refused to sign any declarations that he would never again urge polygamy as the religious way of life or that he would never again practice it himself.

Harold was called before the parole board again in June, 1947. He was offered a parole. He said he would not take it. He wanted a termination of sentence since provisions of a parole would permit him to be taken back to prison if he entered into further plural marriages. It also would have placed him at a disadvantage in resisting attempts to take from him the five children born to the wife who had been killed accidentally.

He won his gamble. He was released on June 26, 1947, after more than two years in prison. His three polygamist colleagues were released on December 15. Harold had trouble getting a job. First he worked in a brick yard, but had to quit after two days because he was unable to endure the physical labor. Then he sold fire extinguishers, and finally sold insurance stock for several years until he and a friend went broke in a land development scheme. Harold had a judgment of $47,000 against him when he took bankruptcy.

The day of the interview he had worked nine hours as a cabinet maker. He was tired that night, but he also felt keenly the opportunity to tell an outsider how he felt about his fundamentalist interpretations of Mormon doctrine and of his resistance to the pressures of the church to which he once belonged.

Harold said he was never excommunicated for polygamy, although he lived right under the nose of the church authorities in flagrant polygamy from the time of his return to Salt Lake City in 1933.

However, he was excommunicated. He said it was because he refused to sign a paper in which he stated he believed that the high officials of the LDS church all were living honorable, monogamous lives.

"I didn't know whether they were or not," he said. Harold was not able to explain why this request was made of him by a bishop and a stake president, but other sources suggested that in those years some polygamists were passing stories that various high LDS officials were secret polygamists.

Harold's voice deepened and his attitude became even more forceful as he began now to explain what he felt about his religion and what had happened to him:

"I just believe all of Mormonism, not just the easy parts," he said. "If it's true at all, it's all true. You can't take plural marriage out and still have the rest be true. We believe it was all revealed by God to Joseph Smith and plural marriage was a part of it as you can see just by reading the book. But they leave it in there and tell you to believe all of it and live your life by it. Then if you follow it, they excommunicate you and get you throwed in jail."

He quoted Brigham Young from a sermon in 1866 when the Saints were being urged by their leadership to go into plural marriage:

"The only men who become Gods, even the Sons of God, are those who enter into Polygamy."

Harold, who had five wives, did his part. So did the wives, for they gave him ten sons, nineteen daughters and one adopted daughter. There were at that time 140 grandchildren and someone, somewhere was expecting Harold's first great-grandchild.

Once he had finished his personal story and begun to attack the present philosophical and theological condition of the LDS church, Harold became even more emphatic and more denunciatory of what he considers to be a betrayal of the doctrines of Joseph Smith and the early LDS leaders. He asserted that the Temple ordinances (rites) had been changed. He went through the Temple twice within five years about forty years ago.

"They had been changed in that five years," he said. "I wonder how much different they are now? If God said how they were to be and the Prophet Joseph put it in *Doctrine and Covenants*, how can man improve on them?"

Harold also found it difficult to agree with the various polygamous cults that abound around Utah and in other Mormon areas. He made it plain that he sees himself as standing alone, not as the leader or a member of any polygamous cult.

"There are two ways you can get intoxicated," he said. "You can get intoxicated by drinking, or you can get intoxicated for the want of power. That's the way I think it is with a lot of those people. I don't belong to any group. I just want to live my life the way it ought to be. There are a lot of people who come here to try to talk to me about things.

But what have I got to tell them about what they ought or ought not to do? Then there are those other knuckleheads! They get people to paying tithes to them! I got no business with people paying tithes to me! I have no right to collect tithes."

If Harold could run the LDS church, how would it be run?

"The ideal Latter-day Saints would be run by revelation. I'm a testimony (proof) that we don't have religious freedom. But we would have to get a group that meant what they said and would live like they were told by God to live."

By the 1930s, Harold believed, there were more people living in polygamy than ever before in the church's history. He thought there were a great many more by the time we talked in the mid-1960s.

He refused again to say who performed his plural marriages. Instead he talked about the Centerville manifestation where he believes Christ and Joseph Smith appeared. He knew three men who were there, he said. One was Louis C. Woolley, one of those "set apart" by President John Taylor to keep plural marriage alive. He also saw John W. Woolley, who once owned the house and who was ninety years old when Harold saw him. He said mysteriously, "Two men are still alive who were called properly by direct revelation to seal in plural marriages." Harold said he would be married only by this sort of authority, never by those he considered to be the haphazard self-anointed who perform rites for some polygamists.

When Harold had finished, Carla, his third wife, answered questions. Had she been married before Harold? She turned to him and asked, "How do I answer that?" He said she had been another man's plural wife in a marriage that failed, and then had become his wife.

Did she find it difficult to move into a home with the

sisters, Alice and Bernice, who were Harold's first wives?
"It was hard for me because their ways were different."
Was a difference made by the mothers between half
brothers and sisters?

"Oh, no. Not at all. I worked then, and I'd leave my little girl with them and I'd take care of their children, just
like my own."

Did she have trouble when Harold went to jail?

"I was three months along, and we went on relief. My
brothers and sisters helped me."

Did she come from a polygamous family? Her face
lighted.

"Oh, I sure did. My grandfather had a plural marriage
and my parents talked of it, but my father was killed before
they did it. My mother remarried and her second husband
—my stepfather—took my aunt, my mother's sister, into
plural marriage. My stepfather was one of those who stayed
in prison and wouldn't sign the paper and get out. My
mother had nine children."

Carla also said that her two predecessors, Alice and Bernice, had remarried after leaving Harold. But she thought
they were separated from their husbands. She and Harold
had a son in the Navy in South Vietnam. They had a daughter of fifteen years and a boy of seventeen years at home.
Four daughters live in the neighborhood, and a son who listened to the interview that night lives with his wife—or
wives, perhaps—in an apartment upstairs.

One of their daughters was involved in the great polygamist raid conducted by Arizona authorities at Short Creek,
Arizona, in 1953, and she came to live with her father's families for a time. But now she is back in Short Creek. Carla
said that Short Creek—now called Colorado City—had
many nice homes, a high school and other public buildings
which she has visited.

She spoke of the polygamous colonists there in tones that

made it plain that she identified with them and supported them morally in the legal troubles they have had.

Between them, Harold and Carla counted up what had happened to the twenty-nine children that four wives had conceived and delivered for Harold.

Twelve were then living in polygamy.

It was late, about midnight, when the talking stopped and Harold walked with me out to the street where we smelled the clean, warm air and looked at the mountains outlined against the starlit sky. After I was in the car I asked him a question that had been nagging at my mind.

"How does a man ask a woman to go with him as a plural wife?"

He smiled and looked at the stars, very proud.

"Those last three asked me. It was the ones I asked who caused me the trouble."

Harold and Carla revealed many things that night. Within them there is a religious determination to continue with plural marriage. They believe that God commanded them to live in this style. They reject completely the easy way out of the trap that Joseph Smith created in 1843 with his plural wife revelation. They will not accept the somewhat ambiguous revelation from President Wilford Woodruff. But neither will they try to organize a separate church based on what they think was the line put down by the Prophet Joseph.

It is remarkable that after his fourth wife died, Harold was no longer a polygamist and could have won his freedom easily by signing the disclaimer. But he would not. He held to the position that he had gone into polygamy as a matter of religious doctrine. He would not abandon that principle on oath because he still believed in it. This effectively answers the argument that Harold's marriages were made merely for the satisfaction of his lusts.

The relations of the wives, as the household grew, was indicative of some of the problems of the plural marriage doctrine. Alice and Bernice, the sisters and first wives, managed cosily, perhaps conspiring to direct Harold so that they controlled the household. But when he brought in first Carla and then Della, their grip on Harold and on the household was broken. Things were different—and stormy.

With so many of Harold's children living in polygamy, and with the wives' families and Harold's family having polygamous backgrounds, we can see how this social tendency grows, as a justification of this type of marital relationship. Certainly, young people who hear polygamy defended and urged from earliest recollection would tend to seek it as a way of life.

They even had a daughter at Short Creek.

At the University of Utah there is an unpublished thesis by John Marshall Day, "A Study of Protest to Adaptation," which examines some of the ways of life at Short Creek. This isolated Arizona community lies north of the Grand Canyon—harsh, dry country, which relies on trade with Utah for commerce, but which is tied to Arizona for law enforcement purposes. In earlier years the authorities seldom came up there.

About 1924 a Mormon there took a second wife, and the rush began. When Utah made unlawful cohabitation a felony in 1933, many other plural families came into Short Creek and by the mid-1930s, there was a large polygamist colony there. By 1960, about 400 adult members of the religious sect lived there. Some of the men had other wives in Canada and Mexico, and they had families perhaps in the places where they worked. One weekend, Day counted 500 adults.

He found that missionaries went out from Short Creek to recruit plural wives. This may sound insane to outside ears, but one must remember that every adult Mormon is well acquainted with the plural marriage doctrine, and each devout Mormon believes that the Prophet Joseph was ordered by God to enunciate it. Many of them no doubt understand the doctrine much better than they understand the twists and turns of theology and realism by which the church has abandoned it.

Remember that the core of Mormon doctrine envisions us as living here in the "mortal existence" with a chance to better our position in the "spirit world." Remember that every Mormon child grows up with a strong feeling—call it a tribal feeling—of belonging to a people who have been much persecuted for religious belief. To such minds an action that can be presented as supporting the tribe's glories and as opposing the persecutions of the non-tribal "they" had a good chance of acceptance.

Remember that rural Utah is a long way from things. A girl might do almost anything that wouldn't endanger her immortal soul if it would get her off that dry, hot, dusty farm.

Day told of one girl in southern Utah who was visited frequently by young men missionaries who persuaded her to come away with them to be a plural wife. A widow said she was recruited from Colorado.

Day found that "high priest apostles" made the decisions in Short Creek. The eldest member in seniority was the patriarch and chief decision maker. The Mormons there quoted Brigham Young's sermons on polygamy over and over, including frequent use of the observation: "A plural wife must overcome weakness."

One man had six wives and twenty children, none of whom was out of the teens. They lived in a large adobe house. Each wife had a separate apartment. The first wife was from Idaho. The second wife was her sister who had been widowed in World War II. Wives three and four were ranch daughters from southern Utah. Wives five and six were college graduates from Salt Lake City who had become impoverished and took to plural marriage to sustain themselves. Day found that the older, more prestigious families had first choice of the young girls for wives.

Almost an iron-clad rule existed that only the first wife was married in a civil ceremony. The others are joined only by religious rites. This enables the husband to escape a bigamy charge. Usually the first wife manages the broad household operation, although each wife has charge of her own quarters. A book, *Rules of Family Conduct*, was circulated among the Short Creek polygamists.

Day found that sometimes other men would say of a polygamist who was unable to control his wives that "he's no king in his own castle."

In 1953 the state of Arizona sent a raiding party that arrested hundreds of persons in Short Creek. Some of the children were taken to Phoenix and Mesa and boarded with LDS church members. The raid was a national sensation, for the staff of Governor Howard Pyle had notified reporters from as far away as Los Angeles and invited them to come along.

It is a part of the political lore in Phoenix that Governor Pyle's defeat at the next election was caused in part by resentment among the regular and anti-polygamous members of the LDS church who live in southern Arizona. They felt, it is said there, that the governor was too anxious for personal publicity. They blame him for the widespread talk about plural marriage. They think his publicity seeking released the ghost that the Mormons have been trying to keep locked up since 1890. The Saints had no objection to Arizona wiping out the polygamous colony, for most of them were as outraged by the practice as are Southern Baptists or Episcopalians. They just thought Governor Pyle could have been a little quieter about it.

The polygamists believe that elements in the LDS church

caused Pyle to come after them. After all, they had been getting along fine in Short Creek for a quarter-century before the raid.

A twenty-six-month investigation preceded the raid. Authorities found that the polygamists were marrying girls of twelve or thirteen years—one at eleven years. Men were swapping daughters. Young girls were under systematic indoctrination to believe that their mission in life was to be a plural wife of a much older man and bear many children for him.

After the raid, the polygamists were quiet for a time, but then they went back to Short Creek. The settlement since has been renamed Colorado City, and now a paved road leads into it in place of the old, dirt and gravel narrow path that was the only entrance when the settlement became infamous. The polygamists thrive there again. Perhaps this time no one will bother them.

The polygamists not only recruit girls and widows into their colony, but they have their missionaries out to try to get whole families or single men as well. One of these interrupted an interview with Jerald Tanner, the LDS apostate in Salt Lake City. He came into the room, and sidetracked the discussion for that time. Later Tanner said the man was a polygamist missionary trying to recruit Tanner and his wife.

The recruitment theory is obvious: Tanner once was a devout Mormon, and he knew all the doctrine but had become dissatisfied with the LDS church. Such persons frequently are dissatisfied with the church in the organizational—as opposed to the doctrinal—sense. They are fertile ground for the polygamists' suggestions and arguments.

When I talked to this fundamentalist missionary by telephone, children were crying in the background, sometimes drowning his voice. He had two wives, he said, and an undisclosed number of children.

"This has been a political football," he said of polygamy. He said 1300 men went to prison in Utah in the 1880s, two more in 1935, and 15 in 1944. "Of course what they're trying to do is abolish polygamy."

He reminded me that the Muslims believe a man may have four wives. Then he told of going to a wedding reception after a Salt Lake City girl married an Iraqui. He asked this man if he practiced his religion's plural marriage doctrine.

"He told me he didn't," the polygamist missionary said. "He said he didn't see how a man could love two women at once.

"I told him 'Don't knock it unless you've tried it.' "

How does the missionary feed his families?

"You work hard and skimp. It just seems like the way opens up for you. I wouldn't advocate it for anybody else, but it's the way for me to live."

He had just been advocating it to Jerald Tanner and would have advocated it to anyone he knew was not a policeman.

His neighbors don't cause him trouble, but he spoke mysteriously of "drunkards and rounders" who hate him bitterly. He was unable to give their names, or even to tell where they existed, and it seemed this was another manifestation of the persecution complex that one finds in many believers in the *Book of Mormon*.

Of polygamy, the missionary said:

"It'll never be accepted. For every convert, we get 100 enemies. People can't understand unless they have the spirit of God within them to make them understand."

In mid-1965 there were no polygamists in jail in Utah, nor were any awaiting trial, officials said. Ernest Wright, the director of the board of corrections for Utah, said that one of the last two to be released asked to have his family visit him in jail. Permission was given and here came thirty-five children. This man had been making about $1000 a month as a salesman before his arrest.

This is one of the mysteries about the polygamists: How do they support their families? The answer is the same as for many large families. They work hard, save their money and do without things that other people have.

The source of the estimate of as many as 30,000 polygamists in Utah was William M. Rogers, a former policeman and an investigator who has studied polygamy for many years. He said there are about 100 "splinter" groups living in various forms of polygamous society. The simplest is a man, his wives and their children, unassociated with others. From this, the practice becomes more and more involved. The most complicated, probably, are the cooperative societies based on polygamy and on commonly owned business and farm operations. These communal forms combine two of the Prophet Joseph's plans for Saintly life which have been abandoned after a trial by the main LDS church.

Rogers worked as in investigator in the late 1950s in the most recent attempt by Utah authorities to cope with the spread of polygamy. This was a grand jury investigation convened in Davis County, adjoining the Salt Lake City metropolis. Rogers produced about 180 witnesses who lived next door to or in the same neighborhood with polygamists. Almost all of these people were LDS church members. None of them would testify against their polygamous neighbors. The investigation collapsed.

Why did they refuse?

One can guess. They might look on the polygamists as true believers in the Revealed Gospel of the Prophet Joseph —perhaps a little out of step, that was all. The regular LDS members might see the polygamists as being just a bit too fundamental for their tastes, but certainly friendly to the faith. Who could say? Perhaps they might even be right. What Saint would then want to answer for having been a hindrance to them? All the tithing and non-smoking and teetotaling of a long lifetime would not weigh positively as much as the negative weight of disturbing the true believers.

Even for those regular Saints who would not believe— even with a corner of their minds—that the polygamists had the true light, there still would be a sympathy derived from the Mormon consciousness of what happened during the late nineteenth century when their church was almost destroyed by a people they looked upon as bigots who opposed polygamy. How could they then add to the problems of the modern polygamists?

Finally, there would be the reluctance to get personally involved in such a messy subject, and a reluctance to see all the old stories trotted out about polygamous Mormons, which would happen if the indictments were voted.

But one thing is certain: If the orders had come down from the men who direct the church in Salt Lake City, the Saints would have lined up dutifully to tell all they truthfully could tell about the polygamists. However, those orders did not come.

When the polygamous Saints were driven to the wall by the federal government in the 1880s and 1890s, they established colonies in Mexico for their plural families. While these—such as Colonia Juarez—now are purely monogamous, the fundamentalist polygamists have established their headquarters in the more lax moral climate south of the border. Rogers said that one branch of these is the Church of the First Born of the Fullness of Times. This group traces its authority back to a secretary to the Prophet Joseph. Many of the missionaries recruiting plural wives in Utah come from these Mexican groups. Rogers said that at one time there were about 200 missionaries from Mexico in Utah, mostly in Salt Lake City.

Another source told of a German convert who came to Salt Lake City as an immigrant. He fell under the influence of the polygamist missionaries. They persuaded him that he was living a perversion of the Gospel. If he wanted the real Gospel, he was told, and the opportunity to achieve real exaltation in the celestial kingdom, he had better come on down south of the border. He went.

(In its European mission a few years ago, the LDS church had an embarrassing thing happen. A number of its missionaries began openly teaching the polygamy doctrine. They were brought to England for a theological trial and were excommunicated. This illustrates the church's ruthless dealings with the polygamists. The death of Heber J. Grant in 1945 brought an end to the line of LDS presidents who had been polygamists, and Grant himself had shown determination in stamping out the practice in the last twenty years of his life. George Albert Smith, who followed Grant, and David O. McKay, who followed Smith, had only one wife each. Both were descended from polygamists, of course.)

Rogers said that one of the most interesting groups he found was the Davis County Cooperative Society, which runs a store on the main street of Bountiful, a Salt Lake City suburb. He said the group owns a cooperative coal mine, a store near Price, Utah, sheep and cattle interests, and does well financially. His interest was in the cooperative aspect of this group's religious practice. It started near Ammon, Idaho, in Mormon country, in the mid-1930s, and traveled to Utah.

An attempt was made to talk to these people, to discover if they practice polygamy as Rogers hinted and as others in that area asserted. At their store—across the street from the tabernacle on Main Street in Bountiful—no one who would discuss these matters was available. The store was piled full of inexpensive clothing—colorful shirts, jeans, shoes, yard goods—and there was a shoe repair shop next door. The shoe repair shop was the first business the group opened there; the store has grown from this beginning.

About a half-dozen full time employees moved around behind counters. A blonde girl in her twenties gave a telephone number and said to ask for "Mr. Kingston." When finally he was reached, Mr. Kingston said he did not intend to discuss the cooperative with outsiders.

Around Salt Lake City this group is called the "Kingstonites." The Davis County grand jury investigation of the 1950s was aimed at it. And missed.

The church's problem with the polygamists is as nothing compared to its problem with Negroes. The narrow channels have been sailed safely by the Saints. The open water lies ahead—just beyond the reef of the appalling Mormon discrimination against Negroes.

VIII

The Anti-Negro Doctrine

THE MOST SERIOUS problem facing the LDS church today is the Negro question. The church has successfully become everyman's church—except it cannot be the African Negro's church. A man can have skin black as a moonless night— and he can be a full-fledged member of the Mormon priesthood. But he can have blue eyes, white skin and blond curly hair and have an African Negro in his ancestry and find himself rejected by the Mormons as an applicant for priesthood. A Negro can join the church. But he may not move a step further. For the African and his children and his children's children the doctrine of eternal progression has little meaning. The doctrine of marriage for time and eternity is for others, not for them. The mortal existence offers lesser opportunity for the improvement of their souls than for other races.

The Negro is barred from the priesthood purely on racial grounds. As we untangle the theology, we must always remember that every devout male Mormon—except the Negro—is expected to become a member of the Aaronic priesthood as a boy of twelve years and a member of the Melchizedek priesthood at eighteen or twenty years. There is no analogy to the priesthood of the Catholic church, for example, with its full-time ecclesiastics who are the members' authorities on religious belief. The Mormons consider that male membership in the priesthood is a requisite for higher place in the Celestial Paradise. But Negroes are barred from this advancement. Priesthood membership is a requisite for an office in management of the church's temporal affairs. So Negroes are barred from office. As we will understand in the unraveling of the theology, the Mormon discrimination against the Negro is the ultimate that can be had on racial grounds. In those states where Negroes were—and sometimes still are—segregated in public places, the theaters used balconies to seat them. These were called "nigger heavens" by the rude and unfeeling. The Mormons do not use this phrase; but their official policies call it to mind.

There are many positions taken within the Mormon world on these matters. The ultra-conservatives look on the problem for Negroes as just one of those things that are inflicted unhappily on other people who should accept their fate humbly—and quietly. The conservatives believe that the Lord has told them that the Africans are not to be taken into the priesthood, and that's that. The ultra-liberals take the position that this interpretation of the scriptures is absolute nonsense. The scholars attempt to reason a way out of it. The vast center of the church just accepts it without question. The apostates, who hate the church anyway, take the position that it's all to the good, that maybe the Saints will wreck themselves, and the rising aspirations of the American Negro will help shove them onto the rocks.

What is this doctrine? How did it come into being? What keeps it alive?

With those questions the curtains part and as the trumpets sound we are in Kirtland, Ohio, in 1835, the time of Andrew Jackson and John C. Calhoun, of western expansion, of slave ships still moving at sea. The slavery question was still balanced delicately on the Missouri Compromise. Dred Scott and Roger Taney were two decades away.

The curiosities looted from the tombs of Egypt were shown

in the remote places. There were mummies, still in their burial wrappings which were covered with Egyptian hieroglyphics. The Rosetta Stone had been found and work was in progress that would use it as the key to unlock the records of the ancient kingdoms of Egypt. Outside scientific circles, this great historical advance was not realized.

Joseph Smith still described his Gold Plates as having been written in "reformed Egyptian" which he translated with Divine help to produce the *Book of Mormon*. There was no one around yet to translate the hieroglyphics. Further, the Angel Moroni had taken back the plates.

In the summer of 1835 a man came to Kirtland with four mummies and some rolls of papyrus covered with hieroglyphics. The official church publication, *Essentials in Church History*, written by Joseph Fielding Smith, the president of the Council of Twelve Apostles, describes it this way:

> Mr. (Michael H.) Chandler had been directed to the Prophet Joseph Smith as one who could translate the characters for him. At his request Joseph Smith gave a translation of a few of them which Mr. Chandler stated agreed with the deciphering of learned men who had examined them. He gave the Prophet a certificate to this effect. Shortly after this interview some of the Saints in Kirtland purchased the mummies and the manuscripts, and, with Oliver Cowdery and William W. Phelps as scribes, the Prophet commenced to translate these records. To their great joy they discovered that one of these rolls contained writings of Abraham, or instructions given to him in Egypt from the Lord. The other contained writings of Joseph, son of Jacob. During the summer the Prophet prepared for the complete translation of the Book of Abraham, as it is called, which now appears in the *Pearl of Great Price*, one of the accepted standard works of the Church.

The papyrus from which the Book of Abraham was translated was destroyed in the Chicago fire. But, unfortunately

for Mormon propagandists, some copies were made of three
figures. These were shown to Egyptologists in later years
when the art of translating the hieroglyphics had moved
further along toward perfection. They said the markings
were only those of the common burial documents, that they
had no relation to anything else and certainly did not carry
the involved historical, philosophical and religious messages
attributed to them by Joseph Smith.

Moreover, the Reorganized Church of Jesus Christ of
Latter Day Saints has never accepted the two books of the
Pearl of Great Price as divinely inspired.

"I guess that you could say that we look on Joseph Smith
as a prophet, and that we also look on him as a man," said
one member of the Reorganized LDS church. "We don't
think that everything he ever wrote was divinely inspired.
Those people in Utah seem to think it was."

With all of this background of controversy, even disbelief,
it is surprising to see that a few verses from the Book of Abraham provide the theological foundations on which has been
built the formalized prejudice that condones the religious
disenfranchisement of the Negro in the Utah Mormon
church.

The passages to which this theological argument is tied
occur toward the end of the first chapter of the Book of Abraham. In the earlier parts of the chapter, Abraham quoted
the Lord's reaction to attempts of the Egyptians to sacrifice
Abraham on the altar of one of their false gods. The altars
were broken up in the Lord's wrath. These six paragraphs
follow, culminating in a clause which Mormons believe
closes to Negroes the gates of the upper reaches of Paradise:

> Now this king of Egypt was a descendant from the loins
> of Ham, and was a partaker of the blood of the Canaanites
> by birth.
> The land of Egypt being first discovered by a woman,
> who was the daughter of Ham, and the daughter of Egyptus,

which in the Chaldean signifies Egypt, which signifies that which is forbidden.

When this woman discovered the land it was under water, who afterward settled her sons in it; and thus, from Ham, sprang that race which preserved the curse in the land.

Now the first government of Egypt was established by Pharaoh, the eldest son of Egyptus, the daughter of Ham, and it was after the manner of the government of Ham, which was patriarchal.

Pharaoh, being a righteous man, established his kingdom and judged his people wisely and justly all his days, seeking earnestly to imitate that order established by the fathers in the first generations, in the days of the first patriarchal reign, even in the reign of Adam, and also of Noah, his father, who blessed him with the blessings of the earth, and with the blessings of wisdom, *but cursed him as pertaining to the Priesthood.*

So there it was set down for those who faithfully follow the Restored Gospel as dispensed in the Utah tradition. They all knew that the Curse of Ham was the black skin and flat nose and kinky hair of the African Negro. Ham's descendants were so marked because he married Egyptus, a Negress, who had carried the Mark of Cain, and it was on Cain that the mark was placed by the Lord in retribution for the murder of Abel. (It fascinates me that the only Negro priesthood member the church admits ever to have had was named Elijah Abel.)

Thus, in 1835, when their church was five years old, the Utah Mormons believe, the pattern was formed that keeps them from having Negroes as full-fledged members.

Yet this was a deviation from the earlier patterns of the religious belief. The *Book of Mormon* speaks plainly in its opening sections in favor of equality of the races at the altar, and this is not surprising. The first Mormons almost without exception were of New England, New York and Ohio stock. They were from abolitionist country almost to a man. So there was no outcry against such sentiments as those in the last paragraph of the 26th chapter of 2 Nephi, where the Angel Moroni and his forebears have been advising men how to order their lives. Then comes this passage:

> For none of these iniquities come of the Lord; for he doeth that which is good among the children of men; and he doeth nothing save it be plain unto the children of men; and he inviteth them all to come unto him and partake of his goodness; and he denieth none that come unto him, black and white, bond and free, male and female; and he remembereth the heathen; and all are alike unto God, both Jew and Gentile.

The Mormons scrupulously follow this today. All men are equal before God. The blessings of the Restored Gospel are equally available to all men. Except the descendants of African Negroes. No matter what they do, no matter how devout they are, no matter how they strive and sacrifice and work for the greater glory of God, the souls that are in their bodies are destined to return to the Spirit World unaccompanied by their earthly families, alone, unloved, foreclosed from the upper levels of the Celestial Kingdom.

Many arguments are used by Mormon theologians to support the basic and fundamental cruelty that this system sets out. One of them told me in great glee how he had vanquished a group of critics who made up a tour of the Temple grounds in Salt Lake City. He said they asked him to defend the church's discrimination against Negroes.

"I asked them if they believed the *Book of Mormon* and they said they didn't, so I told them it didn't really make any difference to them, did it?"

He smiled and continued:

"Then one of them said that for discussion he would say he believed the *Book of Mormon*, so I said to him that if he believed, then he knew why Negroes couldn't have the priesthood, didn't he? And that ended it."

Of course, that did not end it.

Many persons have been perplexed by the shift between the "all men are children of God" position of the *Book of Mormon* (which was translated between 1827 and first publication in 1830) and the passages translated from the papyrus after 1835 and on which the policy of anti-Negro discrimination is based.

Did something happen in those years to change Joseph Smith's attitude toward the question of slavery? Historical research has shown that something did happen.

The first major move of the church was from Kirtland, Ohio, to the Missouri frontier near Independence. Missouri was a slave state. The Missourians of that time and place were a very rough bunch. Their conflicts with the Mormons were quick and deep. There was concern that the inpouring of the Saints would politically overwhelm the Missourians. Economic conflicts were frequent.

In July, 1833, the Mormon paper, the *Evening and Morning Star*, published an editorial designed to warn the Saints against incurring the wrath of the slave-holding Missourians by trying to convert their slaves. The Missourians misunderstood. They took the editorial to be an invitation to free Negroes to settle at Independence. Mormon retractions and explanations were unavailing. The Mormon press was destroyed. Pitched battles were fought. The Mormons eventually were to leave Missouri. The Prophet Joseph and other leaders barely escaped death from a firing squad before it was over.

Not all of this resulted from the editorial about the Negroes, nor was it because the church had no policy of racial discrimination. But this one issue was among the many that helped create the conflict. Some historians argue that it was this memory of turmoil that led to the LDS position on Negroes. By the time the Mormons were situated in Utah, the anti-Negro position became very strong. By 1855, Brigham

Young was declaiming that one drop of Negro blood pre-
vented a man from being a Mormon priesthood member.
Even as he was saying this, Brigham Young knew that the
Negro Mormon elder, Elijah Abel, was living in Salt Lake
City. During the Civil War, Young made a somewhat foolish
prophecy:

"Ham will continue to be the servant of servants, as the
Lord decreed, until the curse is removed. Will the present
struggle free the Slave? No . . . Can you destroy the decrees of the Almighty? You cannot. Yet our Christian brethren think that they are going to overthrow the sentence of
the Almighty upon the seed of Ham. They cannot do
that . . ."

The speeches and writing of the early Mormon leaders in
Utah again and again make it clear that they were running a
white theocracy, and that Negroes were not wanted. They
would accept them, but only as servants—now and in the
hereafter.

Meanwhile, the situation was entirely different among the
members of the Reorganized LDS church. The Civil War
had ended and with it the Negro slavery that had blighted
the American Democracy. On May 4, 1865, Joseph Smith,
III, the son of the first Prophet Joseph, received a revelation
which is recorded in the Reorganized LDS *Doctrine and
Covenants*. It cleared the way for the ordination of Negroes
as priests in that branch of Mormonism. There are many
Negroes in that church. Some of them have had important
positions.

How could the Utah Mormon leaders justify the persecution of a race of mankind because of its color? True, they had
the interpretations of their leaders, dangling over the theological quicksands from the slender thread of the statement
in the Book of Abraham. But how else? How to reconcile
that other souls came into the mortal existence with full opportunity to achieve upward mobility, with a chance to
achieve all sorts of good things for themselves when again

they would go back to the Spirit World? It is one thing to punish the mortal seed of Cain, whose mortal body committed a mortal crime; it is another thing to take a soul from Paradise and sentence it to a mortal existence totally without meaning in the larger scheme.

Again we go back to fundamental Mormon theology. The Heavenly Hosts are the spirits, and these spirits become the souls of men. At a point in time there was a struggle between the Lord and the Devil. Some of the spirits supported the Devil, and these were banished to Perdition with the Evil One. The other spirits stayed in the Celestial Kingdom with the Lord.

But not all of the spirits supported the Lord's side of the argument with equal vigor and tenacity. Some were perilously close to supporting the Devil. When the spirits are dispatched by the Lord to become the souls of mankind, the degree of their support of God in the conflict with the Devil is taken into account in assigning the station of the mortal whose soul the spirit becomes. This is said very plainly by one Mormon writer, John J. Stewart, an associate professor of journalism at Utah State University at Logan. He wrote a short book, *Mormonism and the Negro,* which is sold by the Deseret Bookstores. Professor Stewart wrote:

"The circumstances of our birth in this world are dependent upon our performance in the spirit world, just as the circumstances of our existence in the next world will depend upon what we enjoy in this world."

Thus the doctrine of eternal progression begins for a soul even before it has a body to inhabit. Professor Stewart draws this further picture of the spirit world:

> We were all eager for an opportunity to partake of mortality, knowing that it was a necessary step in eternal progress. And we were willing to come into mortality under those circumstances that we had merited by our conduct in that first estate—the pre-mortal existence, even though un-

doubtedly those who had not been valiant there wished that they had been, just as those of us not valiant in the Gospel cause in this life will have regrets in the next life.

At another point in his discussion of the doctrine that being born a Negro is really a punishment for one of the spirits that has not supported God completely, Professor Stewart wrote:

> Among the Negroid people, as indeed among all the races of the earth, there is infinite variety and degree of circumstances of birth, of goodness, of opportunity or lack of it. There are Negroes born into families of wealth and refinement, others who are blessed with great talents, and there are those born into the lowest classes of society in Africa, in squalor and ignorance, living out their lives in a fashion akin to that of the animals.
>
> Does not this infinite variety of circumstances give further evidence of man's being assigned that station of life which he has merited by his performance in the pre-mortal existence?

At that point in Professor Stewart's paper, there comes a passage which illustrates perfectly the blind spot in the thinking of those devout Mormons who absolutely cannot understand why non-Mormon Negroes resist and oppose and criticize and eventually will concentrate their attacks against this doctrine that Negroes are inherently inferior to the rest of mankind. He wrote:

> . . . Part of Cain's curse was to have as his posterity those spirits unable to bear the Priesthood in this life. In view of the importance that humans rightly attach to their children, their posterity, what greater curse could come upon Cain, as pertaining to this life? And what could be more appropriate than for these spirits to have such a man as Cain as their progenitor?

In all of this there is an argument of racism, of Negro inferiority. But Professor Stewart and those who believe like

him would answer in two ways the arguments that many of
the rest of us would make. First, they would say that this is
the word of God and they can't help what it says. Next, they
would say triumphantly that if the individual Negro does
not believe in the *Book of Mormon* and does not want to be
even a member of the LDS church, it should make no difference to him that the church withholds the priesthood from
Negroes.

However, this misses the point. The LDS church practices
racial discrimination. It clings to that practice in a nation
which is going through terrible struggles to overcome the
pernicious influence of other organizations with anti-Negro
bias. The philosophy is completely unAmerican. It resists
the American view that no man should be penalized for his
race.

So long as the LDS church clings to this racist practice, it
is a political and social cancer.

Here again is Professor Stewart, this time quoting Brigham
Young:

> Why are so many of the inhabitants of the earth cursed
> with a skin of blackness? It comes in consequence of their
> fathers rejecting the power of the Holy Priesthood and law
> of God. They will go down to death. And when all the rest
> of the children have received their blessings in the Holy
> Priesthood, then that curse will be removed from the seed of
> Cain, and they will then come up and possess the Priest-
> hood, and receive all the blessings which we now are en-
> titled to.

It is possible to pile up dozens of quotations from LDS
leaders of the past to show that they consider Negroes to be
an inferior race, and that they consider this to be a divine
decree over which they have no control. For example,
Brigham Young asked a rhetorical question about interracial
marriage:

"Shall I tell you the law of God in regard to the African race? If the white man who belongs to the chosen seed mixes his blood with the seed of Cain, the penalty, under the law of God, is death on the spot. This will always be so."

At another time, he said, "Any man having one drop of the seed of Cain in him cannot receive the priesthood."

Remember that the Mormons are great students of their doctrine and of the speeches of their past leaders. Remember that they strive with each other to be the strongest in understanding and support of doctrine. Remember that a truly devout Mormon looks on his "mortal existence" as just a fleeting moment which offers opportunity to raise his position in the eternal scheme of things.

So what is certain to be the reaction of the Saints to suggestions that Negroes should be treated as equals? Obviously, the response will be that no Saint will feel any obligation to be more than kind to them with that supercilious sort of condescending kindness that chills the soul of the beneficiary. The Saint will know in his heart and believe that God has said Negroes are inferior. True enough, some basically kind and gentle people who are Mormons will find doctrine to quote to show that their church requires them to help Negroes better themselves, and will genuinely feel an equality and brotherhood with them, which is what the American Negro seeks more than anything else.

But the overwhelming Mormon response to the current drive by Negroes to better their condition in American life has been indifference, inattention, irritation and smug self-satisfaction that few Negroes live in the Mormon centers.

It could be argued that the official attitude of the church today is now reflected in the words of Brigham Young. After all, it is equally possible to quote the early leaders in frenzied defense of polygamy, and today no known polygamist is a member of the LDS church.

What do today's Mormon leaders think about Negroes?

In January, 1964, these questions were asked of Joseph Fielding Smith, the heir apparent to the presidency of the church, the nephew of the Prophet Joseph, the aged man who is the official LDS historian, and a widely respected Mormon theologian. In response, he produced a mimeographed sheet, which he said had been prepared for Saints in the armed forces who had trouble answering the rising number of questions about Mormons and Negroes. It begins thus:

During the past decade there has arisen in this country, the United States, a wave of "non segregation," that is, that there should be an equality in all things between the white races and the black or Negro race. This doctrine of social equality and the common mingling of these races is said to be made for the purpose of eventually eliminating the Negro race by absorption through intermarriage. This matter of amalgamation to a great degree has been enforced by the justices of the Supreme Court of the United States. This tendency for "equality" in all things, has brought a flood of correspondence from all parts of the Church asking how it is that the Church of Jesus Christ of Latter-day Saints, stands out in opposition and teaches a doctrine of segregation denying the Negro the right to hold the Priesthood. Some of these letters border on a spirit of resentment and claim that the Church is guilty of great injustice, since "all men were created free and equal." This article is written to place the Church in the right light before its members.

No church or other organization is more insistent than the Church of Jesus Christ of Latter-day Saints, that the Negroes should receive all the rights and privileges that can possibly be given to any other in the true sense of equality as declared in the Declaration of Independence. They should be equal to "life, liberty, and the pursuit of happiness." They should be equal in the matter of education. They should not be barred from obtaining knowledge and becoming proficient in any field of science, art or mechanical occupation. They should be free to choose any kind of employment, to go into business in any field they may choose and to make their lives as happy as it is possible without interference from white men, labor unions or from any other source. In their defense of these privileges the members of the Church will stand.

In the matter of religion they also may choose any faith that they please. The Church does not bar them from membership and we have members of the Negro race in the Church. If a Negro is baptized and remains true and loyal he will enter the celestial kingdom, but it is not the authorities of the Church who have placed a restriction on him regarding the holding of the Priesthood. It was not the Prophet Joseph Smith nor Brigham Young. It was the Lord! If a Negro desires to join the Church we will give him all the encouragement that we can, but we cannot promise him that he will receive the Priesthood.

This might be called the simple, authoritarian position: Don't blame me—blame God! Such an answer pretty well draws the line on discussion. One either accepts that God finds Negroes distasteful and contemptible, not worthy of holding His priesthood, or one does not. Apostle Smith asserts that it is God's will that Negroes be spiritually disabled. Then he turns to the theological side of the argument, with many citations from the books of Moses and Abraham, both from the *Pearl of Great Price*; he suggests a reading of two chapters of one of his own books, *The Way to Perfection*. Then he sums up "the reason why the Negro cannot receive the priesthood." This is "because of transgression in the first estate," i.e., the spirit world, "which deprives him in this second estate," i.e., mortal existence. He continues:

Since Cain slew his brother Abel in order to obtain all the rights of Priesthood to descend through his lineage, the Lord decreed that the children of Cain should not have the privilege of bearing the Priesthood until Abel had posterity who could have the Priesthood and that will have to be in the far distant future. When this is accomplished on some other world, then the restrictions will be removed from the children of Cain who have been true in this "second" estate. We can well imagine that there will be many, after the resurrection, both men and women, who will be assigned to the telestial and terrestrial kingdoms, and that there will be many who will complain and accuse our Heavenly Father of injustice because he will deprive so many of his children of the exaltation? We may well believe that the cry will go forth from some, that God is unjust because he has restricted so many from receiving the blessings of the Priesthood and placed them in these kingdoms notwithstanding they are judged according to their works.

I will confess that to me this is a monstrous doctrine to impose on 2.5 million people. I feel it is a doctrine as far removed from the reality of life in our time as is polygamy or the Blood Atonement of Brigham Young's day. My study of Mormon works, my conversations with Mormon theologians, my observance of the aspects of Mormon life open to a non-Mormon—all of this has convinced me that the anti-Negro doctrine is worthless and useless and not founded properly on the works that the Saints hold sacred. It is a cruel and inhuman doctrine. Candor compels me to make my position clear.

It is plain here that the Apostle Smith believes that Negroes will never be admitted to the priesthood in this world. He hints that there will be another world, at another time, when Abel will have another mortal existence, and will have sons who will become priests. Then these souls condemned in life on Earth to existence within a Negro body will have a chance to become priests.

The foundation on which this whole doctrine of Negro exclusion is based is the clause or so in the Book of Abraham. Yet, of all the works attributed to Joseph Smith, this one is the most thoroughly denounced by the scholarly world. It is not a product of the period when Joseph Smith produced the

Book of Mormon. It was not produced for any purpose of establishing organizational patterns as was much of the revelatory material in *Doctrine and Covenants.* It seems to me to have been just a showing by the Prophet Joseph that he still had the ability to translate "Reformed Egyptian."

This was a mistake.

The Prophet had successfully produced the *Book of Mormon* without ever allowing any of the Golden Plates to be carefully examined, or any inscriptions copied from them to fall into the hands of persons qualified to translate hieroglyphics.

But in the *Pearl of Great Price* the church has reproduced some copies of the hieroglyphics which the Prophet Joseph said he translated. The reproductions are accompanied with detailed statements of what the Prophet said the hieroglyphics shows. It was almost as if the invitation were being extended to scholars to denounce the work. This they have done with gusto.

As an example, in 1912 Rt. Rev. F. S. Spalding, Episcopal Bishop of Utah, published *Joseph Smith, Jr., as a Translator.* The Prophet came off badly in this book. Bishop Spalding took the position that all of the Prophet's works rise or fall on the integrity of any one of them.

I do not take the Bishop's position. Although I do not subscribe to the Saints' religion, the position of the Reorganized LDS church seems much more realistic to me. Perhaps Joseph was a true prophet when he produced the *Book of Mormon* and his revelations. I am unable to produce proof that he was or was not. However, I am convinced by very simple direct evidence that the Book of Abraham is a spurious translation.

Because this evidence is so simple, it is possible to reproduce summaries of it here. The importance of the Book of Abraham as the source of Mormon anti-Negro bias requires that we present this material.

Fig. 1. The Angel of the Lord. 2. Abraham fastened upon an altar. 3. The idolatrous priest of Elkenah attempting to offer up Abraham as a sacrifice. 4. The altar for sacrifice by the idolatrous priests, standing before the gods of Elkenah, Libnah, Mahmackrah, Korash, and Pharaoh. 5. The idolatrous god of Elkenah. 6. The idolatrous god of Libnah. 7. The idolatrous god of Mahmackrah. 8. The idolatrous god of Korash. 9. The idolatrous god of Pharaoh. 10. Abraham in Egypt. 11. Designed to represent the pillars of heaven, as understood by the Egyptians. 12. Raukeeyang, signifying expanse, or the firmament over our heads; but in this case, in relation to this subject, the Egyptians meant it to signify Shaumau, to be high, or the heavens, answering to the Hebrew word, Shaumahyeem.

The translation of the figure by Joseph Smith appears below it, with the numbers keyed to the numbers in the drawing.

Bishop Spalding asked qualified scholars to examine the

reproductions and compare what they read into them with the translations provided by the Prophet Joseph.

On No. 1 (shown here) the birdlike figure, Fig. 1, is the soul, according to the experts; Fig. 2 is a dead person; Fig. 3 is an embalmer or a priest; Fig. 4 is a regular Egyptian bier; Figs. 5, 6, 7, 8 are regular Canopic jars in which were placed the viscera of the deceased; Fig. 9 is a crocodile waiting to devour the dead if he is not properly protected by ritual embalming; Fig. 10 is the regular offering table; Fig. 11 are the pillars of earth; Fig. 12 does not represent heaven.

One scholar told Bishop Spalding that "it is difficult to deal seriously with Joseph Smith's impudent fraud."

Fig. 1. Kolob, signifying the first creation, nearest to the celestial, or the residence of God. First in government, the last pertaining to the

measurement of time. The measurement according to celestial time, which celestial time signifies one day to a cubit. One day in Kolob is equal to a thousand years according to the measurement of this earth, which is called by the Egyptians Jah-oh-eh. 2. Stands next to Kolob, called by the Egyptians Oliblish, which is the next grand governing creation near to the celestial or the place where God resides; holding the key of power also, pertaining to other planets; as revealed from God to Abraham, as he offered sacrifice upon an altar, which he had built unto the Lord. 3. Is made to represent God, sitting upon his throne, clothed with power and authority; with a crown of eternal light upon his head; representing also the grand Key-words of the Holy Priesthood, as revealed to Adam in the Garden of Eden, as also to Seth, Noah, Melchizedek, Abraham, and all to whom the Priesthood was revealed. 4. Answers to the Hebrew word Raukeeyang, signifying expanse, or the firmament of the heavens; also a numerical figure, in Egyptian signifying one thousand; answering to the measuring of the time of Oliblish, which is equal with Kolob in its revolution and in its measuring of time. 5. Is called in Egyptian Enish-go-on-dosh; this is one of the governing planets also, and is said by the Egyptians to be the Sun, and to borrow its light from Kolob through the medium of Kae-e-vanrash, which is the grand Key, or, in other words, the governing power, which governs fifteen other fixed planets or stars, as also Floeese or the Moon, the Earth and the Sun in their annual revolutions. This planet receives its power through the medium of Kli-flos-is-es, or Hah-ko-kau-beam, the stars represented by numbers 22 and 23, receiving light from the revolutions of Kolob. 6. Represents this earth in its four quarters. 7. Represents God sitting upon his throne, revealing through the heavens the grand Key-words of the Priesthood; as, also, the sign of the Holy Ghost unto Abraham, in the form of a dove. 8. Contains writing that cannot be revealed unto the world; but is to be had in the Holy Temple of God. 9. Ought not to be revealed at the present time. 10. Also. 11. Also. If the world can find out these numbers, so let it be. Amen. Figures 12, 13, 14, 15, 16, 17, 18, 19, and 20, will be given in the own due time of the Lord.

The above translation is given as far as we have any right to give at the present time.

Plate No. 2 from the *Pearl of Great Price* was described by all the experts as a facsimile of a hypocephalus. Usually these have a prayer, but the hieroglyphics on this one were so badly copied as to be unreadable. Fig. 1: The word "Kolob" is unknown in Egyptian. Fig. 2: A god with two faces; the word "Oliblish" is not Egyptian. Fig. 3: Horus-Re sitting in his boat with the royal scepter in his hand. Fig. 4: Sokar in his boat; no relationship to the firmament. Fig. 5: The cow of Hathor, behind which a uzat-headed goddess holds a sacred tree. The Egyptian words given by the Prophet are imaginary. Fig. 6: The cardinal points, similar to the Prophet's translation, but not exactly the same. Fig. 7: Nehebka, the serpent-god, presenting an uzat-eye to Horus-Min who is seated. Figs. 8-11: The Prophet numbered these upside down, and the copying of the figures was so poor the experts did not try to read them. Figs. 12-21: Unreadable.

Fig. 1. Abraham sitting upon Pharaoh's throne, by the politeness of the king, with a crown upon his head, representing the Priesthood, as emblematical of the grand Presidency in Heaven; with the scepter of justice and judgment in his hand. 2. King Pharaoh, whose name is given in the characters above his head. 3. Signifies Abraham in Egypt —referring to Abraham, as given in the ninth number of the *Times and Seasons*. 4. Prince of Pharaoh, King of Egypt, as written above the hand. 5. Shulem, one of the king's principal waiters, as represented by the characters above his hand. 6. Olimlah, a slave belonging to the prince.

Abraham is reasoning upon the principles of Astronomy, in the king's court.

The experts told Bishop Spalding that this scene is a very common one. It occurs in most copies of the funeral papyri, coffins, tombs and temple walls of Egypt. But again the copying work is substandard so that the figures are very poor and the hieroglyphics unreadable. Fig. 1: Osiris. Fig. 2: Isis. Fig. 3: An offering. Fig. 4: Goddess Maat of truth or righteousness. Fig. 5: Dead person. Fig. 6: Either Anubis, or the shadow of the dead man.

The men to whom Bishop Spalding turned for advice were scholars at famous institutions. Their names and affiliations: Dr. A. H. Sayce, Oxford University; Dr. William F. Petrie, London University; Dr. J. H. Breasted, Chicago University; Dr. A. C. Mace, department of Egyptology, Metropolitan Museum of Art, New York; Dr. J. Peters, director of the Babylonian Expedition of the University of Pennsylvania, 1888-1895; Dr. S. A. B. Mercer, Western Theological Seminary, Chicago; Dr. E. Meyer, University of Berlin; Dr. F. Baron V. Bissing, University of Munich.

"To anyone with knowledge of the large class of funeral documents to which these belong, the attempts to guess a meaning for them, in the professed explanations, are too absurd to be noticed," said Petrie. "It may be safely said that there is not one single word that is true in these explanations."

The others treated the "translations" as either a maddening fraud or a hilarious joke, depending on the humor of the expert.

The Saints of 1912 did not permit Bishop Spalding's attack on the Book of Abraham—and through it, on all of the Prophet's translations—to go without challenge. They raised hell about it. They wrote letters, made speeches, challenged the Bishop's integrity, accused him of cheating, and did almost everything except prove that the reproduced hieroglyphics said what Joseph Smith said they said.

About a year later a commentator in *The Utah Survey*, Samuel A. B. Mercer, produced a long analysis of the controversy in which he defended Bishop Spalding as a temperate and honorable man, while being gentle also with the Saints. Mercer made these comments:

> The Bishop published the findings of the scholars and the Mormons replied. The replies have been now examined and found wanting. It has been shown that the Mormons failed to concentrate on the point at issue (instead of trying to show that the fac-similes were correctly translated and interpreted, they confined themselves to squabbles about the transliteration of Hebrew words, and to a "symbolical" interpretation of the inscriptions); that they failed to force an agreement between what Joseph Smith said and what we know today about Egyptian and Semitic language, religion, literature, art and culture . . .
> The failure of the Mormon replies is explained by the fact that the unanimous opinion of the scholars is unassailable. In the judgment of the scholarly world, therefore, Joseph Smith stands condemned of self-deception or imposition.

The evidence here seems compelling only insofar as it applies to the Book of Abraham. It may reflect on the character of Joseph Smith, and in this way reflect on the major work, the *Book of Mormon*. But the proof of anything about the *Book of Mormon* is indirect and must be inferred. The Prophet said that the *Book of Mormon* was translated with the aid of two stones which he found with the Gold Plates. He said he followed the instructions of the Angel Moroni and looked through these stones at the plates. The proper translations appeared before his eyes so that he could read them off to the succession of transcribers who served him. But with the papyri brought to Kirtland by Michael Chandler, Joseph presented his findings as a mixture of divine inspiration and scholarly understanding.

The distinction is narrow, but the disproof of the Book of

Abraham is not the disproof of the *Book of Mormon.* In my view, it is intellectually possible for a religious person to be able to accept the one and reject the other, as is done by the Reorganized LDS church.

The Reorganized LDS church has a strong stake in the validity of the works of Joseph Smith, a stake fully as strong as that of the Utah church. Yet, Israel A. Smith, a grandson of the Prophet Joseph, is the author of the following, and wrote it when he was president of the Reorganized LDS church:

> The Book of Abraham is what Joseph Smith said of it, "a translation of some ancient records, that have fallen into our hands from the catacombs of Egypt, purporting to be the writings of Abraham . . ." Joseph Smith was only the translator of this Egyptian manuscript. He did not claim it as an original work of which he was the author. The church has never taken any action to endorse it. We have no record that Joseph Smith, Jr., ever endorsed its contents or teachings. He merely referred to it as a "purported" record. No claim was ever made to include it in the Scriptures of the church during his lifetime. The manuscript was purchased, by some of the Saints, from a traveling showman with some Egyptian mummies.

This examination of the background of controversy on the Book of Abraham is presented because this work alone provides the ground for the exclusion of Negroes. It is here that all the theology ends and begins.

David O. McKay, who as president of the LDS church is the chief prophet, seer and revelator for 2.5 million Saints, wrote in a letter in 1947:

"I know of no scriptural basis for denying the Priesthood to Negroes other than one verse in the Book of Abraham (1:26); however, I believe, as you suggest, that the real reason dates back to our pre-existent life."

In that same letter McKay said:

"Sometime in God's eternal plan, the Negro will be given the right to hold the Priesthood. In the meantime, those of that race who receive the testimony of the Restored Gospel may have their family ties protected and other blessings made secure, for in the justice and mercy of the Lord they will possess all the blessings to which they are entitled in the eternal plan of Salvation and Exaltation."

The inclusion of the phrase "to which they are entitled" gives the game away. That is the nub of the argument. The Saints, acting under a doctrine based on the only factually disproved work among Joseph Smith's translations, hold that the Negroes of the world are not entitled to the same "eternal plan of Salvation and Exaltation" as that held out for all the rest of mankind.

Of course there are Negroes in good standing as members of the LDS church. One of these is Monroe Fleming of Salt Lake City. Over a period of two years he has refused to be interviewed. Once a Mormon bishop urged him to see me. He will not. Sources within the church relate that he stands and gives thanks to God for the opportunity of eternal grace that the church extends to him. He and his wife work around the Hotel Utah, which the church owns.

But on one occasion Fleming is on record as resisting one of the LDS sophistries, i.e., that Negro members who "understand" the doctrinal reasons for their exclusion from the priesthood are not seriously troubled by the circumstance.

Fleming said this was not true. He said, "I know most of the members of the Negro race in the Church and know that they feel that they should have the priesthood if they live a life based upon the principles of the Gospel." The statement was in a letter to Jerald Tanner, the LDS rebel.

The continual LDS insistence on racial bigotry has another serious defect, too, since it assumes that the prohibition is equal to all Negroes and always has been. This is untrue. All Mormons who have ever studied the matter know that

Elijah Abel, the Nauvoo mortician who was a friend of Joseph Smith, was a priesthood member, even becoming a Seventy. He was born in Maryland on July 25, 1810. He was converted and ordained an elder on March 3, 1836. He was ordained a Seventy on April 4, 1841. When he was in his seventy-fifth year, he went on a mission to Canada from Salt Lake City, then much worn out came back to his home to die on December 25, 1884.

Various excuses and misdirections about Elijah Abel are found in LDS literature about Negroes. When all this has been sifted, the fact remains that this Negro was a full member of the Mormon priesthood for almost a half century, that he lived out his life in Salt Lake City during the period when the anti-Negro position of the church was becoming hardened into the condition we find today. Probably the most persuasive explanation is contained in one sentence in the LDS Biographical Encyclopedia. It is this, from the article on Abel:

"In Nauvoo he was intimately acquainted with the Prophet Joseph . . ."

Except for a mysterious Negro barber in Batavia, New York, who may or may not have been ordained by Joseph's brother, William Smith, Abel is the only "official" Negro elder admitted to by the Saints. However, the apostates and anti-Mormons around Salt Lake City have not been satisfied with this. One man has worked on the hypothesis that if Abel lived his life as a devout Mormon, his children also must have been Mormons—at least some of them. This researcher has found that census reports for 1870 showed Abel with six daughters and two sons. From the vast genealogical records of the church, these have been traced, until a string of three generations of Negro Mormon priests had been produced.

Jerald and Sandra Tanner, in a short book they call *Joseph Smith's Curse Upon the Negro*, assert that Enoch Abel, a son of Elijah, was ordained as an elder in Logan, Utah, and that his son, Elijah, a grandson of the first Elijah Abel, was ordained a priest in 1934 and as an elder in Logan in 1935. About the descendants of the pioneer Negro Mormon, the Tanners write:

"At least forty of these live within a radius of 100 miles of Salt Lake City, and, of course, some of them hold the Priesthood and are doing missionary work for the church."

What is it that the church deprives a Negro believer of enjoying? He can be a member; what else does he want?

The answer is as complex as the LDS doctrine and practice, but its fundamental is simple to state: Negro Mormons are shut away from the benefits at the very heart of their religious belief.

This is a church where every man is made responsible for his own salvation. He has certain things set down for him to do, and if he does these things he will achieve great exaltation. The ultimate of this exaltation—Man can become a God.

The first step of this, after joining the church and baptism, is ordination into the priesthood. The priesthood is the central part of the LDS religion. Unless a man enters the priesthood, he has no hope of real exaltation. The Mormons believe that all souls will be redeemed into paradise. The question is only whether one is able to win exaltation in the spirit world by his performance in mortal existence. Thus the doctrine of Negro exclusion from the priesthood means Negro exclusion from greater opportunity for exaltation.

The Negro Mormon can hold no office whatsoever in a church which offers some office to every one of its male members at some time in his life. A gray-haired Negro Mormon who may have spent his adult life in the careful practice of all the complicated and demanding rules set down by the LDS church stands disenfranchised before the altar where a youth whose beard is just beginning to fuzz may preside.

A twelve-year-old boy may become a member of the
Aaronic priesthood, more than this Negro man has been
able to achieve through a lifetime of devotion. To hold any
church office, a Mormon must be a member of the priesthood.

There is an even deeper disability for Negro Mormons.
They are barred from the Temple. This has great significance. It means they cannot have a Temple wedding. Nor
can they have their Temple endowments. Nor can they have
their children and their wives "sealed" to them for eternity.
It means, in fact, that insofar as the religion based on Joseph
Smith's teachings is concerned, the Negro is just able to hold
his own position in the spirit world by joining the church
and suffering all the deprivations expected of him. He gets
no benefit from his mortal existence except the earthly pleasures that preachers of all religions spend so much of their
time railing against. He cannot look forward to better status
in eternity, nor to having his loved ones at his side. Some
Mormon theologians even tell the Negroes that they can
expect only to be servants in the after life.

So the ultimate effect of this aspect of LDS doctrine is as
racist as anything asserted by the Theodore Bilbos and
Robert Sheltons in the bigoted corners of the southern states.
It separates the world into two groups: there are those who
can become full-fledged Saints and thus God's chosen people; there are the African Negroes who are set apart from the
rest of us to occupy a lesser station.

Mormonism is a total way of life. A devout Mormon never
really leaves his religious shell as he goes about his life in the
secular world. So he never really leaves the feeling that
black skin makes a man inferior. This means that the LDS
church actually is one of the most influential organs of racial
bigotry in the United States. All the imposing list of wonderful and truly praiseworthy things about this tremendous
and impressive institution help to conceal this ugly corner
of its theology. When one hears the Tabernacle Choir, one

forgets that no Negro could ever hope to achieve a place in that group. When one listens to the gentle voice and kindly expressions of David O. McKay, one forgets that no Negro can ever hope to become president of the LDS church. Yet throughout the religious institution which produced the Tabernacle Choir and David O. McKay there exists a current of powerful strength that for generations has carried racial bigotry wherever the missionaries carried the Restored Gospel of Joseph Smith.

True, this is all done in a cloak of Christian piety and concern for the brotherhood of man. Seldom is there any surface cruelty. Yet until the federal government outlawed slavery, the Mormons bought and sold Negroes in Salt Lake City. In 1965, Kate B. Carter published a monograph for the Daughters of Utah Pioneers on *The Negro Pioneer*. She traced many of them and told many touching stories of their devotion to the Saints. One of the most touching of these stories was about Venus, who came to Spanish Fork, Utah, as a slave. This is a paragraph from the story of Venus:

> Venus was also a midwife and delivered babies for many of the mothers in Spanish Fork. On April 29, 1860, she presided at the birth of the Gardner twins, Serena and Seranus, who lived to be ninety and ninety-six years old, respectively. Some of the Spanish Fork people remember Venus as being tall, very polite and quiet and always immaculate in her dress. She had a great desire to go to the Temple, and when she found that the Temple was closed to Negroes, she scratched her arm until it bled and said: "See, my blood is as white as anyone's."

But her skin was black and the Mormons tell us they worship a God who finds black skin despicable.

IX

Will the Negro
Doctrine Change?

A FERMENT is working in the Mormon community over the Negro question, particularly among the intellectual element. The mistreatment of Negroes by the LDS church is the reason given by many intellectuals who candidly admit that they have become silent, concealed apostates.

Even among many who cling tenaciously to their belief, there is a swelling opinion that the church is dead wrong on this issue. Mormonism is unusually open to unrest in such a situation, emphasizing as it does the responsibility of every man to be a priest and to be his own repository of knowledge on doctrine. Thus it produces men who can disagree vigorously with some doctrine enunciated at the top, and yet declare themselves in equally positive terms to be faithful believers.

J. D. Williams, the professor of political science discussed in an earlier chapter, is such a man. He can swiftly announce his faithful adherence to the LDS church and just as swiftly reserve his position on the Negro matter. His position has an intellectual fascination to its legalistic structure. He offers it as a way out of the jungle of theology and practicality in which the church today finds itself.

"I've been taught that when there is a conflict of law, the most recently adopted one prevails," he said. "The Book of Abraham represents things that happened about 2100 to

1900 B.C. So that is the date of the statements, the laws, that said the Negroes could not have the priesthood."

He leaned forward, his eyes intent, and presented his points.

"Now the entire twenty-fourth chapter of 2nd Nephi makes it plain that God loves all mankind, all races, equally. This is in about 550 B.C., much later than Abraham's writings."

There was more.

"Then, in the Christian era, we have St. Paul's letter to the Galatians. That makes it very clear."

He began to quote:

"For ye are all the children of God by faith in Christ Jesus."

(It is in the third chapter of Galatians and the remaining applicable material is this:

"For as many of you as have been baptized into Christ have put on Christ.

"There is neither Jew nor Greek, there is neither bond nor free, there is neither male nor female; for ye are all one in Christ Jesus.

"And if ye be Christ's, then are ye Abraham's seed, and heirs according to the promise.")

"You see," said Professor Williams, "the newer statement of God's equal love for all races cancels out the statements in the Book of Abraham."

The odds against this solution being adopted are prohibitively high. It is much more probable that if a change comes, it will be in the manner described by Sterling McMurrin, a distinguished descendant of a distinguished Mormon family.

McMurrin was the Kennedy Commissioner of Education and returned to the University of Utah to become provost in addition to lecturing as a professor of philosophy. In 1960, before his Washington sojourn gave him a wider national reputation, McMurrin spoke at a Negro Methodist church in Salt Lake City. It was a meeting of the National Association for the Advancement of Colored People and McMurrin's remarks were extemporaneous. He spoke on the problem he felt he shared with his audience—the attitude of his ancestral church toward Negroes.

One of the difficulties is that the Mormon church has always been involved in the notion of revelation. It is one thing to have an interpretation of the Bible changed after 50 years or so if you decide some other interpretation is more satisfactory, and thus change the belief, but it is another thing to be a Mormon and in some way or another get it established that this change is a divine revelation. You don't change revelation in the same manner that you change Bible interpretation.

I say this in spite of the fact that I really believe that if I don't die in the near future, I will live to see the time when this "doctrine" is dissolved. I don't mean repudiated. The Mormon church is like the Catholic church. It doesn't repudiate doctrines which at one time or another were held to be revelation or absolute truth. It didn't repudiate the doctrine of polygamy. I use the word "dissolve" and I think by some technique the church will dissolve the "doctrine" on the Negro rather than repudiate it.

This is a very remarkable statement from a man who grew up in the LDS church and is very sensitive to its attitudes, while at the same time as a student of philosophy is very sensitive to the problems of organizational change. In the same speech, McMurrin said of the LDS anti-Negro doctrine:

"It is not only nonsense, but bad nonsense; it is immoral."

Three years later Look Magazine was able to quote Joseph Fielding Smith, the leading theologian of the Council of Twelve Apostles, in these words:

"I would not want you to believe that we bear any animosity toward the Negro. 'Darkies' are wonderful people, and they have their place in our church."

In 1965 Sterling McMurrin said that the LDS church did not have any official doctrine that calls for its anti-Negro position. He insisted that this rested entirely on the interpretations of two or three verses of Scripture and that there are other verses in the Bible and other works sacred to Mormons upon which even the most orthodox could find reason to support the ideal of equality at the altar. But he said that he is all the more deeply troubled that the church has exhibited such anti-Negro prejudices in so many ways even though it has no doctrinal basis for the position.

The roots of this prejudice are deep.

One of the remarkable statements demonstrating this prejudice is in a long speech by Mark E. Petersen, one of the apostles, in a conference at Brigham Young University in August, 1954. In June, 1954, the United States Supreme Court had issued its landmark anti-segregation decision, Brown *vs.* the Board of Education. The winds of change were rising, the storm of Negro protest was building. A convention of LDS teachers of religion at the college level was called together and Apostle Petersen spoke to them on "Race Relations—as They Affect the Church."

To set the stage, the apostle quoted extensively from an interview with Adam Clayton Powell, the Harlem politician and religious leader, in which Powell spoke approvingly of the increase in marriages between Negroes and whites.

"From this, and other interviews I have read," said the man the Mormons consider to be an apostle of Christ, "it appears that the Negro seeks absorption with the white race. He will not be satisfied until he achieves it by intermarriage. That is his objective and we must face it. We must not allow our feeling to carry us away, nor must we feel so sorry for Negroes that we will open our arms and embrace them with everything we have. Remember the little statement that we used to say about sin, 'First we pity, then endure, then embrace.' "

Petersen praised the Chinese, who he understood opposed interracial marriage. He gave the audience a quick run-through of the theory that Negroes carried to earth as their souls the marginally loyal spirits in the struggle between God and Satan. He said:

"We cannot escape the conclusion that because of performance in our pre-existence some of us are born as Chinese, some as Japanese, some as Indians, some as Negroes, some as Americans, some as Latter-day Saints. These are rewards and punishments, fully in harmony with His established policy in dealing with sinners and saints, rewarding all according to their deeds."

Petersen is the fifth-ranking member of the Council of Twelve Apostles. He was born in 1900 and conceivably could one day become president of the LDS church. Consequently, this lengthy statement of his view on the Negro question becomes important.

He asked rhetorically if segregation were wrong, and his answer included these points:

When the Lord chose the nations to which the spirits were to come, determining that some would be Japanese and some would be Chinese and some Negroes and some Americans, he engaged in an act of segregation . . . We speak of the miracle of the preservation of the Jews as a separate people over all these years. It was nothing more nor less than an act of segregation . . . Who placed the Negroes originally in darkest Africa? Was it some man, or was it God? And when He placed them there, He segregated them . . . And He certainly segregated the descendants of Cain when He cursed the Negro as to the Priesthood, and drew an absolute line.

Then he turned to a piece of nonsense aimed to justify the claim that the LDS church really is kind to Negroes.

Think of the Negro, cursed as to the Priesthood. Are we prejudiced against him? Unjustly, sometimes we are accused of having such a prejudice. But what does the mercy of God have for him? This Negro, who in the pre-existence lived the type of life which justified the Lord in sending him to the earth in the lineage of Cain with a black skin, and possibly being born into darkest Africa—if that Negro is willing when he hears the gospel to accept it, he may have many of the blessings of the gospel. In spite of all he did in the pre-existent life, the Lord is willing, if the Negro accepts the gospel with real, sincere faith, and is really converted, to give him the blessings of baptism and the gift of the Holy Ghost. If that Negro is faithful all his days, he can and will enter the celestial kingdom. *He will go there as a servant*, but he will get celestial resurrection. (Emphasis supplied)

Apostle Petersen dipped back into his memory for a story of the church's treatment of a Negro. He told it to show the church's generosity; it will give others a different feeling. But it probably made his point with the white, well-fed, privileged, secure Mormons who heard it.

His story was about a Negro family in Cincinnati, who were Mormons because of the self-conversion of the father, Len Hope. The family belonged to a mission branch, but "some of the members of the church became extremely prejudiced against this Negro family. They met in a group, decided what to do and went to the Branch President, and said that either the Hope family must leave or they would all leave. The Branch President ruled that Brother Hope and his family could not come to church meetings. It broke their hearts. But, the missionaries went out to the Hope home and there conducted Sunday School every Sunday, and served them the Sacrament."

Apostle Petersen told with great praise how Hope, the Negro, paid his tithing all through those years. Sometimes he had to go pick berries in the hills to get any money, but he turned his pennies over to the church which thought more of its bigots than it did of him. His devotion led Petersen to take a great step. Hope wanted vicarious baptism done in the Temple for his family members who had died. Petersen got permission for this—special permission from the then president of the church, George Albert Smith.

"We performed vicarious baptisms for these Negroes," said Petersen, carefully pointing out also—"only the baptisms and confirmations, nothing else, but we did that much. Again I thought of the great mercy of Almighty God, and how He is willing to lift people up if they do their part."

Frequently critics of Mormon segregation are told that the church also believes that Negroes will one day be admitted to the priesthood when the evils of Cain's murder of Abel finally have been cleared away.

"I know of no scripture having to do with the removal of the curse from the Negro," said Petersen. "I think we should not speculate too much about that."

Then he turned back to the question of intermarriage, where he had opened his talk.

"We must not intermarry with the Negro. Why? If I were to marry a Negro woman and have children by her, my children would all be cursed as to the priesthood. Do I want my children cursed as to the priesthood? If there is one drop of Negro blood in my children, as I have read to you, they receive the curse. There isn't any argument, therefore, as to intermarriage with the Negro, is there? There are 50 million Negroes in the United States. If they were to achieve complete absorption with the white race, think what that would do. With 50 million Negroes intermarried with us, where would the priesthood be? Who could hold it, in all America? Think what that would do to the work of the church!"

Apostle Petersen made this revealing statement:

"Now we are generous with the Negro. We are willing that the Negro have the highest kind of education. I would be willing to let every Negro drive a Cadillac if they could afford it. I would be willing that they have all the advantages they can get out of life in the world. But let them enjoy these things among themselves. I think the Lord segregated the Negro and who is man to change that segregation? It reminds me of the scripture on marriage, 'what God had joined together, let not man put asunder.' Only here we have the reverse of the thing—what God hath separated, let not man bring together again."

As in so many statements of the LDS position on Negroes, it comes down here to "God did it, don't blame us."

The apostle had one more question to ask himself:

"What is our advice with respect to intermarriage with Chinese, Japanese, Hawaiians and so on? I will tell you what advice I give personally. If a boy or girl comes to me claiming to be in love with a Chinese or Japanese or a Hawaiian or a person of any other dark race, I do my best to talk them out of it. I tell them that I think the Hawaiians should marry Hawaiians, the Japanese ought to marry the Japanese, and the Chinese ought to marry Chinese, and the Caucasians should marry Caucasians, just exactly as I tell them that Latter-day Saints ought to marry Latter-day Saints. . . .

"I teach against intermarriage of all kinds."

This speech was delivered in a closed meeting. A copy of it came into the hands of James D. Wardle, the Salt Lake City barber who is a member of the Reorganized LDS church. Wardle has enjoyed many years of baiting his Utah Mormon townsmen, and made his copy available to Jerald Tanner, the LDS apostate who specializes in circulating anti-LDS materials. Tanner went to the LDS library, found a copy of the speech and assured himself that it was the same speech he had received from Wardle. But the church would not give him a copy he could take away with him.

Using the Wardle copy as his source, Tanner began to circulate the address. At that time Apostle Petersen was in

England leading the mission there. In early 1965 he wrote to Tanner threatening to sue him if he did not stop publication and recall the previously issued copies of the speech. Tanner gleefully reproduced and circulated the letter. Since then Petersen has returned to Salt Lake City and no suit has been filed.

Another of the apostles, the widely known Ezra Taft Benson, also was in Europe for a protracted assignment at the same time Petersen was there. It was assumed by many observers that both were sent abroad because they had allowed their extreme conservative political views to become involved in their church leadership duties.

Apostle Benson is four chairs away from the LDS presidency. He is best known nationally as Secretary of Agriculture in the eight Eisenhower years. He has had an active church career. He is a great-grandson of an earlier Apostle Ezra Taft Benson who came into the Salt Lake Valley with Brigham Young on July 24, 1847. He was born in Idaho, and was a county agricultural agent there. He was the first head of the department of agricultural economics and marketing at the University of Idaho. He organized the Idaho Cooperative Council and was the executive secretary of the National Council of Farmer Cooperatives when he was named an apostle in 1943.

Around Salt Lake City Apostle Benson is considered to be the most politically conservative member of the Council of Twelve Apostles. He has flirted with the right wing of the Republican party, and his son, Reed Benson, was the unsuccessful right wing candidate for the Republican nomination to Congress from Salt Lake City in 1962. Soon after losing the primary election, the younger Benson identified himself with the John Birch Society for which he became Utah state coordinator. Later he moved to the Society's offices in Washington, D.C. Apostle Benson has supported his son in all of this, although he has never been identified as a member of the semi-secret John Birch Society. (In early 1966, Apostle Benson's flirtation with the Birch Society brought on a crisis in the First Presidency and Council of Twelve. This is examined in a subsequent chapter.)

However, Apostle Benson's attitude toward Negroes (a part of his religion) and his attitude toward all movements for greater liberty and freedom (colored by his right wing political view) have led him into an extreme position. In late 1963 he made a speech at Logan, Utah, where he said that the Southern Negro drive for equality of rights was "fomented almost entirely by the Communists." He said that he thought federal legislation then pending to help Negroes in the South preserve their civil rights was "about 10 per cent civil rights and 90 per cent a further extension of socialistic federal controls."

He made this statement which sounds like the sort of thing one reads in Birch Society pamphlets:

"It is a part of the pattern for the Communist take-over of America."

Then he went to Europe on assignment from LDS President McKay. In 1965, at the April LDS conference, Apostle Benson's speech was reported in the *Salt Lake Tribune* as containing this argument:

Before I left for Europe I warned how the Communists were using the civil rights movement to promote revolution and eventual takeover of this country. When are we going to wake up? What do you know about the dangerous civil rights agitation in Mississippi? Do you fear the destruction of all vestiges of state government?

Now Brethren, the Lord never promised there would not be traitors in the church. We have the ignorant, the sleepy and the deceived who provide temptations and avenues of apostasy for the unwary and the unfaithful, but we have a prophet at our head and he has spoken. Now what are we going to do about it?

Jerald Tanner, who is very tenacious, thoughtfully compared this account from the non-Mormon daily newspaper with the church account of the speech as it was reported in the *Improvement Era*, a church publication. He found that when the apostle's speech was printed by the church, the anti-civil rights paragraphs were deleted.

But this does not conceal the fact that among some members of the Council of Twelve Apostles of the LDS church the opposition to Negroes goes beyond the question of priesthood in the church. Apostle Benson's accusation that the campaigns for the Negro right to vote are Communist motivated is far away from any question of religious brotherhood or any religious dogma about whether the bodies of Negroes must be made to suffer indignity because the souls in those bodies failed to line up properly with the Lord in a struggle with Satan.

The apostle's statement is directly in support of the right wing political view that any attempt of any minority group to gain its rights is somehow inspired by Communists. His doctrine in this sense is an unapproved extension of the church's generally accepted view about Negroes. Elsewhere, the church leaders have carefully spoken out for the preservation of all rights and privileges for the Negro—except the right of holding priesthood in the LDS church. Apostle Benson would not only withhold this from them; he would censure them for trying to achieve their rights in civil society.

Apostle Benson probably is the political spokesman for the right wing elements of the Council of Twelve Apostles. His opposite number, the spokesman for what would be the left wing of the Council (but only the right center of American political thought) is Hugh B. Brown, the first counselor to President McKay, and thus called President Brown in LDS circles.

President Brown was born in 1883 in Salt Lake City, but he

has lived most of his life in Canada. He came back to Salt Lake City in 1953 when he was seventy, an age when most men are closing the books on their active life. However, he was then taking up his important religious work as an assistant to the Council of Twelve Apostles. Then in 1958 he was made an apostle by David O. McKay, and in 1961 became second counselor to President McKay. He became first counselor in 1963 when he was eighty years old.

In this position, Brown has great influence in church affairs, and this influence has been magnified by the inability of the aging President McKay to exercise the control of the church affairs that he once did. The First Presidency, which is made up of President McKay and his counselors, Brown and Nathan Eldon Tanner, makes the decisions on the LDS church's secular affairs. President McKay is the final authority in all matters, for he is the chief prophet, seer and revelator. Whatever he says goes.

Brown has been closer to the aged president than any other apostle. President McKay brought Brown to Salt Lake City in 1953 and "set him aside" as an apostle, then made him a counselor. But when McKay dies, Brown may no longer have a position at the very summit. He could then revert to his position as a member of the Council of Twelve Apostles. The new president would form his own First Presidency, which might or might not include Brown.

Both Brown and Tanner are Canadian in background, although both were born in the United States. Brown lived there from his fifteenth year, Tanner even from a younger age. Brown was a Canadian lawyer and served overseas in World War I as a major in the Canadian army. He served for a time as professor of religion and coordinator of veterans' affairs at Brigham Young University. When he left business life for his church duties, he was president and manager of Richland Oil Development Company of Canada, Ltd.

He has had a run of top level church jobs—stake president,

head of the British Mission, missionary service to Great Britain as a young man. Also, he married a granddaughter of Brigham Young.

This was the man I met first on May 31, 1963. That interview marked the beginning of my lessons in the Mormon doctrine on Negroes. I was checking a report that the LDS church was about to change its position on Negroes.

The first man I saw was Theodore Cannon, Jr., the press spokesman for the church. (Ted Cannon was a tall, rugged, and thoroughly pleasant man who managed with dignity to convey to the non-believer an understanding of LDS doctrine and organization. He never offended by argument and over-zealousness; yet he always managed to maintain the understanding that whatever his questioner might feel, Ted Cannon was a devout Mormon and intended to remain so. He was the son of the oldest son of George Q. Cannon, the nineteenth-century LDS apostle and leader during the polygamous years. I was saddened when Ted Cannon died in February, 1966.)

Cannon said the report of a change in the Negro position was erroneous. But he offered to arrange an appointment with one of the top leaders, and it turned out that only Hugh B. Brown was in town that day. We went to the church Administration building and Brown's office. With us was Jack Goodman, my friend and the *New York Times* representative in Salt Lake City. After Cannon's statements, it appeared that the report to be checked was wrong, and we expected Brown to tell us so.

Instead, Brown stated:

"We are in the midst of a survey looking toward the possibility of admitting Negroes. Believing as we do in divine revelation through the President of the church, we all await his decision."

Cannon looked incredulously at Brown, who continued:

"The whole problem of the Negro is being considered by

the leaders of the church in the light of racial relationships everywhere. We don't want to go too fast in this matter. We want to be fair."

There was more to the interview—for example, Brown said the change, when and if it came, would be a doctrinal upheaval of the magnitude of the abandonment of polygamy. Then it was finished and the three of us walked out into the street. Cannon was distraught. He insisted that I had misunderstood Brown. But Goodman's notes and understanding coincided with mine. I went to my room in the Hotel Utah and wrote an account of the interview. Then Cannon came to look at it. We met in the spacious hotel lobby.

He objected to some of the quotes as not being precisely what his notes showed. I changed them to follow his wording. He asked that I remove a paragraph based on something he had told me, claiming that his account had been off the record and that publication of the paragraph would needlessly embarrass church leaders. I marked it out. When we had finished all this, he agreed that the copy now reflected what he had heard and seen and the background he had given me.

But he implored me not to send it to New York. It would just cause trouble, he said, for the church was not about to make a change in spite of what Brown had just told us. Of course I was not to be persuaded and sent the story.

The *Salt Lake Tribune* is a subscriber to the *New York Times* News Service. On the afternoon of the day the story was to be set in type in New York, it was forwarded to clients of the news service. It was widely printed, but it was never printed in Salt Lake City. The story came in, and was checked for comment with President Hugh B. Brown. He insisted that it not be run. The *Tribune* did not run it. I have never been able to determine whether at that time he denied the story and the quotations attributed to him in it. Later his position was that the story's emphasis was wrong, but that otherwise it was straightforward. Of course, he was in no position to deny what he had said; the quotes attributed to him were those approved by his own press representative.

However, that night two Mormon elders came to the New York Times Building on W. 43rd Street in New York. They argued and tried to persuade the editors of the *Times* to withdraw the story. They did deny that Brown had ever said the things attributed to him in it.

Now I must agree that Ted Cannon was right. Hugh B. Brown did not know what he was talking about. The church was not then expecting a revelation from President McKay to wipe out the discriminatory policy toward Negroes. Perhaps Brown was. But it didn't turn out that way.

The following October at the 133rd annual conference of the LDS church, Brown was the first speaker after President McKay who opened the meeting. He had prepared a talk around the theme of the attack on Mormon morality constantly mounted by the forces of Satan. After his original draft was prepared, for some reason he tacked on at the top a statement on civil rights. He said:

We would like it to be known that there is in this church no doctrine, belief, or practice that is intended to deny the enjoyment of full civil rights by any person regardless of race, color or creed.

We say again, as we have said many times before, that we believe that all men are the children of the same God and that it is a moral evil for any person or group of persons to deny any human being the right to gainful employment, to full educational opportunity, and to every privilege of citizenship, just as it is a moral evil to deny him the right to worship according to the dictates of his own conscience.

We have consistently and persistently upheld the Constitution of the United States, and as far as we are concerned this means upholding the constitutional rights of every citizen of the United States.

We call upon all men everywhere, both within and outside the Church, to commit themselves to the establishment of full civil equality for all of God's children. Anything less than this defeats our high ideal of the brotherhood of man.

Certainly, Hugh Brown believes what he said in these carefully couched paragraphs. However, he also knows that he was not speaking the sentiments of all the members, perhaps not even of a majority of them. He knows, as we have seen in the statements of others of the Council of Twelve Apostles, that there is a disposition among many leading Mormons to consider Negroes a people cursed by God and unworthy of association on equal terms with the rest of mankind.

Every scrap of information I've gathered about Mormons and Negroes points to Hugh Brown as the liberal voice at the top of the church. I suspect that when he told me those things in that interview in 1963, he hoped the change was to come.

However, the odds are all against its coming anytime soon in the terms he described—a revelation by the president of the church. David O. McKay is the most liberal LDS president in sight for a long time to come. Yet, he made it plain in 1964 that he felt it unlikely that any revelation would come that would lift from Negroes their historic disability in LDS doctrine and practice.

He was in Oakland, California, in November, 1964, to appear at the dedication of a new Temple there. He was then ninety-one years old, and greatly enfeebled by a stroke and other illnesses. He was brought to a press conference in a wheelchair, then walked into the room supported by two of his sons. His once powerful voice now was an aged man's squeak. But he was there and we asked him the hard questions.

The Negro matter came up quickly, and he dodged for an answer or so among the underbrush of theological inprecision in the framing of the questions. But then the question was asked directly, in the proper words to discover whether the prophet, seer, and chief revelator thought doctrine on Negroes would be changed to allow them to hold the priesthood. He said:

"Not while you and I are here."

That would seem to end for many years the possibility of a revelation on that subject.

However, there are indications that it does not end the possibility of Negro participation in the Mormon priesthood. There are many straws in the wind that validate the prediction of Sterling McMurrin, the distinguished educator, that sooner or later the church will find a way to dissolve its anti-Negro doctrine and avoid outright repudiation of it.

One indication of potential change is the astounding fact that in the past year or so the Mormons have been ordaining Fiji islanders into the priesthood. It came about gradually. For many years the church maintained missions among the Polynesians, first in Hawaii, then through the Pacific Islands. The Polynesians, of course, are brown but not Negroid in appearance.

The Mormon mission worked through the Polynesians on Tonga and then moved to the Melanesians on Fiji. The Melanesians are black—very black—and are described in reference works as Negroid in appearance except that their noses are not so flat as African Negroes and their hair is more inclined to stand out from their heads than to be coiled closely to it. It was impossible to get a clear-cut answer to questions tracing the background of the decision to make these Negroid Pacific islanders into Mormon priests. But it is obvious that someone advanced the argument successfully that they were not African Negroes and therefore—whatever their skin color—were not the bearers of the curse of Cain.

A different thing is going on in South America where the Mormon missionaires are pushing ahead full throttle. There the former careful selection to keep out "white Negroes" has been allowed to slide a little.

But, sadly, sometimes the missionaries get orders from Salt Lake City to go to a new elder and tell him that he should not try to exercise his priestly authorities, that he has a Negro ancestor and everything was a big mistake.

"There is no question but that in Brazil they have been ordaining priests who are part Negro," said one careful observer.

This is a far cry from a statement recorded as from Zebedee Coltrin, a white Saint, who said it was he who anointed Elijah Abel, the famous Negro priesthood member, when the Mormons were at Kirtland, Ohio. He is quoted as saying, "while I had my hands upon his head I never had such an unpleasant feeling in my life." This was years later when the Saints had reached the Salt Lake Valley.

A similar statement was made by a prominent Mormon in Salt Lake City in 1965. He said that during his missionary duty he was in a ceremony to anoint a convert. He said he lost his power of speech and had to stop. He said he prayed, and then investigated the convert's racial background. He said he found a Negro in the man's family tree. God, you see, had saved him from making a mistake.

However, there is another pressure on the church. Is it to abandon the salvation of the Negroes of the world? What of the obligation that all Saints feel to carry the gospel of Joseph Smith—indeed, the gospel of Christ—to all of mankind? Yet, increasingly the church is coming to the point where the only virgin territories untouched by its missionaries are in Black Africa.

Increasingly the church has found the anti-Negro doctrine

difficult to bear. It leads to ironical events such as occurred in San Luis Obispo, California, Salt Lake City and
Enugu, Nigeria, in 1963, 1964 and 1965.

It all began when a new college student from Nigeria,
Ambrose Chukwu, took an exploratory walk through San
Luis Obispo. He saw the Mormon chapel, was attracted to
it during his first week in town, and went inside to look
further. He attended a service on Sunday, and met the
bishop. As Chukwu told the story in a letter to the paper
back home in Enugu, it was like this:

"We had a very long and friendly chat. But the evening
got ruined when my curiosity again started wandering
away. There was a large map of the world on the wall and
on this map was shown the areas of Mormon activities. An
innocent question popped out: 'Why have you no missions
anywhere in Africa except in South Africa?'"

The Mormons tried to avoid but the African insisted. He
was told that the Negro was cursed by God and could not
be a priesthood member. They continued to talk, and the
Saints finally gave Chukwu a copy of the little book *Mormonism and the Negro*. He read this, and his teeth were
really on edge. He sent along some extracts which were
printed in the *Nigerian Outlook*. He also made some comments on the question of allowing Mormon missionaries
into Nigeria.

"The Mormons could by trickery establish a church in Nigeria and use this as massive propaganda for propagating
and spreading their religion of race hate and race superiority
and discrimination in America," he wrote.

This was really treading on a tender corn. The LDS
church had already designated a man to lead a mission to be
established in Nigeria—the largest nation of Negroes in the
world. He was then in Salt Lake City awaiting final orders
to leave. They never came.

Why was the church to have a mission in Nigeria?

The story and implications are fascinating. In the early 1950s a group of Nigerian Negroes came into possession by chance of a copy of a book describing Joseph Smith's struggles. One of them was interested so he decided to form a branch of the church. He wrote to Salt Lake City and the church bureaucracy more or less automatically sent back the materials to Anie Dick Obot at Uyo, Nigeria. Then the Saints in 1959 sent over Elder Lamar Williams on a scouting trip. There was interest in Salt Lake City in doing something with this group of self-starting Mormons. Williams returned, and was enthusiastic. The plan was mounted to establish a Nigerian Mission. It was at about this time that Ambrose Chukwu sent home his blast at the Saints. He said:

> I think it is the height of impudence for the Mormons even to dream of proselyting in Nigeria, let alone to express it. They are belittling the intelligence of Nigerians, just as they do in everything pertaining to the Negro . . .
>
> There may not be anything wrong for any individual to hold the views the Mormons hold; but there is everything wrong when a group of individuals join themselves together to preach a gospel of race hate and race superiority; and are determined to carry this doctrine into the very portals of the people it is discriminating.
>
> What are we to do? Receive them with open arms and vow to be their servants forever and ever amen?

The *Nigerian Outlook* carried an editorial that day calling on President Kennedy to "ban this anti-Negro organization that preaches heretic doctrines." Of course this was a bit of baying at the moon, just as the description of Mormonism as "godless Herrenvolkism" was a bit of hyperbole. But there was one phrase in the editorial which carried real power: ". . . and must not be allowed into the country."

The Nigerian government simply will not give resident visas to Mormon missionaries and that's all there is to it. Meanwhile, the religious group formed by Anie Dick Obot is spreading among the Nigerians and Obot is its leader. He has not the slightest desire to be allied with the Salt Lake City organization, events have shown.

The ultimate irony would be the growth of a powerful, Nigerian-dominated *Book of Mormon* religious organization that would work among the Negroes of the world. Can you imagine? Nigerian missionaries working among the Negroes of Salt Lake City and Ogden!

X

The Church in Politics

DURING JOSEPH SMITH's life his followers did what he told them almost without reservation. Once he had trouble over a revelation that ordered them to give him—and their church—their property. Another time there was trouble over the suggestion that a follower's wife might want to become the Prophet's plural wife. There were a few other incidents. But the submission to the Prophet's will on political matters was almost total. This was the trouble.

.. When they were in Missouri, some of the conflict with outsiders arose because the Mormons wanted to vote. There was an election day riot when the Missourians tried to keep the Mormons from the polls. The Saints used oak clubs to win the fight and managed to cast their votes—in a bloc of course, which was exactly why the Missourians wanted to keep them from voting. Being Saints, they felt that they had allies in the fight.

"It helps a man a great deal in a fight to know that God is on his side," said John D. Lee who was one of the club swingers.

When the Saints moved to Illinois to build up Nauvoo, Joseph quickly arranged a political base for them. The legislature gave him a city charter that virtually made Nauvoo independent, with the right to raise its army for defense. Joseph was mayor, judge and final authority in all matters.

He was lieutenant general of the Nauvoo Legion, too.
The opposing established political forces in Illinois com-
peted with each other to give the Saints special favors. What
they wanted was the growing block of Mormon votes.

When Joseph was killed and the move came to the desert
redoubt, the political control of the religious colony became
absolute in the hands of Brigham Young. As the Gentile
influences penetrated the Mormon country, control began to
wane. In order to understand what that control is today, we
must understand what it once was and the reasons for the
change. In many ways, the president of the LDS church
today is a more powerful political figure than was Brigham
Young, but this is only because the machine he drives is
bigger. He does not have the control in the absolute sense
that Brigham had it.

In those early days Brigham was both the leader of the
church and the federal governor of Utah Territory (or Deseret as the Mormons preferred to call it). By the time of the
Civil War a succession of federal appointees—Gentiles all
—had come to fill high offices. But the Saints maintained a
shadow government with Brigham at its head.

When an office was to be filled by election, there was really
only one candidate for each position in many of those early
years. This candidate was picked by the church. Stanley S.
Ivins, the Salt Lake City historical researcher, checked returns from eighteen annual elections beginning in 1852. In
1867, the vote was unanimous. In other years a single vote
would oppose the church candidate—or four votes or a
dozen. In two years there was isolated rebellion in two
counties. Over that entire period, said Ivins, there were
96,107 votes cast and 96 per cent of them went to the church-
sponsored candidates.

By 1869 more and more Gentiles lived in the Salt Lake
Valley. There was the beginning of an internal problem
with the rising ambitions of some members. A widespread

heresy developed in 1868 when a group began to publish a magazine opposing church policies. A series of excommunications followed. But in 1870 these ex-Saints became the leaders of the new Liberal Party which for the first time provided a formal opposition year-in-year-out to the Mormon People's Party.

It was in this period also that the church was passing through the most difficult time of its trouble-spotted history. The pressure was mounting year by year from Washington for an end to the practice of polygamy which in those days was the very heart of Mormonism. All but a handful of the bishops, stake presidents, and General Authorities were polygamists. If they expected to have these administrative jobs together with the honor, power and gold stars in Heaven that went with them, the Mormons had to have plural wives. While polygamy was practiced by a minority of the total church membership, it was the standard form of married life among the leadership.

It becomes plain that the political struggles over the plural marriage doctrine were really between the top level of the church and the federal government. The rank and file Saints went where they were led. It became increasingly important to the church leadership to maintain political control in order to support the leaders in their struggle. The church's fights with the Liberal Party became more acrimonious.

By the late 1880s the church leaders realized that no matter what it cost them, they must have statehood. This would rid the Mormons of a law enforcement policy dictated from Washington. Their sheriffs and state courts then would have the right to enforce—or not to enforce, which was more nearly the idea held by the church leaders—any laws against polygamy. As it was in territorial days, the federal government appointed judges, marshals and prosecutors who had no sympathy with polygamy. The jails were full of Saints. The church was creaking under the strain.

One of the arguments posed by apostates and Gentiles against statehood was the monolithic political group controlled by the church—the People's Party. A leading negotiator for the church, Frank J. Cannon, was a son of the leading apostle, George Q. Cannon. Frank Cannon later left the church and described the arguments he used on his father, President Wilford Woodruff and Joseph F. Smith to get them to agree to break up the People's Party. It was dissolved by edict of the church in June, 1891, and its members were told to divide between the Republicans and Democrats.

There was mighty little difference in the political and economic outlook of the men at the top of the church. Their differences were concerned more with personal ambition. So the Democrats and Republicans from the former Mormon People's Party began their "independent" political careers just as firmly tied to the church as they had always been.

In 1892 those local offices to be filled by election had candidates of both major parties. The Democrats won most of them while Grover Cleveland was being elected United States President. It was Cleveland who signed the enabling act that made Utah a state in 1896.

With statehood, the church leaders began to relax. They went merrily along with polygamy, as we have seen, and they also began to reassert their control from the top in political matters. It is obvious to any reasonable person who has watched politics anywhere that the men who were to hold elective office in Utah in those years had to be Mormons or Gentiles friendly to the church. The Saints had suffered through a succession of hostile office holders imposed on them from Washington, and they had suffered through the pressures of the anti-polygamy campaign. They looked to statehood to cure all of these problems, and since they were in the majority within the state it was certain that almost all of the candidates would be Mormons first and Republicans or Democrats second.

The important question was whether the First Presidency and the Council of Twelve Apostles would try to impose its choice in the nominating process and then in the general election. Would the church leaders retreat from their commitments to quit trying to dominate political life as they retreated from their commitments to abandon polygamy? Of course they would! They saw themselves as Christ's representatives on earth and they intended to run things the way Christ wanted them—which was of course the way they wanted them, since they received revelations that guided them.

Stanley S. Ivins has documented the very cruel way the First Presidency destroyed the ecclesiastical standing of one of the apostles who resisted the return to church domination of political life—Moses Thatcher. From the beginning he argued that the church should avoid political meddling. The particular meddling to which he objected was a "political manifesto" in which the First Presidency announced that no church official could take a political office unless the leadership approved it as consistent with his obligations to the church. The announcement of this stand came after Thatcher had been nominated by the Democrats for the senate and Brigham H. Roberts, one of the first seven presidents of the Seventy, had been made the Democratic nominee for representative in Congress.

Thatcher and Roberts refused to accept the dictation. Both were defeated. But the church leadership was not finished with them. They were pressured publicly in editorials in the *Deseret News* which demanded that church members be subject to discipline in temporal affairs. They were pressured in private meetings with the top church leaders. Eventually, Roberts cracked and asked forgiveness. He was restored to the priesthood and later was the church candidate elected to represent Utah in Congress. The House of Representatives refused to seat him because he was a polygamist.

Thatcher was dropped from his position on the Council of Twelve Apostles in 1896, but yet he did not knuckle under. In 1897, he was the Democratic candidate for the Senate. The church opposed him with all its vigor, even though many of the legislators who were Mormons supported him. Finally, after a hard fight, he lost on the fifty-third ballot. He was politically destroyed.

Yet the church leaders were not finished with him.

In the summer of 1897 they formally charged him with apostasy and un-Christian conduct. He was tried before a church group, the High Council of Salt Lake City. The finding was that he must admit he was wrong and most apologize or be excommunicated.

Thatcher wanted to stay in the church so he agreed he had been wrong to oppose the LDS leaders in their political decisions. He lived for twelve more years in Salt Lake City. On his death, his piety and devotion to the Restored Gospel were praised widely. Now he was completely finished and the men who had brought him down could afford to be generous with words.

This case established quite clearly in the minds of all Mormon politicians that they must pay attention to the church leaders. Meanwhile, the leadership had turned to another project very dear to it. What really was needed, it was felt, was a member of the Council of Twelve Apostles in the United States Senate.

Wilford Woodruff, a marvelous old man who saw God's hand in every leaf that fell, and who lived to see the frail colony of Saints grow into the state of Utah, died in San Francisco September 2, 1898. Lorenzo Snow, whose sister Eliza was first the plural wife of the Prophet Joseph and then of Brigham Young, became president of the Saints. He died in October, 1901, and was succeeded by Joseph F. Smith, the son of Hyrum and the nephew of Joseph.

In 1900, perhaps at the urging of Joseph F. Smith, President Snow had appointed as an apostle Reed Smoot, the son of Abraham Smoot who had been sent by Brigham Young to Provo to establish a Stake of Zion and later to open Brigham Young Academy.

Joseph F. Smith had become a Republican when the People's Party was abolished in 1891. Some commentators have argued that his pushing for punishment of Moses Thatcher was in part because Thatcher was a Democrat. Reed Smoot was a Republican.

In 1903 Smoot was elected to the United States Senate from Utah. There was no serious conflict. The Mormons in the legislature accepted the dictation from President Smith that the apostle was to represent the church in Washington and that was that. He was elected.

The problem was in Washington.

Perhaps emboldened by their success in the Roberts case, the anti-Mormon elements in Utah moved immediately against Apostle Smoot. They petitioned that he be denied his seat as Roberts had been denied his. The Senate's hearings on this went on for four years and resulted in shaking the church's new found confidence so that finally the leadership began actually to try to stop polygamy.

It is of great importance that a whole generation of Mormons was wedded politically to the conservatism and Republicanism of Reed Smoot, who became a leader in the writing of protectionist tariffs. Because Senator Smoot was an apostle of the LDS church, the Mormons tended to look upon the attack against him as really an attack on their church. Indeed, it was just that. So they stuck with him from 1903 through the constitutional change when senators became elected by popular vote and did not abandon him until 1932 when he was defeated by a fellow Mormon, but a liberal Democrat, a professor of political science at the University of Utah, Elbert Thomas.

During all those years of the presidency of Joseph F.

Smith, the church leadership had favored the Republican party, perhaps in large part because Smoot was a Republican and could open the church doors for his party friends and the party doors for his church colleagues.

President Smith was in many ways the transitional leader of the LDS church. Before him were the men who had known the Prophet Joseph, who had known Nauvoo, who had suffered the leadership duties of the march to the desert. All the presidents before him had been born before the Restoration of the Gospel. He was born in 1838 during a storm at Far West, Missouri, while his father, Hyrum, was held prisoner by the Missourians who fully intended to kill him.

A mark has been left on the political outlook of the top levels of the church by the fact that during this period of transition, the chief political advisor of the LDS president was the conservative Republican, Reed Smoot.

The three presidents who have followed Joseph F. Smith all were born in Utah and they represent the modern age of the LDS church. The immediate successor was Heber J. Grant. Except for Brigham Young, who ruled for more than three decades, President Grant's tenure from 1918 to 1945 was the longest. It was in his time that the church reputedly achieved its greatest financial success. It also grew rapidly so that by his death there were just under a million Saints. But in President Grant's time, the church was unable to maintain the close political control that it had exercised during the earlier years. The first unmistakable sign of this was the 1932 election of Professor Thomas to defeat the Apostle-Senator Smoot.

Professor Frank Jonas of the University of Utah maintains that the LDS officials never forgave Thomas and that they were intent for the next eighteen years on defeating him, a mission that was accomplished in 1950. Professor Jonas recounts a fascinating story to show the political attitudes of President Grant and the relationship with Senator Thomas. The story:

> Senator Thomas and his daughter, Chiyo, who had served as a missionary for the Church, had just completed dinner with President Heber J. Grant in his home, when Senator Thomas made his request for a blessing. President Grant, who had suffered a severe stroke in 1939, and whose condition had become progressively worse, reasonably declined, saying he had discontinued performing that function. Then something "touched him," for he went into what was described as an hysterical tirade against the New Deal and President Roosevelt. His hatred for both was well-known. Senator Thomas, a Democrat, had become the symbol of the New Deal in Utah, and though he was a loyal and devout member of the Mormon church, he was not considered to be "in line with the thinking of the Brethren," and consequently he inherited by association, correctly, or incorrectly, the hatred the General Authorities held for the Democratic administration in Washington. No one could have felt worse than Senator Thomas himself as the result of this incident in the home of the Mormon President.

This happened in 1942 and President Grant died in 1945. He was then in his eighty-ninth year, another illustration that the church is run by aged men. The rulers—the First Presidency, the leading members of the Council of Twelve Apostles—are always old men, for this is the inevitable result of selection of leadership by seniority. With old men always in control, the pattern of thought and action from the leadership is always more conservative than it might otherwise be. The organizational system also prevents any take-over by the "Young Turks" in some moment of strife. The last take-over was in Nauvoo in 1844 when Brigham Young moved to fill the void left by the murder of the Prophet Joseph and his brother, the Patriarch Hyrum.

The economic, theological and social radicalism of the

days of Joseph Smith and Brigham Young has long since disappeared. Since political radicalism is but the horse that carries these other and really meaningful forms of radicalism, the Mormons have not been political radicals for many, many years.

George Albert Smith, who succeeded Heber J. Grant, was seventy-five years old when he became LDS president. He lived for six years, and was succeeded by David O. McKay in April, 1951, when McKay was seventy-seven. The greatest growth the LDS church has known has been during McKay's administration, and a significant change in political attitude has come about also.

The church has become somewhat more liberal than it was in the days of Heber J. Grant.

Two important political events occurred while George Albert Smith was LDS president. In 1948 a rightist radical from Salt Lake City, J. Bracken Lee, was elected Governor of Utah. He is not a member of the Mormon church. But as will become apparent, Lee has been a dominant figure in Utah politics since 1948. Although he has had more important defeats than victories, he has controlled events and made his weight felt more than any other recent political figure in the state.

The other major political event during the George Albert Smith presidency was the defeat of Senator Thomas by Wallace F. Bennett, a member of an important Mormon family, the son-in-law of the late President Heber J. Grant, and a former president of the National Association of Manufacturers.

Professor Jonas makes a strong argument that the Thomas defeat was engineered through the connivance of some leadership elements of the church. Jonas said that the vehicle was a letter listing church-approved candidates. Senator Thomas was not on this list; Wallace Bennett was. Further, said Jonas, the church had "carefully prepared the stage."

"Briefly, the Mormon church writers and spokesmen identified capitalism with its doctrine of free agency, thereby placing it to the height of a moral plane," Jonas said. "They established atheistic socialism as the opposite of capitalism. Senator Thomas was identified with atheistic socialism and Wallace F. Bennett was made to stand for 'faith and freedom.'"

The man who sent out the letter was a retired Army colonel, Elmer Thomas. Professor Jonas said that Colonel Thomas told him the letter and list had "the blessings of the brethren," i.e., the support of church leaders. However, some of the church leaders denied that they backed the proposal and LDS President George Albert Smith went to some lengths to disavow the attacks on Senator Thomas.

The senator himself credited his defeat principally to the American Medical Association and the Mormon Church. The AMA was out to beat him because he supported a federal medical health insurance bill introduced by the Truman administration. That bill identified for the AMA those political figures who would support such legislation. It went after them hammer-and-tongs and helped to run some, such as Senator Thomas, out of public life. It was not until 1965 that a federal health care insurance plan was passed, and even then it was only for persons over sixty-five years of age.

There was little question that Bennett was closer to the inside "club" of the General Authorities of the LDS church than was Senator Thomas. Bennett had been an official of the Deseret Sunday School General Board since 1938 and his family had extensive marriage and business ties with some of the General Authorities. He was re-elected in 1956 and 1962.

Meantime, J. Bracken Lee as Governor of Utah was reaping a harvest of national publicity as he stood up against almost every liberal thought since the abolition of slavery.

(The record does not show if he was questioned about abolition of slavery.) In 1952 he ran again for governor and sailed into his second term. By 1956 many people in Utah were tired of his antics.

Governor Lee was after a third term, but he was forced into a head-and-head primary runoff with George Dewey Clyde, an engineering professor. Clyde is a very devout, practicing member of the Mormon priesthood. Clyde won, and it appeared that Lee was out of politics. However, this was more apparent than real. He took a deep breath and established himself as an independent candidate. He ran third.

Governor Clyde was elected with only 38.2 per cent of the vote. Lee had made lots of people mad. He had vetoed a Sunday closing bill in 1954, when the church wanted it to help keep the Sabbath holy. The Sons of Utah Pioneers wanted to use the abandoned site of the old Sugarhouse state penitentiary for a museum and park. Lee said they couldn't. Utah pioneers were almost all Mormon; so are their sons. The church wanted to condemn some land near Brigham Young University. Lee would not help. Beyond all of this, he was a 32nd degree Mason. In Utah, Mormons and Masons do not go together.

The final pre-election tipoff that the church was now anti-Lee came when the *Deseret News* dug out details of lax practices of the Utah State Liquor Control Commission which allowed minors to get liquor. The *News* showed that state employees were giving money to Lee's campaign.

But in spite of losing his re-election to the governorship, Lee was not a dead horse in Utah politics. In 1958 he engineered the defeat of Senator Arthur V. Watkins, one of the strongest political figures in the state, and the election of Frank E. Moss, a Democrat. Lee succeeded this time in the tactic that had failed in 1956. By injecting himself into the race as an independent, he was able to defeat the Republican candidate and elect the Democrat.

In 1959 he was elected Mayor of Salt Lake City where he follows the same right wing path and same publicity-seeking activities he used as governor. In 1962, he tried for the Republican nomination for the Senate, but Senator Wallace F. Bennett beat him easily. In 1963 he was re-elected mayor. He travels a lot making speeches at right wing rallies.

Mayor Lee is no Mormon, and has been effectively contained with the help of the LDS church. Yet he is a man of great political talent and may come back to power again. His activities made up just one of the two spectacles in the 1958 election. The competing apostles was the other. Moses Thatcher would never have believed the sight that was run out for the voters of Utah.

First, it should be remembered that Apostle Ezra Taft Benson had been given permission by the First Presidency in 1953 to serve as President Eisenhower's Secretary of Agriculture. He was still an apostle. But he was a Republican apostle. Naturally the Republican party used him frequently in areas where Mormons live. In 1956, he endorsed George Dewey Clyde for governor. He endorsed Wallace Bennett for the Senate. In 1958 he came to Utah again, this time to speak for the re-election of Senator Arthur V. Watkins.

Hugh B. Brown, the most liberal member of the Council of Twelve Apostles, had just been "set apart" as an apostle in April, 1958. In the summer some of the Mormon leaders who also were Democratic party officials called on President McKay and asked that Brown be permitted to go on the stump for the Democrats to match the Republican act featuring Apostle-Secretary Benson. McKay agreed.

Brown was the keynote speaker at the state Democratic nominating convention. He endorsed all the Democratic candidates. He made rude remarks about Sherman Adams, the Eisenhower right-hand man who was accused of taking gratuities from people who had trouble with federal regulatory agencies.

"Brown's presence in the campaign had made it respectable for a Mormon once again to stand up among the members of his church and be counted as a Democrat," said Professor Jonas in his analysis of the 1958 election. "In the meantime, Benson gave several political speeches in Utah. It was apparent that his appeal was gone; the novelty in this election year was not a Mormon apostle in the President's cabinet but a Mormon apostle campaigning for the Democrats, something that had not happened in the state perhaps since shortly after statehood—which came in 1896."

The Benson political appeal was entirely gone, it became obvious in 1962. Reed A. Benson, son of the apostle, tried for the Republican congressional nomination from Salt Lake City. He was badly beaten and soon announced his appointment as a Utah official of the John Birch Society.

Later Reed Benson went to Washington to live, where many Mormons have spent time. George Romney was there for a while before going out to Detroit as the head of American Motors; Stewart Udall currently is the Mormon in the cabinet, having moved in with John F. Kennedy as Ezra Taft Benson left with Dwight D. Eisenhower. There are three Mormons in the Senate, and eight in the House of Representatives in the 89th Congress. The Saints have political strength beyond the borders of Utah. Mormon settlements in the early days formed a crescent across the Mountain West, beginning in the Snake River valley in eastern Idaho, stretching down across Utah into Arizona and Nevada, and into California where it was Mormons who founded the city of San Bernardino.

Today's major Mormon concentrations are along this same line, and it is these concentrations that give the church

Brigham fanned them out to settlements where he thought
the purposes of the church were best served. Those in Idaho
took to the land, irrigated it, raised families, sent their sons
on missions, tithed and prospered. All through those towns
across southern Idaho there are Mormon chapels. The
newspapers carry much news and advertising directed at
the Saints. They advertise genealogy charts made up in the
newspaper printing shop. They carry ads from the J. C.
Penney stores for a sale of "entire stock of LDS garments at
new low prices."

There were in 1965 about 180,000 Mormons in Idaho, and
the state had a population of about 700,000. The legislature
then had forty-four senators and fifty-nine representatives.
Just over a third of the legislature was Mormon with sixteen senators and twenty representatives. The rest was a
mixture of Methodists, Catholics, Presbyterians, Congrega-
tionalists, Episcopalians, members of the Church of Christ,
Baptists, Lutherans, Unitarians and atheists.

The Saints have come a long way in Idaho since the territorial days when they were hated by the Gentiles who
wrote the first constitution and laws of Idaho. Idaho was
admitted as a state on July 3, 1890, at the very height of the
federal campaign to force Mormons to abandon polygamy,
which they did through The Manifesto the following October. Eastern Idaho was full of polygamous families.

The first Idaho constitution carried a section which pro-
hibited people of certain classes from voting, serving as jur-
ors, or holding civil office. The law barred idiots and the
insane, ex-convicts, vote buyers or sellers, prisoners in jail,
Chinese or persons of Mongolian descent not born in the
United States, and Indians who lived on the reservations.
But most of that constitutional provision was devoted to
describing the other single group banned from the voting
place and from public office.

its political clout. Deferring for the moment tl
of Mormon voting strength and political contr
where they are in the majority, it is important to
spread of the church into the surrounding states
important voting bloc that it has built up in the
example in Arizona something approaching 10 per
the vote is Mormon, and this is concentrated in the Ph
Mesa area. Representative Morris Udall, a Democrat,
Saint. In California, the more than a quarter million Sa
are swallowed up statistically in more than 18 million pe
ple. But again there is a concentration, this time in th
San Fernando Valley.

In Nevada, which had 285,278 people in 1960, there were
just under 40,000 Mormons. Of these, about 22,500 are concentrated in the Las Vegas-Lake Mead area of southern Nevada. In 1964, Senator Howard Cannon, a Democrat and a
Saint who had some problems created by the Bobby Baker
case, was opposed in a bitter campaign by the Republican
lieutenant governor, Paul Laxalt, a Catholic and a member
of a prominent Basque family from northern Nevada. Senator Cannon sneaked in with a winning margin that would
have fitted easily around the crap tables of any one of the
Strip casinos. Without 40,000 Nevada Mormons he would
never have made it.

Mormon influence on politics in Idaho best illustrates
LDS political action outside Utah. One of the Mormon
Temples is located at Idaho Falls on the Snake River a few
miles west of the Grand Tetons and Yellowstone Park. The
Snake runs through a broad valley there, and where the ancient lava flows have decayed, an elaborate network of
irrigation supports just the sort of small town and agricul-
ture-oriented society where the Saints feel most comfortable.

From the time of Brigham Young, the Saints have lived
in eastern Idaho. The immigrants arrived in Salt Lake City;

This was the bigamist or polygamist who lived in plural or celestial marriage. It included anyone who taught polygamy. It also included anyone who "is a member of, or contributes to the support, aid, or encouragement of, any order, organization, association, corporation, or society, which teaches, advises, counsels, encourages, or aids any person to enter into bigamy, polygamy or such patriarchal or plural marriage, or which teaches or advises that the laws of this state prescribing rules of civil conduct are not the supreme law of the State."

In modern times the state constitution has been revised to remove these inhibitions on Indians and "persons of Mongolian descent." But persons who teach the doctrine set out in Section 132 of *Doctrine and Covenants* on plural marriage still are covered in the section. The LDS church, of course, no longer teaches that doctrine and excommunicates any member caught teaching or practicing it. But the state constitution of Idaho still carries a provision equating the doctrine of plural marriage with idiocy and criminal activity.

The Saints have become very powerful politically in Idaho, and historically have allied themselves with the Democrats, although in the post World War II period this has changed rapidly. The chief reason for inclining to the Democrats was that the Republicans controlled the constitutional convention in 1889 and wrote the provision barring polygamists from public affairs.

Hamer Budge, the former congressman, was one of the first Saints to break out of Idaho into national politics. His father had been a state supreme court justice. However, in recent years the eastern Idaho congressional seat (the state has two seats) has been a Mormon property. The county offices in eastern Idaho are dominated by the Saints, and Mormons are state auditor, secretary of state and state superintendent of public instruction. Mormons are a majority on the state land board.

In the usual political race where the LDS church itself was not the issue, no candidate who had angered the leaders of the church could win a statewide election in Idaho. The Mormons could be outvoted only when the otherwise divided Gentile majority could be united against them. However, the Saints have not yet elected one of the major state officers. Senator Frank Church, Democrat, Senator Len Jordan, Republican, and Governor Robert E. Smylie, Republican, all are Gentiles.

Elements of the LDS church have tried hard to gain some further political advantage in Idaho. In July and August, 1956, John Corlett, the veteran and respected political writer of the *Idaho Statesman* at Boise, printed the details of a Mormon plan to try to use the church's marvelous organization to nominate Mormons as the senatorial candidates of both parties. Corlett said he doubted that the scheme had the approval of the First Presidency in Salt Lake City. But it had the approval of a large segment of the Mormon leadership in Idaho.

In June, 1956, key leaders of the church were organized as "Citizens for Better Government Committee." They picked directors of their committee in each stake across Idaho. The stake directors then organized ward support. They were to try to capture the precinct committee offices of each party. Registration was to be pushed—among Mormons.

The plan failed. Everybody criticized the backers of the committee. A Mormon editor in Rexburg, John C. Porter, wrote: "No candidate should use a church organization to seek votes. The separation of church and state is too firmly entrenched in the minds of the American public to stand for this, and regardless of the fine purposes, and principles in-

volved, the public will resent and vote against those candidates who are involved."

This was the truth as Porter saw it. My cynical opinion is
that if the plan had worked and through its use the Saints
had elected one of their members as a senator from Idaho,
the men who devised it would have been on the road for
years to other Mormon areas to make talks on the "Keys of
Successful Political Application of the Principles of LDS
Organization."

The Mormon strength in eastern Idaho had reached the
point in 1964 where Mormons could afford to fight with
each other. The result was a fascinating opportunity to
glimpse some of the internal strains in the high levels of the
church, as well as to see how the Saints line up to shield the
sanctity of the First Presidency and Apostles.

These events began in late 1962 and early 1963 after Reed
Benson openly allied himself with the John Birch Society.
His father then answered criticism by pointing to things
about the Birch Society that he thought were laudable. On
September 25, 1963, Ralph Harding, a Mormon who was
the Democratic representative from the eastern Idaho district, stood up in the House of Representatives and criticized Apostle Benson for supporting the radical right. Mr.
Harding wanted to make it plain that the LDS church was
not a branch of the Birch Society.

After his speech he began to get reports of dissatisfaction
among the Saints back home along the Snake River. They
felt it was not very intelligent of the Congressman to wash
the church's linens in public . . . certainly not on the floor
of the House. Of course, Harding also got nice notes from
people who thought he had done well. He even got one
from General Dwight D. Eisenhower who always has resented the attacks made on him by Robert Welch suggesting
that Ike was at the least a Communist dupe. Also, the for-

mer President was hurt that his old friend and cabinet member, Apostle Benson, could give any comfort to such as Welch.

"Your honest and unselfish effort to set the record straight is something that warms my heart," Ike told Harding.

Then in October, 1963, Apostle Benson was exiled to Frankfurt, Germany, to run the European LDS mission. The church said publicly that the assignment had nothing to do with Benson's pro-Birch Society positions. His assignment came within three weeks of his speech at the October, 1963, conference of the church, when he said that church members should "come to the aid of patriots, programs and organizations aiming to preserve the constitution" against threatened socialism and communism. In short, he picked the most prominent forum in the church to enunciate right wing doctrine. David O. McKay sent him out of the country. (Trouble was to resume when he returned two years later.)

This should have satisfied Representative Harding, but his sensitive antennae (and politicians have the most sensitive sort) still detected little pockets of ill will toward him because he had criticized one of the Apostles of Christ. So he sacked up packages of copies of twenty-three letters he had received commending him for his attack on Benson. He sent these to Mormon friends in his district (using government envelopes and his franking privilege, certainly) with a note to show them to "friends" but not to reporters.

"It is obvious that Harding wanted wide circulation of the letters among the members of the (LDS) church," John Corlett wrote in the *Idaho Statesman* in February, 1964, because of course reporters saw the letters.

Three were made completely public, and this really put the fat in the fire for Representative Harding. The one from Eisenhower made no difference. But the other two were disastrous for him. One was from Joseph Fielding Smith, the senior apostle and heir to the LDS presidency. The *Idaho State Journal* at Pocatello said that Apostle Smith's letter contained this revealing paragraph:

"I am glad to report to you that it will be some time before we hear anything from Brother Benson, who is now on his way to Great Britain where I suppose he will be at least for the next two years. When he returns, I hope his blood will be purified."

Now this was just deadly. It showed that indeed the church had exiled an apostle for publicly expressing his political views, and stuck the pin in the balloon of denials that had been floated. It showed a deep division of political thought among the group of men all supposed to receive the Word directly from God. The *Salt Lake Tribune* checked the story with Apostle Smith. He said:

"I don't recall writing 'when he returns, I hope his blood will be purified.' If I did write such a statement, I meant that when he returned he would be free of all political ties."

The apostle also observed that the letter was personal to Harding and was not intended for publication. A child could have seen the axe coming.

Yet there was more.

The third letter revealed by the Pocatello paper was from Robert McKay, a son of the LDS president. It said:

"We shall all be relieved when Elder Benson ceases to resist counsel and returns to a concentration on those affairs befitting his office. It is my feeling that there will be an immediate and noticeable curtailment of his Birch Society activities."

McKay said Harding sent him a copy of the anti-Benson speech of September, 1963, and asked that it be shown to President McKay.

It was apparent that Harding had solicited the laudatory letters, then had produced a limited number of them and had circulated copies among Mormons in his district. They had leaked out and betrayed the church's inner secrets. The next day Harding talked forlornly of retiring from public life. From Geneva, Switzerland, Apostle Benson issued a statement:

"The vicious and unwarranted attack by Congressman Harding is unworthy of comment. I am surprised and disappointed that any responsible person would be duped into giving it notice."

Representative Harding did not leave public office willingly, in spite of his earlier talk of it. He ran as the Democratic candidate in November, 1964, and even though Lyndon Johnson carried the state in the presidential race, Harding lost to a little-known, thirty-three-year-old city commissioner from Pocatello, George Hansen. Hansen is a Mormon and his big margins were in Boise and Idaho Falls.

The presidential election year of 1964 also created troubles for the church in Utah. Early in the game Senator Barry M. Goldwater's supporters sewed up the Utah delegation to the Republican convention. By early spring it was apparent that only the entrance of George Romney, a sort of native son, as a declared candidate, would keep the Utah delegation away from Goldwater. It is apparent in retrospect that the church leaders were not avidly for Goldwater. In 1960, President McKay betrayed an ever-so-slight leaning toward Richard M. Nixon, although John F. Kennedy was able to impress the Mormons just by speaking to them properly. Senator Kennedy knew enough to talk of "the Prophet Joseph" and was able to find some kind things to say about the Saints.

"If we got to have a Catholic, I guess Kennedy is as good as any and better than most," said one Mormon.

The LDS problem in 1964 was the candidacy of Ernest L. Wilkinson for the United States Senate. Wilkinson was a successful lawyer, the director of the church educational system, the president and builder of the Brigham Young University, and a man widely respected in the upper levels of the church. However, he also was a strong conservative, fully at home with the political and economic views of Senator Goldwater. Senator Frank E. Moss, who was elected in 1958 when J. Bracken Lee split the opposition, is a Mormon and a respected man. But he did not have the church credentials of Wilkinson.

However, Moss got the votes and was re-elected.

Some Mormons were offended by what they read of a visit Wilkinson and Goldwater paid to President McKay, then ninety-one years old and just recovering from an illness. It appeared in the accounts that Wilkinson was trying to lead the aged man into some sort of a public endorsement. It did not come.

The Harding case shows that the church can decide— even in Idaho—that a man will not get the Mormon vote if he has been offensive. In the Wilkinson case, it is obvious that mere religious credentials are not enough to cancel out other factors.

But what is the church power to shape the votes of persons in office? Can the LDS First Presidency change the voting paterns of a legislature or a political convention? The answer is mixed and can be read from three stories of political events.

First, consider a matter at the heart of doctrine where the church lost. Here is the way Joseph Fielding Smith tells it in *Essentials of Church History*:

REPEAL OF THE EIGHTEENTH AMENDMENT.—In the year 1918, the people of the United States amended the Constitution of the United States prohibiting the manufacture, possession and sale of liquor. Immediately following this action the liquor interests of the country commenced a vigorous campaign to bring about the repeal of this amendment. Propaganda was carried on vigorously through the press and the people were made to believe that the condition under prohibition was worse than before the amendment was adopted. In the general election of 1933, enough states voted for repeal to make such action effective. Utah, contrary to the wishes of the General Authorities of the Church, joined with the majority of the states in demanding repeal, and the Beehive State held the doubtful, if not disgraceful, position of being the thirty-sixth state of the Union to hold a constitutional convention and thus brought about ratification of repeal. Since that action liquor has been flowing freely throughout the land, crime and drunkenness have increased and the sale of liquor and tobacco has become an outstanding menace to our youth.

The shame of it! Utah gave the final shove that turned the nation back toward the rumpot! Nor could the LDS leaders stop it, even though this was an issue bearing directly on the question of doctrine in the Word of Wisdom. The vote, of course, was in a convention, and we can never know if the electorate of Utah would have stood up against the demands of the First Presidency to vote to continue prohibition.

However, the LDS leadership has not lost entirely. Utah has never had liquor by the drink as it is understood in most other states. In Utah nothing but 3.2 per cent beer is sold by the glass. Hard liquor and wine must be purchased at stores operated by the state. Until 1965 buyers needed a liquor purchase permit for which they paid a fee. There were no real bars in all of Utah. If one wanted to drink in a bar, he took his bottle with him and the bartender mixed his drinks from the bottle.

Frequently over the years as the state's tourism became more important it was pointed out that this system was hardship for the operators of resorts. But no action was taken. In 1965, it was proposed that the state create a system whereby it would license a few places in better hotels, restaurants and resorts to sell those 1.6 ounce miniature bottles so that customers could mix them at their tables.

A careful plan was made. Loyal Mormon members of the legislature wanted to have the bill passed. They took the proposal around Salt Lake City to various power centers for reaction. They wanted to discover if the LDS church would oppose it. The reactions came and none was negative. The bill was introduced and appeared ready for passage. Then the *Deseret News* editorially denounced it as an immoral piece of legislation that would bring the evils of alcohol that much closer to all the people of the state.

That was it. The bill died with scarcely a quiver. The Church of Jesus Christ of Latter-day Saints had spoken. The Mormon-dominated legislature reacted swiftly.

In the final example of the church in political affairs, we have an instance where it went out strongly and was rebuffed.

Section 14(b) of the Taft-Hartley Act specifically permitted the separate states to have laws that outlawed union contracts that required union membership as a condition of employment. The states then could individually outlaw the closed shop. Since we live in a time when the name of a thing is at least as important as the thing itself, these state enactments to hamper union organization and favor employers became known as "right to work laws."

How on earth does this involve the Mormon church? Well, for one thing, Utah was one of nineteen states that passed a right to work law. But more importantly, David O. McKay believes that compulsory labor union membership is an evil thing. He believes that this infringes on the right of free agency, the Mormon religious doctrine. This doctrine holds that God put mankind on earth with the right for each individual to choose his way of life. Each person then has an opportunity to better the condition of his soul if he follows the Restored Gospel. President McKay thinks that compulsory union membership for a laboring man inhibits his exercise of his free agency.

So on June 22, 1965, President McKay and his two counselors, Hugh B. Brown and Nathan Eldon Tanner, wrote a letter to three United States senators and eight representatives in Congress urging them to vote against President Lyndon B. Johnson's attempt to repeal section 14(b) of the Taft-Hartley Act because this would repeal the nineteen state right to work laws. Only the Mormon members of Congress got the letters; the First Presidency ignored the Gentiles there.

The senators to whom the letters went were the two from Utah, Bennett, Republican, and Moss, Democrat, and Cannon, Democrat, of Nevada.

The Democrats in the House who got the letters were John E. Moss, Kenneth W. Dyal and Richard T. Hanna of California, Morris K. Udall of Arizona, and David S. King of Utah; the Republican representatives were Laurence J. Burton of Utah, George V. Hansen of Idaho, and Del M. Clawson of California.

The letter signed by the three members of the First Presidency told the Mormon legislators:

> At the very basis of all our doctrine stands the right to free agency of man. We are in favor of maintaining this free agency to the greatest extent possible. We look adversely upon any infringement thereof not essential to the proper exercise of police power of the state . . .
>
> We respectfully express the hope that no action will be taken by the Congress of the United States that would in any way interfere with the God-given rights of men to exercise free agency in seeking and maintaining work privileges.

Five of the Democratic members—Senator Moss, Representatives Moss, Dyal, Hanna and Udall—all signed a joint letter. They said that they would not heed the attempt of the Mormon president to give them religious instruction on casting their votes. They wrote:

We yield to none of our brothers in our dedication to the protection of the God-given rights of our fellow citizens. While we respect and revere the offices held by the members of the First Presidency of the church, we cannot yield to others our responsibilities to our constituency, nor can we delegate our own Free Agency to any but ourselves. We know that each of you will agree that in this instance we act in conformity with the highest principles of our church in declining to be swayed by the views expressed in the communications.

In signing the letter, Udall also said that he was going to vote the way the First Presidency indicated, but only because Arizona had a right to work law and he felt compelled to uphold it.

If the four Republicans replied to the letter from McKay, Brown and Tanner, the replies were not made public. The Republican position in the Congress was in accord with that of the LDS leadership, and presumably the four would have endorsed the LDS statement.

The repeal passed the House of Representatives by 221 to 203. It died on the vine in the Senate. But it will probably come up again, since President Johnson seems to be obligated to get it passed. Will the church try to use pressure on Mormon members again in order to defeat it?

The ramifications of the LDS attempt to move into national politics on this question could be far-reaching. The election of John F. Kennedy in 1960 brushed away many of the cobwebs of bigotry from the minds of those political manipulators who decide far in advance which men to support for the presidency. If a Catholic can be elected, could not a Mormon? If Kennedy could overcome all the political liabilities of youth, religion, wealth and regional accent . . .

However, during his campaign Catholicism was a tremendous problem for Kennedy. But one can use the First Presidency letter on repeal of 14(b) as a model and concoct an example of something that would have destroyed Kennedy's chances. Just visualize what would have happened if the Democratic nominee in the fall of 1960 had received a publicized letter along these lines:

> DEAR JACK:
> I hope you'll follow the position of your church if you're elected and any questions about birth control come across your desk.
>
> JOHN XXIII

To me the action of the First Presidency of the LDS church to protect the right to work laws is exactly analogous to this somewhat frivolously presented hypothetical example.

However, the way the legislative Saints reacted to the First Presidency letter demonstrates the fundamental relationship between the church and its members in politics today. One man in Salt Lake City said it very well:

"When they can make it a real moral issue, the church leaders can get support for their side from their members. When they can make it a matter of protection of the church, they can win. The rest of the time they get beat."

XI

George Romney—
Latter-day Saint

THIS HANDSOME, DISTINGUISHED man stood in front of his hometown audience and said:

"I believe the constitution and Bill of Rights entitle all persons to equal opportunity in every field. I believe the most urgent national problems are civil rights."

The scene was the dining room on top of the Hotel Utah in Salt Lake City. The time was mid-January, 1964. The audience included most of the business leaders of the area, and three of the apostles of the LDS church.

The speaker was George Romney, home for a visit and for a major tribute to be held that night at a banquet hall at the other end of the business district. He discussed the Republican presidential possibilities of 1964. (In retrospect, he looks even better than he did that day, for he warned that his party had to honor the Negro drive for equality in civil rights or face a crushing defeat in dishonor.)

His audience was not exclusively Mormon, but still it was a place where a co-religionist would ask if being a Mormon had been damaging to Romney's political career. It had not, said the Governor of Michigan, although "it is true that I have been attacked in both my business and political careers because of it."

After his talk, and after the well-wishers had thinned away, I asked him to discuss further the civil rights problem and the companion problem of the LDS theological bias against Negroes. He wanted to duck, and couldn't. He said these things:

"The church dealt with the civil rights question . . . I'm not going to interject religion in politics . . . There is no conflict between church principles and a complete civil rights program . . . There is no concept that a Negro cannot attain as much in the church as I can."

Our exchange was not acrimonious, but he was pressed hard, and after two years as governor of Michigan and eight years as the president of American Motors, he disliked being pressed hard for answers beyond those that he gave the first time the question was asked.

Finally, he said he felt it would be productive of greater understanding to talk to Joseph Fielding Smith, the leading LDS theologian who also was at the breakfast. That day Apostle Smith gave me the statement of the church position on Negroes quoted extensively in an earlier chapter. The essence of this was that God was responsible for the discrimination and that only God could open the LDS priesthood to Negroes.

That night at the testimonial banquet Romney warned of the danger to the Republican party in a campaign in 1964 based on an appeal to the prejudice against Negroes. That speech was ten months before the Goldwater-Miller campaign ended in disaster for the Republicans. Here is a part of what Governor Romney said that night:

"If the Republican party tries to buy the White House with the rights of others, it will become the greatest white elephant in the history of party politics . . . Let me emphasize again, the Republican party must not exploit racial or religious prejudices in order to gain a victory at the polls. To do so would be to disavow the heritage of Abraham Lincoln, to destroy part of the heritage of America, and to renounce the spiritual heritage of the Judeo-Christian world."

In the summer of 1964 when the Republican platform was being written downtown in San Francisco and the party was moving through the dreary disaster of nominating Barry M. Goldwater and William E. Miller at the Cow Palace in suburban Daly City, Romney was one of the brave band of moderate Republicans who fought and lost. They tried to keep the Grand Old Party from running a racist, radical-rightest campaign. They failed.

The heroes of that convention were men like Nelson Rockefeller, the governor of New York; George Romney, the governor of Michigan; John Love, the governor of Colorado; William Scranton, the governor of Pennsylvania; Robert E. Smylie, the governor of Idaho; Mark Hatfield, the governor of Oregon; and a scattered few among the delegates who kicked and fought and refused to be counted, no matter what, in support of a ticket nominated on a promise to uphold the standards of the racists and radical conservatives.

Romney and these others opposed the Goldwater forces not only on the racial bias question, but on the whole matter of the support that was pouring in from the economic and historical illiterates who made up the radical strength at the convention.

Of course, they lost. Remember Nelson Rockefeller, standing on that platform determined to be heard despite the boos of the ill-mannered and power-hungry right wing radicals? Great political courage was demonstrated at the convention; Romney was a part of the courageous group.

These scenes and thoughts came to mind a year later while I was in Lansing, Michigan, waiting to interview Governor Romney about various aspects of his religious faith. This was in the first week in August, 1965, and a cool, cloudy day was at hand. The temperature was 58 degrees and a chill wind blew through a light summer suit. Lansing is not so attractive in any light as is Salt Lake City.

The seat of government is located in a spacious four-block square, surrounded by lawn and trees. The graceful dome and spire seem over-delicate for the blocky buildings and the five floors of offices. A ladder climbs the side of the dome and manages to spoil the effect of those views where it can be seen. Among the trees in the lawn there are statues and memorials to the Civil War, the Spanish War, other wars, but no statue anywhere to Brigham Young.

Across the street is the Plymouth Congregational Church and down the street the Masonic Temple. The skins and hair of the people on the street are a shade darker than the blond, golden Scandinavian look of Salt Lake City street crowds.

Governor Romney and his staff occupy a corner suite of offices in the capital. It was strange to remember that this job was held for twelve years by G. Mennen Williams, the liberal Democrat. Contrasts could scarcely be wider in the backgrounds of two successful men. Williams was born to great inherited wealth, had the doors all open for him from childhood, and needed only to march through them. Perhaps he went into politics because here was a set of doors that only he could open for himself. Romney was born with nothing like that position. His father was never a successful businessman, and Romney has no college degree, except those his renown have brought him in return for speeches at the commencement exercises of others.

Romney was born into the Mormon church. His birthplace was Chihuahua, Mexico, in the Mormon polygamist colony there. He was born in 1907, when plural marriage had passed its peak and after the Reed Smoot investigation by the United States Senate had frightened church leaders into finally acting on their commitments of the 1890 Manifesto to stop plural marriage. Like all Mormons born into the church, Romney has heavily in his consciousness the church's history of polygamy. His father was Gaskell Romney who had just one wife, Anna Amelia Pratt. But behind them his family tree for two or three generations is full of polygamists.

"Polygamists on both sides," he said with a shrug.

The Mormon penchant for genealogy makes Romney's family tree easily traced. In his press secretary's office was a copy of *The Story of George Romney—Builder, Salesman, Crusader,* written by Tom Mahoney and published by Harper and Brothers in 1960. This is one of those friendly biographies. It tells a little of Governor Romney's family tree.

Miles Romney, a carpenter born in 1807, was converted to Mormonism in his native England by the early apostle, Orson Hyde. With his wife, Elizabeth Gaskell, Miles Romney sailed for the United States on February 7, 1841, to join the main body of the church then flourishing at Nauvoo in the last years of Joseph Smith's life.

Their third child, Miles Park Romney, was born in Nauvoo on August 18, 1843. After the church was shattered in 1844 with the martyrdom of the Prophet Joseph and Patriarch Hyrum, the family moved here and there until in 1850 it went to Salt Lake City by ox team. Brigham Young sent the carpenter, Miles Romney, to St. George in Southern Utah to help build things. In 1877, Miles Romney died in a fall from a window while building the St. George Tabernacle.

Meanwhile, in 1862 Miles Park Romney had married his first wife and in 1867 married his second and had a third wife when he went to Mexico in the 1880s to avoid arrest by federal officials. Miles Park Romney was a lively, colorful figure in the polygamist colonies of Mexico.

One of the sons of Miles Park Romney was named Gaskell, in recollection of the maiden name of the English girl who came to Nauvoo in 1841. This was the father of the governor of Michigan. As with so many Mormon families, the Romney story has fascination and scope. But the Romneys of those days were not major figures in the church. However, today one of Governor Romney's cousins, Marion George Romney, is an apostle.

Governor Romney's mother's family had greater historical importance. Her grandfather was Parley Parker Pratt, who ranks as one of the most important martyrs in Mormon history after Joseph and Hyrum Smith.

Parley P. Pratt was an apostle ordained in 1835 by Joseph Smith, Oliver Cowdery and David Whitmer who were in the founding group of the restored Church of Christ. He was in jail with Joseph Smith in Missouri, he made mission trips to England, and when on the twenty-third anniversary of the founding of the church the cornerstone of the Salt Lake City Temple was put down, Parley P. Pratt delivered one of the orations. That was on April 6, 1853. He had a month, a week and four years to live.

Joseph Fielding Smith in his *Essentials of Church History* tells of Pratt's death in this way:

THE ASSASSINATION OF PARLEY P. PRATT.—Another death, occurring May 13, 1857, was that of Elder Parley P. Pratt of the council of the twelve . . . In the spring of 1857, he was in Arkansas. While there he attempted to assist a Mrs. Hector H. McLean, who was a member of the church, to obtain possession of her children, she having separated from her husband because of drunkenness and cruelty. McLean accused Elder Pratt of alienating the affections of his wife and attempting to abduct the children. A trial was held, and Elder Pratt was acquitted of the charge. Shortly afterwards, as he was journeying from Van Buren County where the court was held, intending to join an immigrant company for Utah, he was overtaken by McLean who plunged a bowie knife in his side. After Elder Pratt had fallen from his horse, McLean shot him with a pistol. The assassin was never punished for the foul deed. In this manner died one of the greatest expounders of the latter-day faith, a poet and writer, whose works survive and have done much to bring many to a knowledge of the Gospel. Although their author's voice has long been stilled, his work yet speaks with convincing power.

There was a little more to the story. Richard F. Burton, the English traveling man who was in Salt Lake City in 1860, told it in his account of his trip. He said that the death of Apostle Pratt figured in the accusations then being made against the Mormons over the Mountain Meadow massacre. The Saints at that stage were denying murdering the wagonloads of immigrants from Arkansas. But Burton said the skeptics said the Arkansans were killed by Mormons in revenge for the murder of the Apostle Pratt in Arkansas. Burton also said that Mrs. McLean had become one of the apostle's plural wives; this was the reason McLean had Pratt arrested and was the reason for the assassination.

When little George was five years old, Pancho Villa chased the Mormons out of Mexico. Many of them returned, but not the Gaskell Romney family which went to Salt Lake City—the center of the Mormon universe. George went to Latter-day Saints High School and grew up absorbing into his quick mind the culture, philosophy, moral standards and religious practices of his ancestral church.

He grew up to go on his mission to England and then gravitated to Washington, D.C., to work as a tariff specialist for Senator David I. Walsh of Massachusetts. This was in 1929, and in 1930 he joined the Aluminum Company of America as a Washington representative. In 1939 he became Detroit manager of the Automobile Manufacturers Association, and from 1942 to 1948 was general manager of the association. In 1948 he became assistant to the president of Nash-Kelvinator Corporation, a vice president in 1950 and in 1954 became chairman and president of American Motors which was the product of merger with Hudson

Motor Car Company. He became the "Rambler man" and a symbol of the early success of the American Motors move into the small-car field. After he left the company, competitive pressure from abroad and other United States car companies changed the picture for American Motors.

In his years in Michigan, Romney was drawn into a wide range of activities—clubs, committees, associations. He was drawn also into the outer fringes of politics through interest in creating a new state constitution. After successfully participating in the constitutional convention, he decided to run for governor. The new constitution which he helped to write was adopted during his first term. He was elected the first time in 1962 and re-elected in 1964.

Although he is a relative newcomer in politics and started successfully in the big league as a governor of an important state, Romney has a personality pattern that is typical of his political peers. He has absolute confidence in his ability, but has a tendency to insecurity because of the considerable damage that can be inflicted on his political career by events that he cannot control. Almost without exception, these top bananas of American politics are uneasy and defensive at the beginning of an interview with a writer they have not known well enough before to establish a firm relationship. With those previously built relationships, they know how to act, whether the past has been friendly or unfriendly. The insecurity in these first few minutes arises from not knowing which path to follow. For friends, it is smiling joviality; for non-friends, it is cool, short answers, mixed perhaps with a denunciation of a recent bit of writing, and a careful bit of shadow-boxing when the dangerous areas are approached. Some of these fellows derive more pleasure from dealing with their critics than with their friends.

The Governor was at his desk that day, and a long conference table stretched in front of him, filling the room. He was in shirt sleeves, toying with his glasses, and his hair gave a false impression of total grayness, when in fact it is gray just in front and on the sides, but still dark brown on top. He sat with his eyes slitted as he probed and dodged in the opening rituals of the interview. When it became apparent that the questions were pleasant and that the talk was not full of hidden fish hooks, his eyes came open to show that they were blue-gray which went well with his hair and facial coloring.

What had the church done to him and for him? How much of his accomplishment was due to the church?

He toyed with this for a few minutes, pushing the question this way and that, and explaining, "I want to respond accurately for you."

Then he was ready.

"The church gives you training in group activity, also in public and leadership responsibility from your very early years. Each person is encouraged to accept responsibility."

He leaned forward and pointed an index finger as he talked, and leaned back and looked at the ceiling, twirling his glasses. He remembered his first public speaking, which was in Idaho at a church meeting when he was six or seven years old. He remembered much public speaking in his priesthood work when he was twelve, thirteen or fourteen years old. His work as a young teen-ager in the priesthood quorums provided much public exposure, and frequently he took part in programs.

But the most vivid and meaningful religious experience of his life was his missionary stint in England and Scotland. He leaned forward and pointed, his posture and voice emphasizing his belief:

"There is no training anywhere equal to it. You have full and total personal responsibility."

He leaned back and looked at me somewhat challengingly.

"You know, I am not a college graduate. The best training I ever had was my church training. I do not think there is any college training that is a substitute for my religious training."

At times his voice was penetrating and overpowering, at other times very quiet and conversationally toned. He used these levels consciously and with considerable skill.

He turned to a second point in his discourse on the values to him of Mormonism, which is a word he dislikes. He prefers that he and his co-religionists be called Latter-day Saints or LDS or Saints.

"The religious training gives us a sense of values. A devout member has a sense of personal conviction and this is the big strength we have. The church places great emphasis on knowledge and individual responsibility of a person for his own place in the afterlife. No one else can do it for him. He must do it for himself. He must work for his own exaltation. Salvation comes to everyone, but a person must work for more than that. He must follow the path for his own exaltation."

The Saints draw strength from their association with each other, Romney believed.

"We have a strong sense of obligation to each other. I go out and visit with my youngest son on his home visits when I have time. We believe that when we are in the service of our fellow man, we are in the service of the Creator." (The Romneys have two sons and two daughters.)

There is no feeling for a Saint of having it made.

"There is no concept that you have arrived. The concept of eternal progression is fundamental."

He brought up the free agency doctrine that the LDS church holds in such great esteem. This is the idea that a man may be free to do whatever he wants and that he has complete freedom of choice in whether he will follow an exemplary or disgraceful course of conduct.

Romney turned to government and the position of a

member of the LDS church who holds public office, yet is told by the church to do something that he does not want to do.

For example, if he were in Congress instead of in a governor's chair, he would have received one of those letters from the First Presidency directing him to vote against repeal of section 14(b) of the Taft-Hartley Act and in favor of right to work laws. Presumably, he would have refused to follow the instruction, for he is on record in opposition to right to work laws.

What does he believe is the elected official's proper relationship in the event of such conflcits?

"The church begins with the position that the world is ruled by laws, and that it was created with definite rules. There is no doubt in our minds that the Constitution and Declaration of Independence were divinely inspired.

"Any member of the church in public trust has the right to determine for himself the application of our principles to his official duty. He feels a complete freedom to meet his personal responsibility."

When he decided to run for governor, he was a stake president. Did he ask the church for permission to make the race?

"I asked the General Authorities if there was any 'church reason' why I should not decide for myself to run. I was not asking them to tell me to run or not, but only if there was a reason not known to me that I should not. If they had given me such a reason, I would have considered it along with the other arguments for and against running. But the final decision was personal."

His church's policy on barring Negroes from full participation is really the only major problem the Saints have given to Romney in his political career. But he would never say this, nor did he say it to me, even by indirection.

His problem is the one that every religiously devout and

politically liberal Mormon has: How to reconcile the love of mankind that he holds in his heart as a result of his religious teachings with the deprivation for the Negro of the full realization of the deep religious experience that every Mormon believes his church provides for him?

Many Mormons were interviewed in gathering the material for this book. Some of these were bigots. They thoroughly enjoy the feeling of superiority that it gives them to know that they can have a position in their church that is absolutely unobtainable by a Negro. But for the liberal Mormons, this doctrine is a growing shadow between them and their church.

Governor Romney is deeply troubled by the situation. His acts as a business executive and a public official have shown that he feels deeply the obligation to help Negroes move upward in the social scale.

While he has ready answers to almost all questions in any area of theology or business or politics and is ready to state his position immediately, he has developed a tendency to want to quote someone else when the Negro-Mormon question arises.

When it came up in the interview, he handed over a copy of Hugh B. Brown's civil rights statement at the April, 1965, LDS conference. When we first talked about it in the Hotel Utah in January, 1964, he ended by sending me to see Joseph Fielding Smith.

In the talk in his office, he said, "I have a feeling of obligation to help Negroes far beyond that of people who don't hold my religious convictions."

Then he added: "My views in this regard are so deep that I refused to endorse the candidates of my party for president and vice president in 1964."

And this he did. He incurred the violent dislike of the ultra-right wing of the Republican party by refusing to lend his support to the Goldwater-Miller campaign. While the head of the Republican ticket was losing Michigan badly, Governor Romney was being re-elected by a large majority.

Those who have followed his career are convinced that he wants to run for President in 1968. The concern of some of his advisors in Michigan in 1965 was whether he could win re-election as governor in 1966 by a substantial margin. Their concern was that if he ran much below his high totals of 1964, it would be taken as a sign that he had "peaked too early" to use a phrase made famous by Richard M. Nixon.

Romney has absolutely solid credentials as a moderate Republican. The positions he has taken on issue after issue are those of the liberal Republicans. He has stood up and been counted when the brickbats were flying. He has shown remarkable ability in helping to bring a new and better constitution to Michigan. His administrative accomplishments have won much praise for him.

So how is he going to meet the problem of his church's attitude on Negroes?

More and more as the revolution of rising Negro expectations runs its course, to be labeled anti-Negro is to be a political leper. Romney has escaped this in Michigan, and said that he got 12 to 13 per cent of the Negro vote in his state in 1962 while other Republicans got 7 or 8 per cent. He did much better than that in 1964, of course, but he was the all-Negro-all-moderates-all-liberals anti-Goldwater-Miller candidate that year.

After the interview there was no question in my mind that Governor Romney deeply regrets his church's position on Negroes. He never said this, or hinted it without words. But the impression was inescapable as he talked of the problem.

He is trapped by his doctrine, you see, for it is a far more insidious thing than any other in any major religion in the

United States. As a Mormon he cannot disagree with the church leadership in a matter of doctrine such as this.

Remember the second question on the "Bishop's Temple Recommend form" which was: "Will you and do you sustain the General Authorities of the Church, and will you live in accordance with the accepted rules and doctrines of the Church?"

Governor Romney's position is difficult beyond that of such critics as Professor J. D. Williams, a devout Mormon who still disagrees with the anti-Negro practices. If Romney were to begin to criticize, he would be expected to lead a campaign to change the practice, and this he could never do.

Certainly George Romney is not going to lead an apostasy movement on the Negro question, and he is not going to criticize publicly the church leadership for the position which it—and he—inherited from men long dead. He will go along and attempt to let people know that he stands foursquare for civil rights for all races and religions. He also will work carefully within the LDS church for some solution to the deadlock.

Romney's influence already has been felt on this question. In 1962, for example, it was widely believed in higher Mormon circles that at the April Conference in the Tabernacle, some adjustment would be announced in the position on Negro membership activities. Of course the announcement did not come. This flutter of reconsideration of the traditional position was built on the growing realization that the church was out of step with modern thought on race relations; but it was prompted at that particular time by the Romney plans to run for governor of Michigan. Among the Mormon intellectuals, Romney is looked upon as a liberal within the church.

He also is a representative of the great number of Mormons who have roots in Mormon country but who have moved away for the pursuit of opportunities and the life that can be found away from the traditional home of their religious faith.

The twentieth century has seen a reversal of the "gathering" that went on under Brigham Young's leadership when the faithful poured into the Salt Lake Valley so they could help the Saints overcome the cruel environment. Now they are born and grow up and are educated there, then leave to produce branches, missions, then wards and stakes as the Restored Gospel encircles the globe.

For there are Mormons almost everywhere—even in Nigeria where the missionaries could not go, there are Mormons teaching in colleges and working for the Nigerian government. The scattered Saints are becoming more important in the total numbers of the church, also.

When George Romney became president of the Detroit stake of his church, it had about 2500 members, and when he resigned to run for governor, it had 5000. In places where ten years ago there were one or two Mormon families, in the mid-1960s there are new chapels and thriving ward organizations.

One of the problems for Utah has been the heavy expenditure to educate the youngsters—most of them Mormons—and the loss of this investment as they left the state to go all over the world for their hunt for a place in life.

Would George Romney have become governor of Utah if he had stayed at home? Probably not. The skills that his church found and hardened and sharpened in him are duplicated in many men who live and scramble for places in life in Salt Lake City today. The patterns of life and social organization that produced Romney produced many others of similar ability, drive and direction.

But the places where Romney went he found few men

who had the peculiar combinations of genes and religious-
social belief that he inherited from Parley Pratt and Miles
Romney and the others in his background.

"I am completely the product of the Church of Jesus Christ
of Latter-day Saints," said Governor Romney.

That is his assessment and there is no reason to challenge
it. But he is a product of the out-of-Utah LDS society, and
this has made him different from those who stayed at home.
He has been able to continue in his church, where others
much like him have dropped away.

He also has a much more free approach to doctrine and
scripture, a feeling of his relationship to his religion that
must be much closer to what was felt in Nauvoo than what
is felt in Salt Lake City today.

As we got up to end the interview, he began one of those
syllogisms that students of theology love to use on people
like me. It was now my turn to twist and squirm and avoid.

"You believe the Old Testament, don't you?"

"Well, Governor, I don't know whether I do or not."

"Oh, come on now, of course you believe the Old Testament," and his voice had taken on that harsh quality.

Inspiration saved me.

"Well, I suppose I do believe it, insofar as it's properly
translated."

His long, jutting jaw dropped, and then he broke into un-
controlled laughter. The tossing back of one of the Prophet's
Articles of Faith to break up his attack was so audacious that
he was delighted with it.

We shook hands and I left, reassured about George Romney.

XII

The Rightists and
the LDS Church

A MAN sits in a lovely room in a faculty club on a famous campus and comments on the future of his ancestral religion, the church of the Latter-day Saints:

"We must make an impact. We must bring about a discussion. We must have these points of view examined. The church must evolve and meet the world."

Another man sits in a beautifully paneled office and discusses the hopes of some of his intellectual peers to bring about a change in the direction of the LDS church.

"They're whipped before they start. There is no way for them to get control. The system is all against them."

Major problems in two levels of time confront the church. The first of these is the Negro question, which is far and away the major problem in the short term. The second is the need for an accommodation for the growing numbers of intellectuals. In the long run, this may be the greatest problem the LDS church faces.

The Saints have had their greatest growth under the presidency of David O. McKay, and this was one of the most liberal presidencies in the church's history. McKay was born September 8, 1873, on a farm at Huntsville, Utah, and has been an important figure in the church since he was thirty-two years old, when he was appointed one of the apostles. He was selected and named by Joseph F. Smith and it is perhaps symbolic that he was one of three men named in April, 1906. Two of the vacancies filled at that time had been created in the purge from the Council of Twelve Apostles of two polygamists, Matthias F. Cowley and John W. Taylor.

McKay's place in the apostolate was created as a by-product of the solution of the polygamy problem, and in the last years of his life the church has been faced with the Negro problem. He has not found a way to solve it.

The organizational pattern of the LDS church gives the president a control that well could be envied by the political figures that have served as President of the United States. The president of the Saints sits at the peak of his church's control structure. He is the chief in all matters that touch the church. The gospel is what he says it is. He is the chief prophet, chief seer, chief revelator. He is the inheritor of the supernatural powers of the Prophet Joseph and all that remains of the temporal powers of Brigham Young.

President McKay has spent almost his entire adult life in the day-to-day service of his church. He became a teacher at a church school when he was twenty-six, after having served his mission. He held that job until he became an apostle. He was first the assistant, then the general superintendent of the church Sunday school. He became a counselor to President Heber J. Grant in 1934.

Each LDS president names two (or more) counselors to help him and this collection is called the First Presidency. Usually, these counselors are themselves apostles, but not always. Almost all of the administrative activities of the church are taken in the name of the First Presidency.

Until the fall of 1965, McKay's two counselors were Hugh B. Brown, born October 24, 1883, and Nathan Eldon Tanner, born May 9, 1898. As McKay gradually became more and more feeble with his advancing years, Brown and Tanner came to exercise more control over church affairs.

When two more persons were added to the First Presidency in late October, 1965, it was taken by outsiders as a device for lessening this control by Brown and Tanner.

One of the two added was Joseph Fielding Smith, the senior member of the Council of Twelve Apostles who presumably would succeed to the presidency if he outlived McKay. Smith was born July 19, 1876. He is the only Smith now of importance in the LDS church, except for Eldred G. Smith, the patriarch, a position traditionally held by the family.

Yet the family founded the church, and a half century ago Frank J. Cannon could say that Joseph F. Smith (father of the present man) "notified the world that his branch of the Smith family had been designated by divine revelation to rule in the affairs of all men, by an appointment that had never been revoked."

Cannon described the Smiths in the church of that day in terms of their relationship to the then LDS president:

> He has since made his cousin, John Henry Smith, his first counselor; and he has inducted his son Hyrum into the Apostolate by "revelation." This latter act roused the jealousy of the mother of his son Joseph F. Smith, Jr., and the amused gossip of the Mormons predicted another revelation that should give Joseph, Jr., a similar promotion. The revelation came. So many others have also come that the Smith family is today represented in the hierarchy by Joseph F. Smith, President, "Prophet, Seer and Revelator to all the world"; John Smith (a brother) presiding Patriarch over the whole human race; John Henry Smith (a cousin) apostle and first counselor to the president; Hyrum Smith and Joseph F. Smith (sons) apostles; George A. Smith (son of John Henry) apostle; David S. Smith (son of Joseph F.) counselor to the presiding Bishop of the Church in line of succession to the bishopric; and Bathsheba W. Smith, president of the Relief Societies.

In these years of service to his family's religion since his appointment to the Council of Twelve in 1910, Joseph Fielding Smith has become the conservative theologian of the church. He has been a prolific author on the theology and history of the church. But he also has been waiting for the time when he would become the head of the church that his family founded.

The other man who was added to the First Presidency in 1965 was not an apostle. He was one of the twelve assistant apostles when he was named, but presumably will be elevated when a vacancy occurs. He is Thorpe B. Isaacson, born September 6, 1898, a successful insurance man. Isaacson also is a conservative Republican who has been mentioned as a candidate for governor or for United States senator, but probably will never make a campaign for either job. (He became seriously ill a few months after his promotion.)

The public explanation for the appointments was not clear-cut. Sources close to the church suggested that they were made because the more conservative members of the Council of Twelve felt that the liberal Hugh Brown was able to take more and more of the responsibility from President McKay and to exercise this authority in ways displeasing to some of the other apostles. It also was pointed out that only a few months before, the church had brought Ezra Taft Benson back from his political exile in Europe.

In a sense, what appears to have happened here in the 1960s has been the creation of a regency in which the divergent voices have spokesmen. It includes the heir apparent, even though he was past eighty-nine when he was named to the First Presidency.

The practice has been that when the LDS president dies, the First Presidency is dissolved and the Council of the Twelve Apostles elects a new president, who always has been the senior member in years of service as an apostle. On

three occasions there have been intervals before the appointment of a new president, and in these times the Council of
the Twelve Apostles has directed the church. The first of
these was after Joseph Smith's murder in 1844 when the
presidency was vacant until Brigham Young filled it in 1847.
After Young died, the presidency was not filled until 1880,
three years later, with the election of John Taylor. After Taylor died, it was not filled until two years later in 1889 with
the election of Wilford Woodruff. Since then Lorenzo Snow,
Joseph F. Smith, Heber J. Grant, George Albert Smith and
David O. McKay have been selected in a formality of endorsement when the presidency became vacant.

There is no rule that holds that this must be done. Joseph Fielding Smith will be ninety years old—or beyond.
What if his colleagues on the Council of Twelve decided
that this was the time to break the chain of custom? There is
slight chance they will decide this, and if he outlives David
O. McKay, the grandson of Hyrum Smith probably will come
at long last to the position that he undoubtedly considers
to be his birthright.

Who will follow Smith to the First Presidency? Certainly,
the days of strong influence for Hugh B. Brown would be
past. Nathan Eldon Tanner might remain on as the chief
financial advisor to the presidency. The other top counselor
position probably would go to Isaacson or one of the other
conservatives in the Council of Twelve.

The seniority list of the apostles becomes important, as
well as their ages, for no matter how senior they may be, advanced years may keep one from achieving the presidency.

One must remember, in assessing this list, that really
there are fifteen apostles, counting President McKay. The
president and his first and second counselors also are apostles. In addition to the senior member, Joseph Fielding
Smith, born in 1876, the thirteen are as follows in order of
seniority:

HAROLD B. LEE, born March 28, 1899, former educator and businessman, once a Salt Lake City commissioner.

SPENCER W. KIMBALL, March 28, 1895, reared in Arizona, an insurance and banking executive.

EZRA TAFT BENSON, August 4, 1899, farm cooperative leader, Secretary of Agriculture under Eisenhower, 1953-1961.

MARK E. PETERSEN, November 7, 1900, successively reporter, city editor, general manager of *Deseret News*.

DELBERT L. STAPLEY, December 11, 1896, wealthy businessman with varied interests, merchandising, banking, utilities.

MARION G. ROMNEY, September 19, 1897, former lawyer, took up fulltime church work in 1941.

LEGRAND RICHARDS, February 6, 1886, member of prominent church family, former realty business.

RICHARD L. EVANS, March 23, 1906, former radio announcer who has been producer, writer, and "voice" of the Tabernacle Choir broadcasts since 1930.

HUGH B. BROWN, October 24, 1883, lawyer, educator.

HOWARD W. HUNTER, November 15, 1907, attorney and businessman in Los Angeles.

GORDON B. HINCKLEY, June 23, 1910, businessman, then longtime employee of the LDS church.

NATHAN ELDON TANNER, May 9, 1898, industrialist, pipeline executive, speaker of Alberta legislature.

THOMAS S. MONSON, August 21, 1927, manager of Deseret News Printing Department.

Beginning with the appointment of Marion G. Romney in April 1951, eight of these men have been named to the council of apostles during McKay's presidency. The earlier appointees at the top of the list are looked upon by observers as the conservatives who will be running the LDS church for the years it takes the calendar to catch up with them.

What hopes do the liberal, intellectual Mormons have of changing their church's attitudes and action patterns during these years of conservative leadership?

"You got to have faith," was the hopeful expression of one devout Saint as he thought of this.

Meanwhile, on the political front the church must stand off the current attempts of the right wing organizations to capture that marvelous organization and turn it to their dark political purposes.

J. D. Williams, a devout Mormon and professor of political science at the University of Utah, sketched some of the connections that he has observed.

He said that in 1961 the moves from the right began with anti-Communist schools, Birch Society organizer visits, and special meetings attended by some of the top leaders of the church. Then Reed Benson was identified publicly as an organizer for the John Birch Society.

"So we wake up one day to find the John Birch Society among us, led by the son of the apostle," said Professor Williams.

However, he insists that thus far the church leadership has resisted the attempts to enlist it in the right wing cause.

There is substantiation for Professor Williams' judgment in the way a great, flapping crisis was resolved after it gripped the church's top leadership in early 1966. The issue was Apostle Benson's relationship to and work in behalf of the John Birch Society.

This was such an important disruption that we must take the time to understand it fully. It came about because of the April church conference in 1966 and reached its climax at about the time the conference opened. The LDS church was founded on April 6, 1830, and the Saints maneuver so that their April conference includes meetings on that day every year. They also like to have meetings on the weekends. Since April 6, 1966, was a Wednesday they opened the conference that day, then recessed until Saturday and Sunday. Non-conference meetings were scheduled in the interval.

In early March a letter from Dr. J. Reese Hunter, a Mormon and an optometrist, announced that Robert Welch, the John Birch Society founder, would speak in Salt Lake City on Thursday night, April 7, and that apostle Benson would introduce him. The letter noted the dinner was in a "free night" during the conference. It was addressed to "Dear Brethren" and was an outright attempt to draw on the LDS church as a recruiting ground. When he came to town to make the speeech, Welch made no denial. He said he found the church "a very good recruiting ground to go to."

"If we are looking for conservative, patriotic Americans of good character, humane consciences and religious ideals, where would you go looking for them any more hopefully than among the Latter-day Saints?" he said. "The Latter-day Saints are as individuals the kind of people we would like to have in the John Birch Society."

However, by the time Welch was making those remarks in the President's Room of the Hotel Utah (pictures of LDS presidents hang on the walls) the plans for apostle Benson to introduce him were down the drain. The exact details of what led to the change in plan will never be known, unless some leak in high church councils lets them out.

But I was told by two members of the Council of Twelve Apostles that Benson pulled out of his plan to introduce Welch when he was pressured by his associates on the Council. He appeared at the banquet, sat at the head table and received a thunderous applause from his co-religionists who made up perhaps two-thirds of the audience of 600. But he kept his mouth shut.

These events were at the end of the crisis which had been some months in the building. Their origins were in 1962 when Reed Benson went to work for the Birch Society. There were roots in the action in 1963 that sent apostle

Benson to Europe, and in the publication of the letters from
Joseph Fielding Smith and others supporting Representative
Ralph Harding's attacks on Benson. Soon after Benson returned to Salt Lake City in late 1965, his resumption of association with the Birch Society became apparent.

In early 1966, a right wing group called the Utah Forum
for the American Idea rented the Assembly Hall, an old
stone meeting house which shares the Temple Block with
the more famous Temple and Tabernacle. The speakers for
a series of meetings included W. Cleon Skousen, a Mormon
conservative; Clarence Manion, conductor of the conservative Manion Forum on radio and television; and John
Stormer, author of None Dare Call It Treason which is an
attack on various liberal persons and institutions in American
life.

The opening meeting on February 11, 1966, was addressed
by apostle Benson in a speech titled "Stand Up for Freedom." This talk was recorded on video tape by television
station KSL, owned by the Mormon church. It was not broadcast at that time. Ken Curtis, manager for television of KSL,
told me the standard fee of $500 was charged. The speech
was attended by many conservative thinkers, in and out of
the LDS church. No voice was raised that criticized holding
it on church property, for the Mormons frequently make
their Assembly Hall available to other groups.

For a while the public didn't know what happened next.
The talk manuscript was sent to the Church News Department of the Deseret News. The Church News Department
actually is an arm of the church's propaganda and internal
communication system. It produces a special section that is
distributed locally each Saturday with the News but also
is distributed independently of the newspaper to Mormons
throughout the world. It carries much information of internal interest to the Saints.

The plan was to have the Benson speech printed in the

church newspaper, thereby emphasizing further the apostle's view that the Birch Society was a fine, patriotic organization. In the body of his speech, he had defended the Society in words like these:

"The Communists had intended to confuse the American people and they did. The tar brush tactics smeared the image of the new, small, but rapidly growing John Birch Society to the point where many people thought it must be a group of neo-Nazis or a revival of the Ku Klux Klan. Some prominent, highly respected men were so deceived that they declared that the infiltration of the John Birch Society was equally as bad as the infiltration of the Godless Communist conspiracy."

He also said:

"Now, in the light of what I have just related, you will understand my feelings when people would ask how I felt about the John Birch Society. Because of the amazingly effective propaganda against them, it has been very unpopular to defend this group. I can remember when it was unpopular to defend my own church. Nevertheless, as soon as I learned what the Communists and liberals were doing to the John Birch Society, I felt a deep indignation that this should happen to any non-political, patriotic group of American citizens. I felt it was dishonest, immoral and crass hypocrisy. I still feel that way."

However, he said he was not a member.

When this speech came into the Church News Department, it soon found its way to the desk of Earl Hawkes, the manager of the *Deseret News*. He objected to printing it. He carried his objection to the highest levels of the church. Then he was told to run it, but was allowed to take out the sections that praised the John Birch Society. This amounted to twenty-seven paragraphs and did not disturb the Benson denunciation of Communism or praise of the American Constitution, nor his denial of membership in the society. When the speech was printed, the liberal elements of the Mormon community were outraged. The story of how it came to be printed gradually seeped out. The outrage was heightened on March 30, 1966, when the full speech was broadcast from the video tape by KSL-TV, the church station. This time the apostle was able to say all the good things about the Birch Society that had been edited from the reprint of the speech.

Meanwhile, another cause for concern had come to the attention of the Council of Twelve Apostles. They learned that the April issue of *American Opinion*, the Birch Society magazine, had scheduled a cover photo of President McKay. The apostles sent David Lawrence McKay, a son, to ask their president to withdraw his permission for the picture's use.

The old man agreed, and the apostles notified the Birch Society not to use the picture. When the April issue of *American Opinion* appeared, its cover carried a picture of J. Reuben Clark, Jr., a member of the LDS First Presidency from 1933 until his death in 1961. A page of tribute to Clark was signed by Robert Welch.

When the letter announcing apostle Benson's plans to play a leading role in the Welch banquet burst on the apostles in early March, they were flabbergasted. First they caused the *Deseret News* to carry an announcement that contained this paragraph:

"In order to avoid any misunderstanding we wish to notify bishops, other church officers, and members of the church in general, that the church is not involved in this dinner in any way, and furthermore, that the church has no connection with the John Birch Society whatever."

Then on the Saturday before the Welch banquet, the Church News Section carried a long editorial written by Mark E. Petersen, the apostle who ranks immediately behind Apostle Benson in seniority. The editorial noted that "good citizens wonder what may be done to steady the ship of state." Members of the LDS church must "avoid extremes and extremists," and "the great men of our nation have never been extremists," apostle Petersen wrote. He also wrote:

"Some have wondered if the church is involved in such groups as the John Birch Society, but it is no more a part of that group than of any other political aggregation. The church has nothing to do with Communists, nothing to do with racists, nothing to do with Birchers, nothing to do with any slanted group."

Sometime early in the first week of April, 1966, the apostles got down to business with Elder Ezra Taft Benson. He agreed not to introduce Robert Welch. But he sat at the head table, silently, while a speech titled "A Touch of Sanity" was rattled off by Welch. As a sample of the nonsense being peddled that night by the former candy maker, he argued that the anti-war demonstrations of 1965-66 were operated by Communists who really want to keep the United States involved in Vietnam.

"All they needed was merely to have a few thousand of their agents and dupes and stooges stage some parades and establish some picket lines, protesting our being in Vietnam, and demanding that we withdraw," Welch said. "This ruse, of getting what they want by the principle of reversal applied in this manner, is so old and so familiar to the Communists that they did not even have to give it a second thought."

But while his colleagues had persuaded Benson to hold his endorsement of Welch to a minimum level, they did not stop his flirtation with the Birchites. A month later William J. Grede, a Milwaukee, Wisconsin, industrialist who is a leading member of the Birch Society, said that he wanted Benson to run for the Republican presidential nomination in 1968. This would hold together the conservative coalition constructed in 1964 to help Barry Goldwater. In Salt Lake City, apostle Benson's reaction was to avoid comment at this time on his possible candidacy.

It seemed to me, as I interviewed dozens of people that week, that the seriousness of this deep conflict at the top of the church was not recognized in Salt Lake City in early April, 1966. Lower-level Saints tended to joke about Welch and Benson. Only among the students of Mormon affairs and in the very top levels did one get the full flavor of crisis.

Sterling McMurrin, the educator and former U.S. Commissioner of Education, recognized it. He said that "this is the first major crisis in the church since its decision to abandon polygamy in 1890. What is involved here is a typical Mormon abhorrence of extremism. The leadership of this church is politically conservative, but it is not extremist."

There seemed to me to be a little more to it even than that. One of the apostles told me, as he was confirming that indeed the Council of Twelve had influenced Benson to drop his plans to speak for Welch, that it was not the Benson association with the Birch Society that was at issue.

"If Elder Benson on his own wants to work in it, that's his business. Elder Benson, I hope, is not involving the church."

This was what worried his colleagues about Benson's actions. He had spoken in the Temple Square to what was fundamentally a right-wing political meeting. He had praised and defended the Birch Society. He had arranged to have his remarks published in the Church News Section. He had arranged to have the entire speech broadcast over the church television station. He had cooperated in an attempt to draw an audience from top church leaders to fill a banquet room to hear the founder of the John Birch Society.

His colleagues were not resisting the Birch Society connections Benson might have; they were resisting his use of his membership on the Council of Twelve to further the aims of the Birchites. They want him to be an apostle first; they feared he was tending to place the Birch Society ahead of his churchly duties.

To anyone who has studied the 1964 presidential campaign, the civil rights movement, and the emergence of such things as the Birch Society, a pattern becomes apparent. That pattern, very rich and varied, includes one element that is disturbing to many Saints and to others who are not members of the LDS church but admire their organization and many of the things it stands for.

That element is this:

The bigots and race baiters who make up much of the radical right want to make common cause with the LDS church in regard to the Negro.

For example, in 1964 California political life was disrupted by one of those issues that divide political parties and families and longtime friendships. This was over whether the state was to have a law that would forbid racial discrimination in real estate transactions. The liberals, of course, favored having such a law. The conservatives were against it. Naturally, it was aimed at helping Negroes to break out of the patterns of slum housing, one-race schools and other manifestations of the discrimination that afflicts them in the big cities.

The Mormon church in California opposed the law. It was voted out. The bigots were loudly triumphant. But the LDS church kept its mouth shut afterward, perhaps somewhat ashamed. Those Mormons willing to defend their church's doctrine will attempt to explain it in terms of theology, and argue that the Mormons as individuals really love and cherish the Negro and want to help him establish a better place in American life. The action in California in 1964 shows differently.

A Negro who practiced law in Utah for a long time, D. H. Oliver, had some comments on Saints and Negroes. He published them as *A Negro On Mormonism*. Here are to things he said:

"Different from the general concept of race prejudice, Utah has one distinctly all its own, designed to nullify the Constitution of the United States, reverse the decisions of the United States Supreme Court, ignore the mandates of the Presidents of the United States, and degrade Negroes to a position of servitude and economic slavery by their religious doctrines . . ."

Also:

"Because of the doctrines . . . and constant pressure from Church leaders, employment opportunities for Negroes in Utah are confined to menial labor and positions of servitude and, thus, they find themselves faced with greater difficulties in securing employment commensurate with their qualifications than Negroes in the deep South."

This racial view, which the segregationists would recognize as a common purpose between them and the LDS church, may cause the Mormons more trouble in the future. In 1965, Dr. Glen W. Davidson wrote in the *Christian Century* that his interviews with new LDS converts in the southern states turned up a surprising number who joined because they accepted the Mormon anti-Negro position.

It is possible, but unlikely, that the Mormon church could become the religious refuge of the anti-Negro bigots. It also could become a bastion of the right wing, reactionary political forces who are allied with the southern racists in many common purposes. The church is founded on authority at the top, and unquestioning faith at the bottom. All sorts of strange structures have risen on these foundations in the past—polygamy, communal colonies, "blood atonement," to name three. There is no organizational guarantee that would prevent the construction of a right wing, racist church on those foundations in the future.

The safeguard that is most visible is the growing number

of liberally oriented Saints produced by exposure to the life outside Utah and by the Mormon drive for education for the young. Again and again as one moves through Mormon country, there appears a liberal spokesman who at the same time is a devout member of his church. The collective pressure of these men is felt at the top of the church. Also, they are able to stand outside the church structure and survive almost untouched. This was an unusual position in the years gone by; in Brigham Young's day, one needed a hide of cold-rolled steel and independent means to be able to stand up against the church on its home grounds. But there are more and more of these men today. As one surveys Mormon thought away from Salt Lake City and the desert redoubt, one finds a different orientation. The emotional ties to the church many times are stronger, and frequently are more rational since they are not the effect of social pressure so much as of personal choice. But there is less willingness to submit to a lot of foolishness from the top leaders of the church; the direct control is less.

So the struggle will continue between the various philosophies. The rightists probably will not be able to gain complete control in the foreseeable future. Nor is it likely that the liberal elements will gain control and turn the church radically away from the traditional positions it has held.

There is indication that new lines of communication between Mormons in different areas may begin to appear. This could have remarkable effects. As things have stood for more than a century, there has been no means of talking over problems internally except face to face, or in publications produced under control of the General Authorities— the *Deseret News*, the *Improvement Era*. One could write a book and some Mormons did. But this is a limited means of communication.

At the end of 1964, plans were announced by a group of

Mormon intellectuals to publish a periodical under the title *Dialogue* that would circulate among a Mormon audience. It was not presented in any sense as a rebellious publication, but as a means of exploring subjects of broad interest among the Saints.

The attitude of the church leadership did not become apparent immediately, and probably will not until later when the General Authorities have had a chance to see what the magazine intends to be. If they dislike it, a little mimeographed notice will go out to each bishop and stake president telling them to pass the word that the magazine is not the sort of thing that Mormons should spend their money to buy or waste their time in reading.

Control would be exercised in negative terms, which is the usual pattern when the LDS church deals with the advance of ideas. Usually by the time a Saint achieves an important church position he is of an age when his creative years are far behind him. Joseph Smith, Jr. was seventeen years old when the Angel Moroni told him of the Gold Plates. He was twenty-one on September 22, 1827, when the Angel finally turned the plates over to him for translation. When the church was established on April 6, 1830, Joseph was twenty-four years old. He was but thirty-eight years old when he died in the thunder of gunfire at the jail in Carthage.

That age—thirty-eight years—is the age of the youngest and newest member of the Council of Twelve Apostles at the end of 1965. There are now sixteen men in the First Presidency and in the Council. Their average age in late 1965 is over sixty-eight years. The oldest is David O. McKay, born in 1873, and the youngest is Thomas Monson, born in 1927.

The Mormons have had an impact on the rest of the United States just as they have in turn been shaped. When they left Florence, Nebraska, for the valley of the Great Salt Lake in 1847, they were leaving the United States. There had been hints they might go to some other place. Vancouver Island was discussed.

Had they gone to some other place, where their chances of winning representation and full participation in a national government would have been so much less, their development undoubtedly would have been along more harsh, more reclusive lines.

But they settled in the desert where they could carve out and occupy an area that in the nature of things political, geographical and historical had to become a part of the United States. When it did, the Mormons were assured of representation in that government. That achievement of political representation also has made them a part of the social and economic structure of the United States. In joining, they changed it slightly, and in a way that made it more receptive to them than it would have been before. The hard campaign for statehood changed the Saints very much, and the acceptance of the responsibilities of statehood changed them even more.

They have become thoroughly and completely America, which they certainly were not when Brigham Young had them organized for the Mormon War of the late 1850s. They are never completely in step with the national stride; but who is?

From all the forces that churn around within it, the nation develops a stride all its own. None of us is completely in step.

If the Mormons can somehow solve their problem about the Negro, their major short term trouble will be out of the way. Certainly their problem will be met in some fashion, just as an earlier church met the much more difficult problem of wiping out polygamy within the membership. Dr. Sterling McMurrin suggested that the anti-Negro doctrine will somehow be dissolved, as the polygamy doctrine was dissolved. Just how this could be done is not clear, not even to McMurrin, but he probably is right. Sometime in the future, the pressure for equality at the altar for Negroes will become so great that the Saints will find a way to give it to them.

What of the longer range problem of the tendency among the more highly educated young people to drift away?

There really are two parts to this problem. First, there is the shift in the attitude that must come as a young Mormon leaves the highly controlled atmosphere of his home, his stake and his flurry of church-related activities on moving from Mormon country to college. Next, there is the increasing problem of maintaining relationships on the traditional pattern between the central church in Salt Lake City and the larger and larger world that the church occupies.

From its earliest days the church has been closely knit. Joseph Smith moved the church around with him as he shifted from Kirtland, Ohio, to the Missouri frontier to Nauvoo, Illinois. In a sense, it is still that way—the church is located wherever the LDS president happens to be. But the church also is a growing bureaucracy in Salt Lake City.

When the ideal of The Gathering was still in vogue, it was easy to maintain a close relationship between the top and the rank and file. Converts could be brought to Mormon country and everybody lived there.

In those early days the First Presidency and Council of Twelve Apostles could make personal visits to all the Mormon areas at frequent intervals. It became a custom to hold quarterly conferences in each stake. With about 2500 to 5000 members in each stake, this was a manageable group. The custom grew up that one of the General Authorities would be present at each stake conference. By 1921, there were 100 stakes, which meant 400 conferences to be divided among the leaders, which was within the reasonable limits of demand on the ability of the older apostles to travel.

But by 1965, there were 400 stakes, and this means 1600 conferences a year. Today, there are more men among the General Authorities, too. Through addition of twelve assistant apostles, the use of the presidents of the First Council of Seventy, the three men in the presiding bishopric, and the patriarch there are thirty-eight men available to provide the "spiritual feast" the faithful look for at the quarterly conferences.

For various reasons, the conferences cannot be held on some weekends, so that about forty to forty-five dates are open. Then some of the General Authorities are unable to be away so much for reasons of health, or age, or press of duties in Salt Lake City. The end of all this is that not for long can the faithful look forward to a visit from an apostle or other high leader every three months. It is rapidly approaching the point where some places will get a General Authority for no more than one conference a year.

While the world gets smaller in so many ways, Salt Lake City gets further away as the church expands in size. To the outsider, it appears that some new administrative procedures must be worked out that will facilitate maintenance of the close relationship of past years from the top down. There have been indications within the church that this need is recognized.

With the college students, the church long ago recognized the problem and took steps by building LDS centers around many big schools to counter the tendency of college life to whirl young Saints away from their church. As a result, it has managed to hang on to many of its young intellectuals in the period since the end of World War II when so many thousands of young Mormons have been able to pursue the ideal expressed in the Mormon scripture: "The glory of God is intelligence."

The church has been uncannily able over the years to meet the needs for change thrust on it by the change in the outside world. The devout, of course, will hold that this is the result of the special relationship between the Saints and the Being that orders us all.

While I do not believe this, it would not trouble me to find that it is so. For some years now I have drawn great pleasure and no little inspiration from visits to that beautiful capital city of the Saints. Almost without exception they have been courteous, informative, pleasantly challenging and yet mysteriously—tantalizingly—secretive about things in the back corners of Mormon life.

The Mormons are a fine people. Their contribution to American life has been considerable. With a few exceptions, which are very plainly set out in these covers, I find their doctrine to be humane, productive of progress, patriotic, wholesome and praiseworthy. It has the further advantage of requiring such sacrifice from those who follow it that most of the religious charlatans are weeded out. If a man passes himself off in serious circumstances as a Mormon, one can know how he will react in most situations. Being a Mormon is too demanding a job for one to be able to pose at it successfully.

There is a whole pattern of life which exists in these cities along the western slope of the Wasatch Mountains that would not be known were it not for the religion founded on the writings and speeches of Joseph Smith. There are weaknesses in that pattern of life; but there are strengths that far out-balance the defects.

The Mormons have contributed much to the modern United States. They will contribute more. After all, God has told them to progress.

Index

334